Case Studies
in
Perinatal Nursing

Contributors

Diane Angelini, EdDc, CNM, CNA
Christine Williams Burgess, DNSc, RN
Mary Ellen Burke, MSN, RN
Jeanne Watson Driscoll, MS, RN, CS
Harriet W. Ferguson, EdD, RNC
Sandra Friedman, MSN, CNM
Susan Givens, MPH
Meredith Goff, MSN, CNM
Carol J. Harvey, MS, RNC
Dana Jolly, MS, CNM
Jane McManus Kenslea, MS, CNM
Cheryl Kirkland, MS, RN
Christine Whelan Knapp, CNM, MS
Vanda R. Lops, MS, CNM
Gayle L. Riedmann, MS, CNM
Ava R. McCarthy Sauer, MEd, CRNA
Kathleen Sullivan, MSN, CNM
Ruth Tucker, PhD, RN
C. Patrice Valle, MS, CNM
Tina Weitkamp, MSN, RNC

Case Studies
in
Perinatal Nursing

Edited by

Diane J. Angelini, EdDc, CNM, CNA
Director
Nursing Education and Research
Women and Infants' Hospital of Rhode Island
Providence, Rhode Island

Christine M. Whelan Knapp, CNM, MS
Nurse Midwife
Boston, Massachusetts

An Aspen Publication
Aspen Publishers, Inc.
Gaithersburg, Maryland
1992

Library of Congress Cataloging-in-Publication Data

Case studies in perinatal nursing / edited by Diane Angelini, Christine
Whelan Knapp.
p. cm.
Includes bibliographical references and index.
ISBN: 0-8342-0227-1
1. Maternity nursing—Case studies. I. Angelini, Diane J., 1948—
II. Knapp, Christine M. Whelan, 1951—[DNLM: 1. Obstetrical Nursing.
2. Perinatology. 3. Pregnancy Complications—nursing.
WY 157.3 C337]
RG951.C37   1991
610.73'678—dc20
DNLM/DLC
for Library of Congress
91-25953
CIP

The authors have made every effort to ensure the accuracy of the information
herein, particularly with regard to drug selection and dose. However, appropriate information sources should be consulted, especially for new or unfamiliar drugs or procedures. It is the responsibility of every practitioner to
evaluate the appropriateness of a particular opinion in the context of actual
clinical situations and with due consideration to new developments. Authors,
editors, and the publisher cannot be held responsible for any typographical or
other errors found in this book.

Editorial Services: B. Mangus

Library of Congress Catalog Card Number: 91-25953
ISBN: 0-8342-0227-1

Printed in the United States of America

2   3   4   5

To David and my Dad—DJA

To Bob, Michael, and Andrew—CWK

Table of Contents

Preface

Case study methodology is utilized by major academic disciplines including law, business, and medicine. Nursing, too, has found the use of case studies to be a helpful and informative way to present clinical findings and materials relevant to patient care. The clinical arena provides rich patient situations from which to draw case studies.

There is a positive effect on learning, both in the formal educational setting and in continuing education, when information is presented to nurses in a case study format. The analysis of each case presentation draws into play current clinical skills and knowledge.

It is hoped that this selection of perinatal case studies will broaden the knowledge base and clinical level for both the novice and the expert perinatal nurse. While this text is not comprehensive in all avenues of perinatal care situations, it does encompass a unique array of subject areas including postpartum vulvar edema, the pregnant spinal cord injury patient, multiple sclerosis in pregnancy, support systems and preterm birth, and cardiomyopathy, among others. Additionally, thought-provoking cases concerned with access to perinatal care and cognitive strategies for coping in labor are included. The editors have chosen a potpourri of topics to enrich the clinical practice of the perinatal nurse.

Chapter 1

Fetal Alcohol Syndrome

C. Patrice Valle

Fetal alcohol syndrome (FAS) is the number one cause of mental retardation in the Western world, with an incidence of 1.9 per thousand births.[1,2] Ranking second and third are Down's syndrome and spina bifida (1.25/1000 and 1.1/1000, respectively).[1] Interestingly, fetal alcohol syndrome is the only one of the three that is preventable.

FAS is characterized by all of the following for definitive diagnosis:

1. prenatal and/or postnatal growth retardation (weight, length, and/or head circumference below the 10th percentile when corrected for gestational age)
2. central nervous system involvement (signs of neurologic abnormality or developmental delay)
3. characteristic facial dysmorphology with at least two of the following signs: microcephaly (head circumference below the 3rd percentile); short palpebral fissures; poorly developed philtrum, thin upper lip, and/or flattening of the maxillary area[3,4] (Fig. 1-1).

In addition to the above listed criteria, there may be associated features,[5,6] but they are not required for the diagnosis.

4. physical deformities (limb deformities, cleft palate/lip, genitourinary abnormalities)
5. cardiac defects (such as tetrology of Fallot)
6. ocular problems
7. hyperactivity.[5]

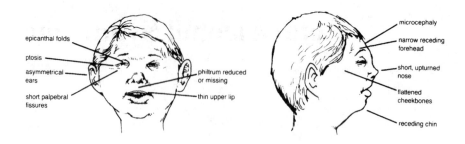

Figure 1-1 Features of the Fetal Alcohol Syndrome. *Source:* From Jones and Smith (1975), Plant (1985), and National Women's Health Report (1988).

HISTORICAL PERSPECTIVE

Alcoholism has been linked to defective offspring since the Greek and Roman times. Plato stated that "children shouldn't be made in bodies saturated with drunkenness."[7] In Carthage and Sparta there were laws forbidding newly married couples below the age of 30 to drink so that defective children might not be conceived.[7-9]

Warner and Rosett summarized a group of research findings between 1900 and 1918. They were especially impressed by MacNicholl's research in New York City in 1905, in which it was found that, of 6,624 children of drinking parents, 53% were "dullards"; among the 13,523 children of abstainers studied, however, only 10% were dullards.[7]

Many quasiconclusive and ill-conceived studies explaining defective children obscured the alcohol-fetal damage picture until the 1960s, when Lemoine et al. from France reported on a study of 127 children of alcohol-dependent parents.[8] Although it was not distinguished which parent was at fault, the study concluded that these children had a cluster of common features. The average IQ of the children was 70. The facial features were characteristic: short upturned nose, receding chin, and deformed, sunken nasal bridge. The overall growth showed low birth weight, slow growth, delayed psychomotor and language development, short height, and hyperactivity.[7,9,10]

Not too long after this, in 1969, Ulleland, a pediatric resident, noted that a small group of six children she was following somehow would not respond to the best of medical care and attention and seemed not to be thriving.[11] All six had mothers who were diagnosed to be alcoholic. Shortly thereafter, Ulleland et al. documented another ten similarly affected children.[11] She presented these discoveries at the American National Council on Alcoholism in 1972.

Smith and Jones, two dysmorphologists at the University of Washington, continued research to find the link between maternal drinking and fetal injury. Their work, published the following year, conclusively illustrated and named the disorder "fetal alcohol syndrome."[3] (See Fig. 1-1 for Jones/Smith pattern of malformation.)

Smith and Jones had a small sample of 11 children, and some of their medical and scientific colleagues viewed this work with skepticism because much of the data about the mothers was limited (such as nutritional information, other drug use, smoking, etc.). Although Jones and Smith addressed the nutritional factor,[3] poor socioeconomic status, a risk factor shared by all the mothers, should not have been so readily dismissed.

Finally, between 1977 and 1980 a few researchers attempted controlled studies to document clearly the differences between patients with alcohol-induced defects and controls.[7,12] The numbers remained small, and it was still unclear whether light or moderate drinking induced the same effects that heavy drinking did. It was clear, however, that large scale research with tighter controls was needed.

Kline et al. in 1980 produced a well-controlled retrospective study on 616 women on welfare assistance who spontaneously aborted.[13] They considered other factors such as smoking and other drug usage. They demonstrated a correlation between moderate drinking (one ounce of alcohol per day) and spontaneous abortion. Interestingly, the same group of researchers repeated this study with a group of private patients and did not find an obvious correlation between moderate drinking and abortion or even low birth weight.[13]

In 1981, the Surgeon General issued his recommendation regarding alcohol usage during pregnancy: "Even if she does not bear a child with full fetal alcohol syndrome, a woman who drinks heavily is more likely to bear a child with one or more of the birth defects included in the syndrome."[7,14]

Kunitz and Levy in 1974 documented the social science and epidemiologic literature on Native Americans and alcohol use.[15] It seemed that tribes with a loose, band-level social organization tended to have a higher incidence of alcohol-related problems than did those with a strict, highly structured tribal organization. May and Hymbaugh stated in 1983 that fetal alcohol syndrome distribution and incidence actually followed this pattern.[16] The more highly structured tribes had fewer drinking mothers and therefore a significantly lower incidence of fetal alcohol damage. Unfortunately, certain tribes (Apache and Ute) demonstrated a very high incidence of fetal alcohol syndrome, making the overall incidence of fetal alcohol syndrome in the southwestern tribal areas as high as 28.9%.[2,16] If all fetal "effects" are accumulated, the incidence jumps to 44%.[2,16] Pueblo and Navajo tribes have the lowest incidence of fetal alcohol syndrome in that region.[2,16]

RESEARCH LIMITATIONS

Unfortunately, it seems that the limitations of retrospective research have plagued the efforts of many researchers in the search for the key to fetal effects and alcohol. Alcohol histories are usually obtained or conducted at the end of pregnancy, which can be distorted by bias or vague due to poor recall. In addition, assessment of other confounding polydrug use, smoking, or caffeine ingestion can be hampered.

Prospective research has its share of problems. In Plant's prospective research the ethical problems of knowing the effects of heavy drinking and not letting the client be informed of these effects were readily acknowledged.[7] She decided to inform patients only if they requested the information that evidence from America suggests that heavy drinking during pregnancy is harmful and the current study was being undertaken to ascertain at which levels of alcohol consumption damage might occur.[7] She also decided not to bias the research. When patients seem to be consuming "dangerous" levels of alcohol, no advice was given by the research team. Clinic staff were informed only on the best methods to record consumption histories.

RECENT LITERATURE

Plant was not the only one who recently pointed out the distinct difficulties of conducting human research in this very controversial area. A pediatrician and an epidemiologist at the Boston University School of Public Health reviewed all of the literature and research on alcohol consumption during pregnancy.[4] They looked at the three areas upon which most of the research had previously been based: the dysmorphology itself, intrauterine growth retardation, and neonatal neurobehavioral dysfunction. They concluded the following:

1. The dysmorphology of fetal alcohol syndrome may reflect a common pathway of numerous agents or a combination of agents, rather than a specific teratogenic effect of alcohol.

2. Unless confounding variables are controlled, study findings may either overestimate the magnitude of a specific substance or demonstrate a significant association where none exists.

3. Studies on the neurobehavioral effects of alcohol need more extensive controls for and examination of interrelated factors such as concomitant drug use and indicators of maternal health.[4]

It is clear, now, that fetal alcohol syndrome cannot be explained in the simplest of terms.

Foster suggested in 1986 that, although ethanol and/or its metabolite may be directly teratogenic, an alcoholism-induced autoimmune response in the mother may cross-react with and interfere with the development of the fetal brain and possibly other tissues, thus contributing to severely abnormal brain formation and other congenital deformities.[17] He supported this hypothesis by quoting numerous studies, most of which documented hypersensitivity of chronic alcoholics to S-100, one of the brain proteins. This protein is involved in the process of organizing neurons into the complex architecture of the brain. The brains of victims of fetal alcohol syndrome, it has been noted, are characterized by chaotic migration and structural organization of neurons during fetal development.[17,18] It is also known that the blood-brain barrier, which protects the brain from autoimmune damage, is not fully intact until approximately the time of birth.[15] Foster and others went further to suggest that the incidence of FAS may be more clearly related to the stage (chronic) of the alcoholic disease than to the quantity of alcohol consumed during the pregnancy.[17] He suggested further research on all of the brain proteins in chronic alcoholic and nonalcoholic pregnant women.

Interestingly, in separate research conducted by O'Connor et al., a significant linear relationship between drinking *prior to* pregnancy and infant mental development was found. Studying a group of 25 older (more than 30 years of age) primiparous women, she discovered that the 1-year-old infants of women who consumed >30 ml of absolute alcohol per day demonstrated a significantly lower mental development score than did those who consumed 3 or fewer milliliters per day.[19] None of the women smoked or abused drugs, and caffeine intake was controlled. Two other researchers demonstrated that older pregnant animals exhibit higher blood alcohol levels than do younger animals in controlled studies.[20,21]

Friedler documented studies of a possible relationship between paternal drinking and low infant birth weight and of neurophysiologic alterations in the sons of alcoholic fathers and abstinent mothers.[22] Nelson et al. documented clear neurochemical deviations in the offspring of rats after prolonged paternal inhalation exposure to ethanol.[23] Although the origin of the effects of paternal exposure to alcohol is unknown, Freidler suggested that morphine-related alteration of reproductive function should be investigated. He suggested that drug-induced changes in paternal reproductive function may somehow affect the process through which sperm are "selected" for fertilizing the female. This mechanism, nonetheless, still remains obscure.[22]

Abel has now begun to document fetal alcohol syndrome in families.[24] He noted that the incidence of fetal alcohol syndrome among older siblings is as high as 170/1000; among younger sibs, however, the incidence has been 771/1000. (The U.S. experience is 1.9/1000.)

Despite the wealth of research with animals and humans, the actual mechanism by which fetal alcohol syndrome occurs is still unknown. As we have seen, the theories have ranged from dose-response, autoimmunity mechanisms and the timing factor (first vs. second vs. third trimester) to maternal age, family genetics, and paternal exposure. A new term in the research into prenatal alcohol exposure, fetal alcohol effects, refers to alcohol-related birth defects in infants and children which do not meet the diagnostic criteria.[5,14]

Nonetheless, it is important to keep in mind that, whatever the cause of the syndrome, whether it is fetal alcohol syndrome or fetal alcohol effects, mental retardation is involved in the majority of the cases. And mental retardation can be a tremendous social and financial burden. Abel and Sokol stated that, conservatively estimated for the United States, the economic cost of anomalies, treatment of sensorineural problems, and mental retardation is $321 million per year.[2] Fetal alcohol syndrome–related mental retardation alone may account for as much as 11% of the annual cost for all mentally retarded and institutionalized clients in the United States.[2]

* * * * *

CASE STUDY

This 30-year-old gravida IV, para II Native American (13/16th Sioux) woman presented for nurse-midwifery care at the local urban Indian Health clinic at 23 weeks gestation with a reasonably good dating of pregnancy per history of 22 May 1984 and estimated date of confinement (EDC) of 27 February 1985. At the first visit she was size equivalent to dates. Her obstetrical (OB) history was as follows: 1971, normal spontaneous vaginal delivery of a viable 8-lb 13-oz girl, induced in hospital; 1973, spontaneous abortion at 24 weeks, secondary to "drug addiction"; 1981, therapeutic abortion at 6 weeks gestation. Her past medical history included a seizure history since 1982 secondary to a "blow on head, cerebral bleeding," now on Dilantin; heroin addiction for 20 years, with present $20/day use since June 1984; methadone maintenance program 1975–76, 1981; consumption of four or five bottles of Night Train (cheap red wine) per day; hepatitis in 1973; tuberculosis with isonicotinoylhydrazine (INH) treatment in 1962; multiple emergency room admissions for stabbings, urinary tract infections, and seizures; multiple drop-in visits to the emergency room and the Indian clinic for tranquilizers (Valium and Benadryl). Her family history included an insulin-dependent mother (unknown number of years); hypertension and heart disease in the mother; father and brother who are twins. She lived with her mother and 14-year-old daughter and occasionally lived on the street. The father of the baby was in and out of the picture and was also an alcohol abuser.

The woman, on her first visit, requested that she get assistance in "finally getting clean." Arrangements were made with the local county hospital and the obstetrical department for admission for detoxification. She was admitted 2 days later and discharged 14 days after treatment was initiated. Dilantin was switched to phenobarbital after an initial seizure 8 hours after admission. She was discharged after having made verbal and written agreements about chemical dependency and prenatal care. This took place after two multidisciplinary sessions that involved social services in both the clinic and the hospital, methadone maintenance program workers, public health nurses, the obstetrical service, the nurse-midwife, and pediatric teams. She refused care in the "white-man doctor hospital" and chose to continue prenatal care at the Indian clinic with the nurse-midwife and nurse practitioner there.

She was found at the entrance to the emergency room at the county hospital 7 days after discharge from detoxification with the diagnosis of alcohol withdrawal seizure. During the following 3 months she made it to one prenatal appointment and dropped in without appointments for the rest (four more). Each time she was seen her uterine size correlated to dates. Although clinic and hospital charts stated otherwise, she reiterated closer to the due date that she "did not drink until I was 6 months pregnant." The plan of management was to begin nonstress tests at 32 weeks gestation. Arrangements were made for her at the hospital, but she never showed. Finally, at 35 weeks gestation, she was physically transported by the clinic staff to her nonstress test and taken back to the clinic for a prenatal examination. By 37 weeks she had 3+ pitting edema and a borderline blood pressure (118/86). By the 38-week visit, the Child Protective Services procedure was explained to her and the father of the baby, at which point she became tearful and stated that she did not want her baby taken away.

On 21 February 1985 she delivered a 2420-g girl (Apgars 8,9) over a second degree perineal laceration. The baby was noted to have the facial characteristics of fetal alcohol syndrome (Fig. 1-1) and microcephaly on admission to the nursery. The baby had withdrawal behavior the following day and was displaying seizure activity the next day. The infant received Valium once that night.

The baby remained in the hospital for a total of 8 days until foster care could be found. The infant was placed (after much local Native American community controversy) under the care of the father's family in an adjacent city and was subsequently placed in an infant development program. Three years later, case workers documented a questionable mild delay on the Denver Developmental Scale. She was referred to ENT specialists for oral motor problems (excessive drooling, which the case worker noted had resolved by her third birthday), expressive delay, and a hearing assessment. She was 25-months size by the time she was 34 1/2 months old, and by 36 months she weighed 22 lb.

The mother continued to binge drink and was seen on numerous occasions in and out of the emergency room and the Indian clinic. She was admitted for fever of unknown origin a year later. She died 7 days after admission; the diagnosis was ethanol withdrawal and endocarditis.

* * * * *

CASE ANALYSIS

This case is a clear example of much of the recent literature. Alcohol and polydrug (heroin, Dilantin, Benedryl, and tobacco) use is common among alcohol-dependent pregnant women, as was explained by Jessup and Green,[6] and cannot be overlooked when managing the care of a chemically dependent woman. Because of this, it is difficult to ascertain that alcohol in and of itself was the cause of the outcome. One can readily see the difficulty in isolating alcohol when studying this drug as it pertains to pregnancy.

It was interesting for the staff to hear the woman restate that she had not taken any alcohol until the sixth month despite the recorded knowledge that she was seen in the county hospital on two occasions for binge drinking and withdrawal during her fourth and fifth months. This also demonstrated the woman's inability or reluctance to tell the truth about how much she drank and when she drank.

This case history also served as a springboard for ideas via city hall in this particular city about how and what can be done to assist these types of pregnant women to remain in a drug-free support system. It was obvious that this was the major follow-up problem for this patient and that, had she been discharged to housing that supported "clean" living, she may not have had as much opportunity to return to binging. As it was, there was nowhere to send her in the city, as all of the halfway houses or drug programs were not equipped to take pregnant women or families.

PREVENTION AND CARE OF FETAL ALCOHOL SYNDROME AND FETAL ALCOHOL EFFECTS

Because fetal alcohol syndrome and its effects are preventable, it seems appropriate to review current prevention strategies. It has been over a decade since defects have been known to occur when a pregnant woman consumes large amounts of alcohol. In 1981 the Surgeon General did not know the minimal threshold for these birth defects. Many have since concurred that no threshold of "safe" drinking during pregnancy has been established.

Seegmiller et al. stated that health warning labels on alcoholic beverages are long overdue.[25] Some cities, counties and states have individually set precedents and post health warning signs for pregnant women in restaurants and at point-of-purchase wherever liquor is sold.[26] The United States Senate is presently considering a measure to demand health warning labels all over the U.S.[25]

In caring for the pregnant woman, Jessup and Green recommended early identification and interventions.[6] (Table 1-1 displays some of the medical, historical, and behavioral cues that any practitioner can begin to use with all pregnant clients.) Because alcohol dependence can be frequently associated with polydrug use, Jessup and Green recommended that the drug and alcohol history be used in conjunction with alcohol-oriented questionnaires (the 10-Question Drinking History, or TQDH, by Rosett et al. or the Michigan Alcohol Screening Test [MAST]).

Table 1-1 Medical, Historical, and Behavioral Indicators of Alcohol Abuse and/or Alcohol Dependence

Medical Indicators

Liver disease; hepatomegaly
Pancreatitis
Hypertension
Gastritis; esophagitis
Hematologic disorders
Poor nutritional status
Cardiac arrhythmias; other cardiac disease
Alcoholic myopathy
Ketoacidosis
Neurologic disorders
Intrauterine growth retardation

Historical Indicators

Depressive disorder
Psychiatric treatment or hospitalization
Reference to alcohol or other drug-abusing
  partner
Physician prescription or other procurement
  of psychoactive drug
Multiple emergency room visits
Complicated perinatal history
Low birth weight
Prematurity
FAS or FAE
Foster or other caretaker placement of
  children
Learning disability or hyperactivity in other
  child

Behavioral Indicators

Smell of alcohol on breath
Mood swings
Memory lapses and losses
Difficulty concentrating
Blackouts
Inappropriateness
Irritability or agitation
Depression
Slurry speech
Staggering gait
Bizarre behavior
Loss of job
Decreased job performance
Suicidal feelings, gestures, or attempts
Sexual dysfunction
Conflicts with spouse, family, or friends
Domestic violence
Child abuse and neglect
Automobile accidents or citation arrests
Children with scholastic or behavioral
  problems
Secretiveness or vagueness about personal
  or medical history

Source: Reprinted with permission from *Journal of Psychoactive Drugs* (1987; 19[2]:193–203), Copyright © 1987, Haight-Ashbury Publications.

In addition, pregnant women who have a history of intravenous drug use should be evaluated for their risk for acquired immune deficiency syndrome (AIDS).[6]

Jessup and Green warned against using self-reporting because most addictive women deliberately conceal use or cannot remember the amount used.[6] One experienced Native American social worker learned to double mentally the number given by a woman responding to the question of "How much?" she uses (whether alcohol, cocaine, or heroin).

The suggested intervention for the alcohol-dependent woman is as follows:

1. Statement of the problem. ("I am concerned that you may have a problem with alcohol.")

2. Statement of the indicators of alcohol abuse or dependence. ("Your liver is enlarged; you have been hospitalized for pancreatitis, and you have told me that you were picked up off the street and taken to the hospital. Last week I could smell alcohol on your breath.")

3. Explanation of the possible effects on the fetus and the benefits of abstinence. ("The alcohol that you drink may cause your baby to grow slower and cause other problems in development, like mental retardation. You can reduce or eliminate those problems by stopping drinking . . . .")

4. Expression of concern and a willingness to support recovery efforts. ("I am concerned about your baby and you, and I would like to support you in a decision to stop drinking. Here are some materials to read and then we can talk further . . . .")

5. A referral for treatment of the drinking problem. ("Here is the phone number for the women's alcohol treatment program. You can talk with them about your drinking. Please make an appointment to see them this week or today."[6]

Ideally, both alcohol dependence treatment and perinatal services should be provided in a comprehensive care setting that offers obstetric, pediatric, social work, nutritional, and alcohol-dependence treatment services or referral. When a specific case arises, a member of this multidisciplinary team (the obstetrician, nurse-midwife, or social worker usually, but not always) should serve as a case manager, assuring that services are coordinated and that open communication continues among the providers.

One must also remember the ethical consequences involved in caring for such women. Prenatal noncompliance, child abuse, and neglect have often been documented in this group of women, and ethical dilemmas have recently emerged on whether to report noncompliant women to child protective agencies before delivery. One must decide where one stands on the issues of fetal rights and maternal rights before caring for these women.[6]

Richman, from Toronto, asserted that primary prevention includes (1) health protection (the use of public direct regulatory activities such as regulations regarding the sale and availability of alcohol, warning labels, etc.); (2) disease prevention (services directed to helping reduce the occurrence of fetal alcohol syndrome); and (3) health promotion (activities that can foster positive behavior and good health practices). He believed that attention given to psychologic and sociologic approaches can change attitudes toward drinking more than can just alcohol education, per se.[27]

IMPLICATIONS FOR PRACTICE

Penticuff stated that adaptation or maladaptation to the developmental tasks of pregnancy in the face of the diagnosis of fetal jeopardy is affected by four balancing factors: realistic perception of the pregnancy events, adequate situational supports, adequate problem-solving strategies, and eventual resolution of the high-risk situation.[28] This case is a clear example of maladaptation. Some researchers have concluded that learned helplessness occurs when repeated failure to achieve goals or to reduce stress in spite of one's best efforts produces detrimental behavioral, cognitive, and emotional patterns that eventually arrest problem-solving and produce fatalism.[28,29]

It was clear that the woman was already adapting ineffectively during everyday activities and that this behavior had existed long before the pregnancy. The patient's existence was one of denial, inappropriate affect, resistance, drug use, and impulsive behavior. Many of the behaviors exhibited by this woman are also listed by Jessup and Green as medical and historical indicators of alcohol abuse (e.g., physician prescription for other psychoactive drugs, alcohol on breath, slurry speech, etc.; see Table 1-1). Nevertheless, this woman did initiate a verbal desire for recovery. Pregnancy is marked by motivation to change,[30] but this may prove to be an enormous task for the alcohol/drug-dependent pregnant woman.

The focus for care should be on the self, and discussions around recovery should center on the concept of self-fulfillment rather than self-sacrifice.[6] Jessup also suggested that guilt-inducing language should be avoided and that the expression of hope for the unborn child may be instrumental in the woman's decision to seek treatment.[6] Involvement of the family, especially the father of the baby, may also positively influence the pregnant woman to recovery.[6]

Because denial is such a great part of the pregnant alcohol/drug-dependent woman, compliance can become a major barrier to successful care, as was seen in the case above. Nevertheless, it is the obligation of the health care provider to carry out the treatment-oriented program.[6]

In this era of seemingly growing chemical dependence in our society, it seems fitting that we as obstetrical and primary care practitioners fine-tune our focus to the growing numbers of women who are addicted to drugs of *any* sort for whatever reason. We should assist them in viewing their own self-worth, educate them, and continue to support them as they succeed in producing offspring with a minimum of society-dependent defects.

REFERENCES

1. Abel EL, Sokol RJ. Fetal alcohol syndrome is now leading cause of mental retardation (letter). *Lancet*. 1986;2:1222.

2. Abel EL, Sokol RJ. Incidence of fetal alcohol syndrome and economic impact of FAS-related anomalies. *Drug Alcohol Depend*. 1987;19:51–70.

3. Jones KL, Smith DW. Recognition of the fetal alcohol syndrome in early infancy. *Lancet*. 1973;2:999–1001.

4. Zuckerman BS, Hingson R. Alcohol consumption during pregnancy: a critical review. *Dev Med Child Neurol*. 1986;28:649–661.

5. Breast NT. Fetal alcohol syndrome educator's guide. California State Department of Alcohol & Drug Programs, California Women's Commission on Alcoholism, Fetal Alcohol Syndrome Demonstration Project, October 1985.

6. Jessup M, Green JR. Treatment of the pregnant alcohol-dependent woman. *J Psychoactive Drugs*. 1987;19:193–203.

7. Plant M. *Women, Drinking and Pregnancy*. London, England: Tavistock Publications; 1985.

8. Lemoine PH, Harousseau JP, Borteyru, Menuet JC. Children of alcoholic parents: abnormalities observed in 127 cases. *Quest Med*. 1968;25:476–482.

9. Dobbie J, Philippa B. *Fetal Alcohol Syndrome*. Toronto, Canada: Addiction Research Foundation of Ontario 1978.

10. Hill LM. Effects of drugs and chemicals on the fetus and newborn (second of two parts). *Mayo Clin Proc*. 1984;59:755–765.

11. Ulleland C, Wennberg R, Igo R, Smith N. The offspring of alcoholic mothers. *Pediatr Res*. 1970;4:119–122.

12. Rosett HL. A clinical perspective of the fetal alcohol. *Alcohol Clin Exp Res*. 1980;4:119–122.

13. Kline J, Shrout P, Stein Z, Susser M, Warburton D. Drinking during pregnancy and spontaneous abortion. *Lancet*. 1980;2:176–180.

14. Drinking and pregnancy: not a compatible marriage. *Natl Women's Health Rep*. May/June 1988;9:1–3.

15. Kunitz SJ, Levy JE. Navajos. In: Harwood A, ed. *Ethnicity and Medical Care*. Cambridge, Mass: Harvard University Press; 1981.

16. May PA, Hymbaugh KJ. A pilot project on fetal alcohol syndrome among American Indians. *Alcohol Health Res World*. Winter 1982/1983;7:3–9.

17. Foster JW. Possible maternal auto-immune component in the etiology of the fetal alcohol syndrome. *Dev Med Child Neurol*. 1986;28:649–661.

18. Hammer RP. Alcohol effects on developing neuronal structure. In: West JR, ed. *Alcohol and Brain Development*. Oxford, England: Oxford University Press; 1986.

19. O'Connor MJ, Brill NJ, Sigman M. Alcohol use in primiparous women older than 30 years of age: relation to infant development. *Pediatrics*. 1986;78:444–450.

20. Vorhees CV. Maternal age as a factor in determining the reproductive and behavioral outcome of rats prenatally exposed to ethanol. *Neurotoxicol Teratol*. 1988;10:23–34.

21. Abel EL. Fetal alcohol syndrome: Behavioral teratology. *Psychol Bull*. 1980;87:29–50.

22. Friedler, G. Effects on future generations of paternal exposure to alcohol and other drugs. *Alcohol Health Res World*. Winter 1987/1988;11:126–129.

23. Nelson BK, Brightwell WS, Mackenzie-Taylor DR, Burg JR, Massari VJ. Neurochemical, but not behavioral, deviations in the offspring of rats following prenatal or paternal inhalation exposure to ethanol. *Neurotoxicol Teratol.* 1988;10:15–22.

24. Abel EL. Fetal alcohol syndrome in families. *Neurotoxicol Teratol.* 1988;10:1–2.

25. Seegmiller RE, Carey JC, Fineman RM. The hazards of drinking alcoholic beverages during pregnancy: should the public be warned? *Teratology.* 1987;35:479.

26. Prugh T. Point-of-purchase health warning notices. *Alcohol Res World.* Winter 1987/1988;11:36.

27. Richman A. Prevention of alcohol-related problems: introduction to a symposium. *Drug Alcohol Depend.* 1987;20:9–11.

28. Penticuff JH. Psychologic implications in high risk pregnancy. *Nurs Clin North Am.* March 1982;17:1, 69–78.

29. Martin EP, Seligman WH. *Helplessness: On Depression, Development, and Death.* San Francisco, Ca.: W.H. Freeman and Co.; 1975.

30. Colman L, Colman A. *Pregnancy: The Psychological Experience.* New York, NY: Seabury; 1971.

Chapter 2

Reproductive Loss and Pregnancy Factors

Harriet W. Ferguson

From the beginning of time, women have conceived and carried a pregnancy only to have it terminate in abortion or stillbirth. The cause of many such events may never be known, but the sadness and pain that accompany such losses are well known to women. To embark upon another pregnancy after repeated losses is an effort that blends tentative anticipation with fear and anxiety.

REVIEW OF THE LITERATURE

Historically, stillbirth and pregnancy loss have been described in several passages of the Bible. However, discussion of these topics has been absent from much of the early nursing literature. Older nursing textbooks virtually ignored the topic of pregnancy loss. A review of the index of a standard nursing textbook (Bookmiller and Bowen 1954) shows a brief discussion of abortion, but the book fails to address stillbirth at all.[1] By the next decade the same authors addressed abortion in a similar manner and listed stillbirth in the index. A careful review of the content refers the reader to information about perinatal mortality but excludes specific information regarding the actual event of fetal death.[2] Lerch noted that "an intrauterine fetal death may occur as a complication of placenta insufficiency, maternal diabetes, or accidents to the feto-placental circulation, such as separation or a compressed cord."[3] In 1975, Dickason and Schult provided a somewhat greater discussion of fetal death, but physiologic explanations and nursing care priorities are obvious in their absence.[4] Jensen and Bobak dealt sensitively with issues of loss and grief, but specific scientific information dealing with the causes of pregnancy loss were not included.[5] Most textbooks adequately address the often fatal outcome of cord accidents, placental dysfunction, hemorrhagic complications, and anoxia as rationales for fetal death late in pregnancy.

With the development of a more holistic orientation toward the consumer of health care, nursing literature related to pregnancy loss has gradually emerged with a significant focus toward understanding both the phenomena of loss and grief and the need to provide emotional support for the family. Much of the nursing literature today consists of case studies describing individual patient scenarios experienced by the nurse-author in clinical practice.[6–8] Other pertinent nursing literature describes effective after-the-fact nursing intervention strategies[9–12] or stresses the need for family or maternal support.[13–16] Although these writings were helpful to the nurse's clinical practice, the nursing literature, including textbooks, is devoid of writings that provide insight into the scientific explanations regarding pregnancy loss.

For better understanding of the physiologic events that contribute to pregnancy loss, a review of the literature is helpful. Inasmuch as up to three-quarters of fertilized ova terminate in abortion[17] and 15% of all recognized clinical pregnancies are lost,[18] the issue of pregnancy loss is substantial. Of even more significant concern is repeated pregnancy loss in the same woman.

Chromosomal Abnormalities

Chromosomal abnormalities are one of the factors contributing to pregnancy loss. As gestation time increases, the frequency of chromosomal abnormalities decreases proportionately. Among embryos the frequency is 38 to 75/1000, in fetuses of 15 to 20 weeks gestation the frequency is 27/1000, and among newborns the frequency is 6/1000.[19] This decrease occurs because various chromosomal abnormalities affect the growing pregnancy at different times, some causing early pregnancy loss and others causing stillbirth or birth defects in live-born neonates. DeWald and Michaels reported selected facts regarding the role of chromosomal defects in pregnancy loss.[20] The numerical defect, aneuploidy (any chromosome number greater or less than 46 but not a multiple of the haploid chromosome number of 23), as in Turner's or Kleinfelter's syndromes, is rarely associated with recurrent miscarriages. Another numerical defect, polyploidy (chromosome numbers that are greater than 46 but always exact multiples of the haploid chromosome number of 23), similarly contributes rarely to recurrent abortion. Structural defects such as deletions (the loss of a portion of any chromosome) and duplications (replication of two or more copies of one or more genes within the same chromosome) are not implicated in recurrent miscarriages. However, an inversion, a structural defect in which there are breaks within the same chromosome, is sometimes related to recurrent miscarriages. Translocation is another structural defect wherein two chromosomes become attached and act as one chromosome; this constitutes the most common type of chromosome abnormality in women who have repeated miscarriages. Of significance, then, is the need for extensive genetic counseling in women who have had repeated miscarriages and adequate laboratory analysis of the products of conception after the miscarriage.

Structural Defects

Long recognized as a cause of repeated pregnancy loss is the structural defect of cervical incompetence. The incidence has historically been cited as 3/1000 deliveries.[21] Rock and Murphy reported that a recent rise to 5/1000 seems to be unrelated to the increasing numbers of elective abortions.[22] In addition to traditional cerclage procedures, these clinicians cite the use of the Smith-Hodge pessary to change the weight distribution of the pregnant uterus and bedrest as useful interventions.

Structural uterine defects, congenital in nature, have been recognized as a factor contributing to midtrimester pregnancy loss. In the unicornous or didelphic uterus, each successive pregnancy is sustained longer than the previous one until a viable outcome results.[22] However, since the septum may be the site of implantation in the bicornous uterus, Rock and Murphy found an increase in early pregnancy loss; unlike other researchers, they also described repeated early pregnancy loss in the presence of a double uterus. Because research has reported mixed findings about how uterine structural defects contribute to pregnancy loss, it seems appropriate that evaluation of other contributing factors be conducted before any surgery.

The presence of intrauterine adhesions may contribute to early pregnancy loss because of diminished uterine capacity or because of insufficient endometrium to support fetal growth.[22] Often a hypoestrogenic environment following birth or miscarriage fosters the growth of such adhesions. In 1981, March and Israel reported an 87% subsequent term pregnancy rate when the woman was treated with hysteroscopic lysis of adhesions.[23] However, other researchers have found a 50% subsequent success rate when the treatment was lysis of adhesions followed by the insertion of an intrauterine device or Foley catheter and a course of exogenous estrogen.[24]

Repetitive pregnancy loss related to the presence of uterine fibroids is estimated at 18%.[25] In the presence of fibromyomas, diminished blood supply to the growing fetus and placenta may contribute to pregnancy loss. Buttram and Reiter stated that successful pregnancy after myoectomy may be dependent, in part, on the location and size of the tumors removed.[26] Babaknia et al. reported a 50% term pregnancy rate after myomectomy for repeated pregnancy loss.[27]

Infectious Processes

Known to contribute to potentially fatal chorioamnionitis are numerous bacterial or viral organisms, perhaps the most infamous of which is ß-hemolytic streptococcus. Certain other organisms have been studied in an attempt to link their presence to the causes of repeated pregnancy loss. Mycoplasmas, small nonviral organisms often found in both male and female reproductive systems, were recovered from amniotic fluid samples via intrauterine pressure transducers by Cassells et al.[28] Thirty-five percent of women with overt symptoms of amnionitis and 8% of women with unsuspected infection were positive for *Mycoplasma hominis*, and 50% of both groups were infected with *Ureaplasma urealyticum*.[29] Research supports the belief that the presence of either *Mycoplasma* or *Ureaplasma* places the expectant mother in a high-risk category for a poor outcome.[30] Until an absolute cause-and-effect relationship can be established, an assessment for the presence of both organisms should be conducted in couples who have experienced two or more pregnancy losses.

When *Toxoplasma gondii*, a protozoan, infects the healthy adult the results are usually mild. However, its propensity for congenital transmission in the acute primary phase makes this disease of great concern. During early pregnancy, the trophoblast constitutes a fairly effective resistant barrier but, when the fetus is affected, the results are often severe.[30] The fetus is more often affected when the infection occurs during the third trimester and, while the fetus is often spared, the effects can be devastating. No certain link has been made between this infection and recurrent pregnancy loss, but any woman who has had recurrent abortions should be serologically evaluated. If abortion occurs, careful laboratory analysis of the products of conceptions should be conducted if the woman has had a positive serologic test.

Hormonal Factors

Recurrent pregnancy loss has often been ascribed to "hormone problems." Pernoll et al. stated that studies from the 1950s and 1960s seem to support the notion that one of the leading causes of repeated early pregnancy loss was hypothyroidism.[31] However, Maxson contended that this is a rare event, believing that research design flaws may have caused bias in the findings that led to the earlier conclusion.[32] Serum thyroid-stimulating hormone (TSH) and free thyroxine measurements can readily detect thyroid dysfunction and are appropriate tests for women who have had two or more spontaneous abortions, although the link between the two is minimal.

Although professionals often connect carbohydrate intolerance with recurrent miscarriage, Rock and Zacur found no data to support the belief that subclinical or adequately controlled diabetes is implicated.[33] There is, however, clear evidence that insulin-dependent women whose glucose levels are out of control do have an increased spontaneous abortion rate.[34,35] Maxson suggested that, unless a woman has had an unexplained second or third trimester pregnancy loss or has signs of diabetes, a routine glucose tolerance test is not warranted.[32] However, in practice, this test is often done as a routine screen and serves as an early warning to client and health care provider alike.

The hormonal problem most closely related to pregnancy loss is luteal phase inadequacy. Research by Grant et al. in 1959 and by Botella-Llusia in 1962 indicated that between 38% and 60% of women with consecutive abortions had a poorly developed secretory endometrium.[36,37] Of women with luteal phase inadequacy, Daly et al. found that 16% had hyperprolactinemia.[38] Luteal phase inadequacy can be produced by hyperandrogenemia; although the link between this state and pregnancy loss is unclear, Maxson suggested assessment of androgen levels in women who have overt symptoms of androgen excess.[32]

Environmental Concerns

In recent years the relationship of environment to human health and subsequently to pregnancy outcome has emerged as an issue. Pregnancy loss because of exposure to potential fetotoxic substances in the expectant mother's home, workplace, or community has spurred the interest of consumers and health care providers alike. Substances known to be potentially lethal are chloroquine, antineoplastic agents, and heavy metals; those that are suspect are anesthetic gases and oral antidiabetic agents, while polychlorinated biphenyls may possible be linked to fatal fetotoxicity.[39]

Autoimmune Disease

Finally, the relationship between recurrent intrauterine death and autoimmune disease has been investigated. Studies reported by delJunco resulted in confounding findings regarding the role played by systemic lupus erythematosus (SLE) in pregnancy loss.[40,41] There is an increase in intrauterine death in women following the onset of SLE,[42] but the rates vary from study to study. In research on both spontaneous abortion and stillbirth, the rate of intrauterine death ranges from 11.2 to 46.2%; SLE is known to result in other adverse pregnancy outcomes such as intrauterine growth retardation, prematurity, and neonatal lupus.[40,41] How women with lupus anticoagulant are predisposed to pregnancy loss warrants future research; currently, suspicion has been raised about its contribution. Additionally, while the relationship of anticardiolipin antibody to pregnancy loss is suspect, the reported research may have sampling and design flaws so that no cause and effect conclusions can be drawn.[40,41] No relationships between rheumatoid arthritis and pregnancy loss has been established.[40,41]

* * * * *

CASE STUDY

With understandably mixed feelings, D.H. sought early prenatal care for this pregnancy. She was in good health at the time and, aside from having been treated at age 16 for gonorrhea, gave no significant personal history. A family history revealed one aunt with hypertension. She was gravida VII, full term pregnancies II, premature births III, abortions I, living children II.

At age 17 D.H.'s first pregnancy had ended with a spontaneous vaginal birth of a small-for-gestational-age male infant. During the next year, an early pregnancy loss terminated her second pregnancy at 13 weeks. Eighteen months later she delivered a stillborn female at 31 weeks following a placental abruption. The fourth pregnancy 2 years later produced another small-for-gestational age male delivered vaginally after successful hospitalization for preterm labor. Two years later the fifth pregnancy ended at 31 weeks gestation with the birth of a stillborn female via emergency cesarean section for placental abruption. Two years later the scenario repeated itself with the sixth pregnancy ending exactly as had the fifth—the birth of a stillborn female via emergency cesarean section for placental abruption at 31 weeks.

Although it was evident that D.H. had mixed feelings about investing energy in hopes of a positive outcome for this pregnancy, she was extremely compliant and came for prenatal visits to her private obstetrician faithfully every 2 weeks. Weekly nonstress testing began in the third trimester with two reactive tests at 31 and 32 weeks gestation. In week 33, however, several spontaneous prolonged decelerations were noted; when the test was repeated the next day, the same decelerations appeared. A biophysical profile scoring was then performed, which demonstrated a small amount of amniotic fluid present, yielding a total score of 6 (Table 2-1). Further findings showed a fetus that was small for gestational age. D.H. was admitted to the hospital for observation and for further studies to determine which intervention strategies would provide the optimal outcome for mother and baby.

Table 2-1 Patient's Biophysical Profile Scores by Weeks

	Week 33	Week 34	Week 35
Fetal breathing movements	2	2	2
Fetal activity	2	2	2
Fetal tone	2	2	2
Amniotic fluid volume	0	0	2
Fetal heart reactivity	0	2	2
Total score	6	8	10

Source: Patient data

The initial nursing history provided data that were helpful in planning D.H.'s care. She stated, "It's hard to have a good outlook when you've had so many disappointments at the time of birth. I'm so worried about my children and my husband, too. You know, he has to work and there's no one to help care for the children. He doesn't even know how to cook." On physical examination D.H. measured 64 in. She began the pregnancy at 172 lb, but she now weighed 199 lb. She denied the use of cigarettes, alcohol, or unprescribed drugs. A review of systems was normal but showed a trace of edema in both ankles, +3 deep tendon reflexes, and blood pressure of 131/82. No history of infectious processes during the course of pregnancy was elicited.

Laboratory testing revealed a slightly low red blood cell count at 3.8, a hemoglobin level of 12.3 g, a hematocrit of 36.1%, and a normal differential; coagulation studies were all satisfactory. Serology was negative; electrolytes and liver enzymes were within normal limits. A 24-hour urine showed satisfactory volume, was negative for creatinine, and had a trace of protein. A routine urinalysis showed the presence of 3+ bacteria, and a culture and sensitivity demonstrated the presence of more than 100,000 *Escherichia coli*. Immediate intravenous ampicillin therapy was begun.

Monitoring of D.H.'s blood pressure showed vacillating readings throughout the day, ranging from 98/68 to 140/92. Bed rest in the left lateral position was maintained with consistent compliance by the patient. Fetal heart tones were recorded every 4 hours and remained between 130 and 150 beats per minute. Fetal activity has long been the benchmark of fetal health, with at least 10 fetal movements in 12 hours predictive of a positive outcome.[43] D.H. counted more than 15 movements daily. Daily nonstress tests demonstrated good fetal heart reactivity in response to fetal activity as well as good variability. Only an occasional uterine contraction was noted. A daily biophysical profile score showed a rise from 6 in week 33 to 8 and finally to 10 in week 35 (Table 2-1). Amniocentesis on admission showed the L/S ratio to be 1.5:1.

Nursing strategies gleaned from the nursing literature were aimed at promoting safety, providing an opportunity for D.H. to discuss concerns, and involving her actively in care by counting fetal movements and recording intake and output. Support for the nursing staff's efforts was provided by the social worker, who spent at least one-half hour per day with the patient. Mr. H. was a military career person and was able to arrange for an emergency leave to be at home with his children during their mother's hospitalization. Even so, D.H. felt uneasy and anxious about the children, so arrangements were made for several afternoon visits. At these visits D.H. helped the children with their homework and seemed pleased with the pictures and posters that they made and placed on the walls in her room.

After a hospital stay of 8 days during which her blood pressure was stable and the biophysical profile score improved (see Table 2-1), D.H. was discharged to be followed twice a week as an outpatient. At 35 weeks gestation, another amniocentesis was performed and lungs were noted to be mature. Repeat ultrasound studies indicated that the fetus was not severely growth retarded, so D.H. was subsequently readmitted to the hospital for a repeat cesarean section the next morning.

DeVore and Platt provided a differentiation between two types of intrauterine growth retardation.[44] Symmetrical intrauterine growth retardation occurs before the last trimester and is related to delays in both body and brain growth. It is most commonly seen in the fetus with a congenital infection, chromosomal or structural anomalies, or early environmental insults. Asymmetrical growth retardation (as seen in D.H.'s fetus) is known as head-sparing, is typically encountered during the third trimester, and is related to compromised uteroplacental blood supply.[45]

At the time of this admission, D.H.'s anxiety had mounted and her blood pressure had increased to 140/90. D.H. had delivered her other babies at various hospitals throughout the country as she accompanied her husband in his mobile military career; no previous hospital records were readily available. A record review might have provided insight into her blood pressure as a primigravida, whether preeclampsia was related to the growth retardation seen in her children who survived, and whether the abruptions that occurred with the first two fetal deaths were related to hypertension.

Spinal anesthesia was administered for the cesarean section; however, D.H. was able to feel pain upon incision. General anesthesia was then administered. A low transverse incision was performed and a 1720-g male neonate was delivered with Apgar scores of 7 and 7. No gross abnormalities were observed; oxygen was given to the newborn, and he was immediately transported to the newborn intensive care unit because of his small-for-gestational age (SGA) status.

The surgery was completed uneventfully, and the patient was moved to the recovery room, where her blood pressure stabilized at about 136/90 and all other vital signs were satisfactory. At the end of 2 hours she was able to return to her room.

*   *   *   *   *

CASE ANALYSIS

Considering the nature of D.H.'s prenatal course, her recovery was remarkable. She encountered no complications. However, early assessment of the newborn detected what was believed to be tetralogy of Fallot. He was quickly transferred to the nearest children's hospital where further evaluation revealed that the defect was transposition of the great vessels. This posed the greatest challenge to the nursing staff as they supported the family through this new crisis.

D.H. had periods of tears and sadness and self-blame. She stated several times that "there must be something wrong with me—I can't even have a baby like other women can." The primary nurse offered many opportunities for D.H. to ventilate concerns. Physicians and the social worker worked cooperatively with nurses to assure D.H. that assigning blame for such an outcome was inappropriate. The family was involved to the extent possible to foster D.H.'s attachment to her new son. Mr. H. traveled back and forth between the two hospitals bringing news of the baby's condition. Telephone conferences between D.H. and the baby's physicians and photographs of the baby helped to promote D.H.'s ability to cope with the stress. Although it was important for the children to see their new brother, D.H. believed that they would be frightened to see all of the equipment surrounding the tiny baby. Instead of a visit, selected photographs were shared with the children and a visit would wait until D.H. could accompany them to the hospital to see the new baby.

On the fifth postpartum day, D.H. was ready for discharge; her husband and children came to the hospital for the big event. An early morning phone call to the children's hospital indicated that the baby was stable, so the family planned to visit the baby on the way home. The family would await continued medical evaluation of the baby regarding the need for surgical intervention. Since the newborn's care was being provided by a children's hospital unrelated to the mother's institution, the nursing staff was never apprised of the final outcome for the baby.

IMPLICATIONS FOR PRACTICE

Although this pregnancy resulted in a more positive albeit not perfect outcome, repeated pregnancy loss poses a serious dilemma for clients and health care providers alike. Nurses are in a unique position to provide health counseling in a variety of settings. When women with a history of repeated pregnancy losses are encountered, referral for complete evaluation and follow-up is crucial. In this case, because D.H.'s husband was in the military, frequent moves about the country were the norm and no liaisons were developed with a family physician or a personal obstetrician until this time. For this reason the details of the past obstetrical history were unclear. No connections were ever made between factors that may contribute to pregnancy loss and D.H.'s circumstances. Therefore, it is essential for this young woman to have further on-going evaluation by an obstetrician skilled in high-risk care and that access to past records be possible. A referral was made to the community health nurse for home visits to reinforce D.H.'s continuing care and to support the family as the new baby's needs evolve.

REFERENCES

1. Bookmiller MM, Bowen GL. *Textbook of Obstetrics and Obstetric Nursing.* 2nd ed. Philadelphia, Pa.: W.B. Saunders Co.; 1954.
2. Bookmiller MM, Bowen GL, Carpenter D. *Textbook of Obstetrics and Obstetric Nursing.* 5th ed. Philadelphia, Pa.: W.B. Saunders Co.; 1967.
3. Lerch C. *Maternity Nursing.* 2nd ed. St. Louis, Mo: C.V. Mosby Co.; 1974.
4. Dickason EJ, Schult MO. *Maternal and Infant Care: A Text for Nurses.* New York, NY: McGraw-Hill Book Co.; 1975.

5. Jensen MD, Bobak IM. *Maternity and Gynecologic Care: The Nurse and the Family.* St. Louis, Mo: C.V. Mosby Co.; 1985.

6. Floyd CC. Pregnancy after reproductive failure. *Am J Nursing.* 1981;11:2050–2053.

7. Whitaker CM. Death before birth. *Am J Nurs.* 1986;157–158.

8. Herbert WNP, Stuart NN, Butler LS. Electronic fetal heart rate monitoring with intrauterine fetal demise. *J Obstet Gynecol Neonatal Nurs.* 1987;16:249–252.

9. Kowalski K. When birth becomes death. *AORN J.* 1983;38(1):57–61, 64—65.

10. Sadler ME. When your patient's baby dies before birth. *RN.* August 1987;28–29.

11. Grabauskas P, Neithercut C, Pacek C, Sparks M. Helping the parents after a baby's death. *RN.* August 1987;31–32.

12. Hutti MH. A quick reference table of interventions to assist families to cope with pregnancy loss or neonatal death. *Birth.* 1988;15(1):33–35.

13. Mina CF. A program for helping grieving parents. *Am J Maternal Child Nurs.* 1985;10(2):118–121.

14. Ilse S, Furrh CB. Development of a comprehensive follow up care plan after perinatal and neonatal loss. *J Perinatal Neonatal Nurs.* 1988;2(2):23–33.

15. Kavanaugh K. Infants weighing less than 500 grams at birth: providing parental support. *J Perinatal Neonatal Nurs.* 1988;2(2):58–66.

16. Maguire DP, Skoolicas SJ. Developing a bereavement follow-up program. *J Perinatal Neonatal Nurs.* 1988;2(2):67–77.

17. Miller JF, Williamson E, Glue J, Gordon YB, Grudzinskas JG, Sytces A. Fetal loss after implantation: a prospective study. *Lancet.* 1980;2:554.

18. Poland BJ, Miller JR, Harris M, Livingston J. Spontaneous abortion: a study of 1,961 women and their conceptuses. *Acta Obstet Gynecol Scand Suppl.* 1981;102.

19. Hook EB, Porter IH. *Population Cytogenetics: Studies in Humans.* New York, NY: Academic Press; 1977.

20. DeWald GW, Michels VV. Recurrent miscarriages: cytogenetic causes and genetic counseling of affected families. *Clin Obstet Gynecol.* 1986;29:865–885.

21. Baden WF, Baden EE. Cervical incompetence: current therapy. *Am J Obstet Gynecol.* 1960;79:545.

22. Rock JA, Murphy AA. Anatomic abnormalities. *Clin Obstet Gynecol.* 1986;29:886–911.

23. March CM, Israel R. Gestational outcome following hysteroscopic lysis of adhesions. *Fertil Steril.* 1981;36:455.

24. Schenker JG, Margalioth EJ. Intrauterine adhesions: an updated appraisal. *Fertil Steril.* 1982;37:593.

25. Robbins SA, Shapira AA. Uterotyboplasty. In: Robbins LL, ed. *Golden's Diagnostic Roentgenology.* Baltimore, Md.: Williams & Wilkins Co.; 1967;3.

26. Buttram VC, Reiter RC. Uterine leiomyomata: etiology, symptomatology and management. *Fertil Steril.* 1981;36:433.

27. Babaknia A, Rock JA, Jones HW. Pregnancy success following abdominal myomectomy for infertility. *Fertility-Sterility.* 1978;30:644.

28. Cassells GH, Davis RO, Waites KB, et al. Isolation of *Mycoplasma hominis* and *Ureaplasma urealyticum* from amniotic fluid at 16–20 weeks of gestation: potential effects on outcome of pregnancy. *Sex Transm Dis.* 1983;10:294.

29. Blanco JD, Gibbs RS, Malherbe H, Strickland-Cholmley, St Clair PJ, Castaneda YS. A controlled study of genital mycoplasmas in amniotic fluid from patients with intra-amniotic infections. *J Infect Dis.* 1983;147:650.

30. Byrn FW, Gibson M. Infectious causes of recurrent pregnancy loss. *Clin Obstet Gynecol.* 1986;29:925–940.

31. Pernoll ML, King CR, Prescott G. Genetics for the clinical obstetrician-gynecologist. *Obstet Gynecol Annu.* 1980;9:1.

32. Maxson WS. Hormonal causes of recurrent abortion. *Clin Obstet Gynecol.* 1986;29(4):941–952.

33. Rock JA, Zacur HA. The clinical management of repeated early pregnancy wastage. *Fertil Steril.* 1983;39:123.

34. Crane JP, Wahl N. The role of maternal diabetes in repetitive abortion. *Fertil Steril.* 1981;36:477.

35. Miodovnik M, Sillman C, Holroyde JC, Butler JB, Wendel JS, Siddiqui TA. Elevated maternal glycohemoglobin in early pregnancy and spontaneous abortion among insulin dependent diabetic women. *Am J Obstet Gynecol.* 1985;153:439.

36. Grant A, McBride WG, Moyes JM. Luteal phase defects in abortion. *Int J Fertil.* 1959;4:323.

37. Botella-Llusia J. The endometrium in repeated abortions. *Int J Fertil.* 1962;7:147.

38. Daly DC, Walters CA, Soto-Albors CE, Riddick DH. Endometrial biopsy during treatment of luteal phase deficits is predictive of therapeutic outcome. *Fertil Steril.* 1983;40:305.

39. Pernoll ML. Abortion induced by chemicals encountered in the environment. *Clin Obstet Gynecol.* 1986;29(4):953–958.

40. DelJunco DJ. Association of autoimmune conditions with recurrent intrauterine death. *Clin Obstet Gynecol.* 1986;29:959–975.

41. DelJunco DJ. *The Relationship between Rheumatoid Arthritis and Reproductive Function.* Houston: The University of Texas School of Public Health; 1986. Thesis.

42. Syrop CH, Varner MW. Systemic lupus erythematosus. *Clin Obstet Gynecol.* 1983;26:547.

43. Sadovsky E, Yaffe H. Daily fetal movement recording and fetal prognosis. *Obstet Gynecol.* 1973;41:845.

44. DeVore GR, Platt LD. Diagnosis of intrauterine growth retardation: the use of sequential measurements of fetal growth parameters. *Clin Obstet Gynecol.* 1987;30(4).

45. Hadlock FP, Deter RL, Harrist RB. Sonographic detection of abnormal fetal growth patterns. *Clin Obstet Gynecol.* 1984;27(2).

ADDITIONAL BIBLIOGRAPHY

Borg S, Lasker J. *When Pregnancy Fails—Families Coping with Miscarriage, Stillbirth and Infant Death.* 1981.

Chapter 3

Abruptio Placenta Complicated by Disseminated Intravascular Coagulopathy

Ruth Tucker

Disseminated intravascular coagulopathy (DIC) is a secondary pathologic state caused by excessive thrombin activity.[1] DIC is defined as a state where there is rapid, inappropriate intravascular consumption of procoagulants.[2] Multiple disseminated thromboses block the microcirculation, causing ischemic tissue damage.[3] DIC is manifested by varying degrees of bleeding and is known by other terms such as defibrination syndrome; hypofibrinogenemia, consumption coagulopathy, and intravascular coagulation and fibrinolysis (ICF).[4]

REVIEW OF THE LITERATURE

Pathophysiology of DIC

Activation of a cascading series of clotting factors maintains normal hemostasis.[3,5] The coagulation cascade is a sequence of enzymatic reactions that result in fibrin formation.[6] Various checks and balances exist within the body to regulate the blood-clotting mechanisms. In DIC, this delicate balance fails, with a resultant systemic rather than local generation of thrombin and plasmin. Release of procoagulant substances into the blood by a primary source initiates the general coagulation activity.[7]

DIC may result from activation of either the extrinsic or the intrinsic coagulation pathway, or a combination of both. Obstetric conditions believed to initiate the extrinsic pathway include abruptio placentae, retained dead fetus syndrome, and pregnancy-induced hypertension (PIH). These conditions release thromboplastin into the maternal bloodstream (Fig. 3-1).[8]

Sepsis, which damages the endothelial cells, activates the intrinsic coagulation pathway. Intra-amniotic saline infusions and amniotic fluid emboli trigger both pathways.[8] DIC seems to occur in normal labor as a transitory state peaking at the time of birth.[9]

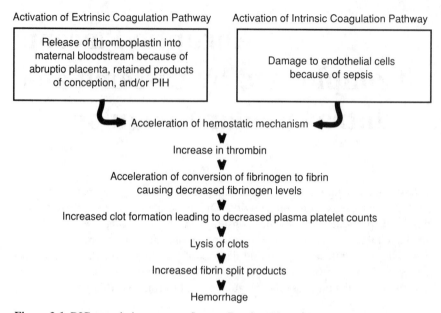

Activation of Extrinsic Coagulation Pathway   Activation of Intrinsic Coagulation Pathway

Release of thromboplastin into maternal bloodstream because of abruptio placenta, retained products of conception, and/or PIH

Damage to endothelial cells because of sepsis

Acceleration of hemostatic mechanism

Increase in thrombin

Acceleration of conversion of fibrinogen to fibrin causing decreased fibrinogen levels

Increased clot formation leading to decreased plasma platelet counts

Lysis of clots

Increased fibrin split products

Hemorrhage

Figure 3-1 DIC coagulation process. *Source:* Reprinted from *Maternal Newborn Nursing,* ed 3 (p 778) by SB Olds, ML London, and PA Ladewig with permission of Addison-Wesley Publishing Company, © 1988.

Blood levels of plasma coagulation factors and platelets are determined by their relative rate of consumption and production. The rate of consumption is governed by the intensity of thrombin generation and the particular mechanism that initiated the DIC. The rate of production is determined by the ability of the liver and bone marrow to replace the depleted plasma coagulation factors and platelets.[4]

The clotting cascade is always accompanied by a concurrent plasmin generation. Thrombosis occurs when the intravascular clotting process dominates in the presence of minimal fibrinolysis. This process consumes the coagulation factors and platelets. Hemorrhage occurs when fibrinolysis dominates and the fibrin/fibrinogen degradation products (FDPs) are elevated. The antihemostatic effect of FDPs interferes with the formation of firm fibrin clots. A vicious cycle results, followed by further bleeding. Occasionally, hemorrhage and thrombosis will occur simultaneously.[7] DIC may be graded according to severity from stage 1 to stage 3, with stage 3 being the most severe.[10]

Tissue damage from ischemia, either localized or generalized, is due to thrombi in the microcirculation. Impaired blood oxygenation, decreased urine output, and impaired liver function may result from organ dysfunction caused by tissue damage.[11] Microcirculation blockage coupled with the production of kinins (potent vasodilators) seems to be responsible for the hypotension and shock present in some cases of DIC.[4] The kinins have a direct relationship to the contraction of smooth muscle tissue and to the dilatation of blood vessels as well to blood coagulation and fibrinolysis.[12]

Abruptio Placenta and DIC

Not only is pregnancy suspected of predisposing a woman to DIC, but pregnancy also presents unique triggering mechanisms (i.e., abruptio placentae, PIH, amniotic fluid embolus, dead fetus syndrome).[13] The most prevalent cause of DIC in obstetrics is abruptio placentae, or premature separation of a normally implanted placenta. Approximately 50% of maternal deaths due to hemorrhage occur after abruptio placentae. The frequency of abruption is 1 of 85 to 1 of 250 deliveries.[14,15]

The maternal compartments of the placenta (intervillous spaces) have a blood flow of approximately 600 ml/min near term.[16] Severance of the arteries and veins responsible for carrying blood to the intervillous spaces occurs with abruption. The pregnant uterus is unable to contract and retract, which are the usual controls of bleeding after delivery. If the abruption encompasses more than 30 to 40%, severe fetal hypoxia occurs, which often leads to lethal consequences for the fetus.[16] If fetal death does occur, the maternal blood deficit may be estimated to be at least 1000 to 2000 ml.[4]

The site of separation has clinical importance. Marginal placental separations bleed from the veins at the edge of the placenta or from the intervillous space. This is usually less serious than central separation, which involves disruption of the arteries causing a high-pressure arterial bleed. An expanded retroplacental hemorrhage results.[4]

Abruption may be graded based on severity from I to III. Grade I, the mildest, is usually diagnosed retrospectively. Grade II, considered intermediate, has the classical symptoms, with signs of uterine hypertonicity. The fetus is still alive. Grade III is the most severe, and fetal death has occurred. It may be further designated as grade IIIa, no coagulopathy present, or grade IIIb, in which coagulopathy is present.[16,17] There is a direct correlation between the severity of the clinical picture and the degree of placental separation.[16] Severe coagulation defects are more common with grade III abruption.[13]

Pathologically, three forms of abruption have been described: revealed, concealed, and mixed. Free vaginal bleeding occurs with revealed. In concealed, blood is trapped among the placenta, membranes, and uterine wall. Blood may pass into the amniotic fluid, causing a port-wine staining, or into the uterine musculature, causing uteroplacental apoplexy (Couvelaire uterus). Couvelaire uterus is caused by an accumulation of blood in the myometrium and results in a purplish discoloration and uterine rigidity.[8] Hemorrhage that is partly revealed and partly concealed is considered mixed.[16]

In addition to vaginal bleeding, symptoms for revealed abruption include backache or abdominal discomfort and localized uterine tenderness. With concealed bleeding, there is the sudden onset of abdominal pain and a boardlike uterus, which is tender and enlarged. Tetany of the uterus with abruptio placentae may result from excessive bradykinins. After delivery in the presence of DIC, uterine atony may occur as bradykinins are consumed.[18] Fetal parts may not be palpable, and fetal heart sounds may be absent. Signs and symptoms of hemorrhagic shock may be present.

The placenta itself contains inhibitors of both coagulation and fibrinolysis. These inhibitors are essential for the efficient functioning of the uteroplacental unit. With placental separation in abruption, these usual safeguards against coagulation are gone. Thromboplastins and fibrinolytic activators enter the maternal circulation, and the DIC cycle begins.[16] The highest concentration of tissue thromboplastin isolated in mammalian tissue is found in trophoblastic cells.[14]

Significantly lower adenosine diphosphatase activity in women with abruptio placenta than in control groups has been identified.[19] A trend toward intrauterine growth retardation (IUGR) was also noted. These findings suggest that an abnormal retroplacental circulation exists in pregnancies complicated by abruptio placentae and IUGR before there are clinical symptoms.[19,20]

Blood coagulation factors, the majority of which are produced by the liver, increase as gestation advances.[21] The hypercoagulabile state of pregnancy is designed to compensate for blood loss and to provide rapid hemostasis after delivery. However, this protective mechanism leaves the pregnant patient vulnerable to DIC and thromboembolic complications.[22]

Overt coagulopathy due to DIC and fibrinolysis occurs in approximately 10% of patients with abruption. The uterus becomes hypotonic in 20% of those cases.[16] The levels of FDPs are extremely elevated.

Hemostasis at the placental site is dependent on myometrial function and adequate amounts of clottable fibrinogen. Intravenous fluids, oxytocics, and bimanual compression of the uterus will usually control uterine atony. Surgical intervention is rarely necessary.[2,16] However, a rare form of uterine dysfunction that is resistant to oxytocics may ensue.[16]

Smaller placental separations may pose no particular problems in labor. However, more extensive separations are associated with uterine hypertonicity, which may cause rapid cervical effacement and dilatation.[2,16]

The systemic microvascular circulation is compromised by shock and DIC. Tissue hypoxia, metabolic disturbances, and increased vascular fragility result. Potential complications of DIC for the obstetric patient include postpartum hemorrhage, renal and hepatic failure, pulmonary hypoperfusion (shock-lung syndrome), and intracranial hemorrhage.[16]

In patients with abruption and a live fetus, the development of fetal distress is a constant concern. Blood loss and uterine hypertonicity are primary contributors to fetal heart rate changes.[23] In addition to fetal tachycardia, a loss of beat-to-beat variability may be noted.[15]

Aggressive management for placental abruption may increase the neonatal morbidity associated with prematurity. With abruptio placentae, DIC can be self-limiting.[24] If the fetus is alive and obviously immature, a cautious, conservative approach may be considered if there is evidence of maternal and fetal stability.[25] Duration of the gestation, birth weight, and the degree of separation of the placenta are critical factors to be considered in determining neonatal outcome. Aggressive intervention is necessary if both the mother and fetus are in jeopardy, even if the fetus is immature.[26,27]

Diagnosis of DIC in Obstetrics

Ecchymoses, hematuria, or oozing at the intravenous insertion site are early signs of DIC.[28] Specific laboratory findings from rapid screening tests will confirm the diagnosis. Platelet count, partial thromboplastin time, prothrombin time, and fibrinogen are assessed when DIC is suspected. FDPs are useful for the assessment of fibrinolysis.[2] Elevated FDPs confirm the presence of DIC but are not considered diagnostic.[29]

Antithrombin III (AT III), a major inhibitor of thrombin and thrombin generation, is the most sensitive laboratory parameter for diagnosis. When consumption exceeds production of thrombin, AT III levels decline. During normal pregnancy, AT III levels remain unchanged. AT III "reserves" seem to be reduced during pregnancy. Therefore, the predictive value of finding a low AT III value increases during pregnancy.[7]

Ultrasound may be helpful to rule out placenta previa and to identify larger hematomas. An important indication of retroplacental bleeding is a bulging of the placenta into the uterine cavity.[30,31] However, small abruptions may be missed. Special function tests (renal, pulmonary, liver) assess the effects of DIC on target organs.

Treatment of DIC in Obstetrics

Vigorous restoration of the circulation is stressed.[32] With adequate perfusion of major organs, the reticuloendothelial system is better able to remove the activated coagulation factors, circulating fibrin, and FDPs. Removal of these substances aids in the restoration of normal homeostasis. Death, in most cases of hemorrhage, results from poor tissue perfusion due to hypovolemia rather than from a lack of circulating red cells.[29,33] Saline solutions, such as lactated Ringer's, are widely acceptable plasma expanders. Whole fresh frozen plasma, providing fibrinogen, antithrombin III, and coagulation factors V and VII, as well as maximal volume, is recommended for plasma replacement with obstetric hemorrhage. Sufficient control of symptoms of DIC in the field of obstetrics may be obtained with AT III concentrate without the risk of increased bleeding.[34]

If no liver damage has occurred, plasma factors usually reach normal levels within 24 to 48 hours, with spontaneous resolution of coagulation defects. Two to 7 days may be needed for platelet counts to return to normal.[32] The process of producing and releasing mature platelets by the bone marrow is a slower process than platelet production.[11] Healthy women have a bone marrow reserve capable of providing compensatory increased output of platelets in this instance. Large amounts of stored blood used in a short span of time may result in a temporary dilution of platelets. Cryoprecipitate may be used if fibrinogen levels are very low.

Heparin therapy is rarely indicated in obstetric hemorrhage. Heparin may significantly increase the potential for life-threatening hemorrhage in the presence of abruptio placentae.[4,32]

Efforts should be made to eliminate the cause of excessive generation of thrombin. Vaginal delivery places less stress on hemostatic mechanisms than does cesarean delivery. The benefits of uterine stimulation with an oxytocic to provide a vaginal delivery override the risks.[32] Regional anesthesia (caudal, epidural, or spinal) is contraindicated because of the risk of hematoma formation, which may cause permanent nerve damage.[4]

* * * * *

CASE STUDY

A 27-year-old white woman, at 35 weeks gestation, gravida IV, para I, abortus II, was admitted to the observation area of the labor and delivery unit for conservative management of possible premature labor. Her first and second pregnancies had been aborted electively. The third pregnancy had been delivered by cesarean section because of cephalopelvic disproportion. An amniocentesis to determine fetal lung maturity had already been scheduled in preparation for a repeat cesarean delivery and bilateral tubal ligation.

This was an unplanned pregnancy. The patient was separated from the father of the baby, whose whereabouts were unknown. No family members were living in the area. Financial aid had been refused by the patient, who received room and board for housekeeping chores.

Gestational age was determined to be 35 weeks by size and 38 weeks by dates. This size-date discrepancy of 3 weeks was consistent with earlier antepartum examinations. Other than this finding, the pregnancy had been unremarkable. Recent antepartum laboratory studies had showed a hemoglobin level of 13.4 and a hematocrit of 38.8.

Contractions had begun 3 hours before admission. The membranes were intact. There was no reported vaginal bleeding or pain. The patient had noticed a decrease in fetal movements over the past 12 hours. Electronic fetal monitoring was planned for several hours to assess uterine activity, fetal movement, and fetal heart rate. The baseline fetal heart rate was in the 150s. After 3 hours, the baseline fetal heart rate dropped to the 110s for about 2 minutes. The monitor strip revealed a hyperstimulated pattern of contractions. The patient was hydrated with 500 ml of lactated Ringer's solution and sedated with morphine. Contractions decreased in frequency to every 5 to 10 minutes and were less intense.

The patient was admitted and transferred to the high-risk labor and delivery unit. On admission, stat blood work for type and screening, hemoglobin, hematocrit, and platelet levels was done. Reports indicated that all were within the normal ranges.

One and a half hours later, fetal tachycardia developed. The patient was placed on her left side, and oxygen was started by mask without resolution of the problem. The patient complained of unrelenting abdominal pain and uterine tenderness. The fetal heart rate continued to increase, with a decrease in short-term variability. Tetanic contractions were noted. Ultrasonography revealed an abruption.

An emergency cesarean delivery under general anesthesia was performed secondary to fetal tachycardia and uterine tetany. Rupture of membranes released bright red amniotic fluid. A 5-lb 8-oz female infant was delivered with Apgar scores of 1 at 1 minute and 4 at 5 minutes. The neonate's condition stabilized after transfer to the Infant Special Care Unit and administration of oxygen by hood for tachypnea. Admission hemoglobin/hematocrit for the infant was 16/45, respectively. The neonate continued to do well.

Delivery of the placenta revealed a greater than 50% abruption with a 500-cc blood clot. Uterine atony after delivery was not responsive to Pitocin, Methergine, or prostaglandin. Approximately 40 ml of nonclottable blood was aspirated from the uterus. Hematocrit levels dropped from 35 to 25. A hysterectomy was performed.

Intraoperative clotting studies showed a drop in prothrombin time (PT) from 14.3 to 11.4 and of partial thromboplastin time (PTT) from 40 to 28. Fibrinogen levels were also decreasing. FDPs were extremely elevated. Laboratory study results strongly supported the diagnosis of coagulopathy. Rapid volume replacement was obtained with 6 liters of lactated Ringer's solution. Plasma replacement followed with 4 units of packed red blood cells (PRBC), 3 units of fresh frozen plasma (FFP), and 2 units of albumin. Final estimated blood loss was in excess of 2500 ml. The postdelivery hemoglobin was 9.2 and hematocrit was 12.6.

The patient was transferred to the recovery room, where petechiae were noted on her abdomen several hours later. Hemoglobin/hematocrit levels dropped to 5.7/16.7, respectively. A steadily decreasing urine output was noted with a low of 25 ml per hour. Additional blood and blood products were infused. Four hours later the hematology consultants noted that fibrinogen levels were rising and that platelets were low but stabilizing. The low platelet reading was attributed to a dilutional effect.

The patient's condition remained stable during the remainder of the recovery room stay. Total plasma replacement during hospitalization included 14 units of PRBC, 3 units of fresh frozen plasma, and 4 units of albumin. After 2 days in the recovery area, the patient was transferred to the postpartum unit. Mother and daughter were discharged home after a 7-day uneventful postpartum course.

The pathology report noted a large clot, extremely dilated uterine vasculature, and intramural hemorrhage in the lower anterior uterine wall. These data confirmed the diagnosis of abruptio placentae and provided the rationale for the persistent uterine atony after delivery.

*   *   *   *   *

CASE ANALYSIS

A patient with abruptio placentae complicated by the development of DIC requires intensive nursing care. The continuous multifaceted monitoring requires a nurse-patient ratio of 1:1.

In this case, two admission indicators of increased obstetric risk were the reported decrease in fetal movement by the mother and the size-date discrepancy. Indicators of serious status were the change in fetal heart rate baseline from the 150s to the 110s and the spontaneous uterine tetany. After medical interventions, these symptoms disappeared for a brief time. Uterine tenderness, severe abdominal pain, tetanic contractions, fetal tachycardia, and loss of beat-to-beat variability followed, indicating a critical situation. Ultrasound identification of an abruption was further confirmed intraoperatively by blood-stained amniotic fluid and a large placental clot at the separation site.

Nursing assessment is directed at noting bleeding tendencies, measuring blood loss, preventing or minimizing further blood loss, assessing and treating shock, monitoring fluid replacement and physiologic responses to it, assessing vital organ functioning, and providing emotional support and education to the patient and the family.[11,18,35–39]

Bleeding tendencies may be evidenced by bleeding gums, oozing from venipuncture sites, easy bruising, epistaxis, and hematemesis. Laboratory studies measuring clotting parameters and organ functioning must be monitored. Facial edema may occur because of the increased capillary permeability.[18]

Knowledge about the administration of fluid and blood replacement products and the recognition of adverse responses are imperative. Adequacy of fluid replacement is evaluated via a central venous pressure line. Kidney damage may result from vasospasm created by hypovolemia rather than from DIC alone.[36] Urinalysis and hourly intake and output reports serve as indicators of the adequacy of kidney functioning.

The patient must be protected against further blood losses. Side rails may be padded to prevent bruising. Placement of the blood pressure cuff should be rotated. Gentle handling for comfort measures such as positioning and oral hygiene is important. Blood clots should not be cleaned from puncture sites. The number of venipunctures may be minimized by coordinating this with administration of medications through existing intravenous lines or by mouth as permitted.

Blood loss may be monitored by peripad count. A blood clot in the vagina may cause the lochia to be watery and pink (serosa) rather than red (rubra).[11] The dressing over the abdominal incision should be checked for evidence of oozing, and blood stains should be marked to assist in future evaluations.

Emotional support for the patient and family is essential. Fear and anxiety may be overwhelming during this potentially life-threatening event. Mood swings, depression, and anger may follow such a traumatic and unexpected pregnancy outcome. Procedures and treatments should be explained, as should the disease process of DIC. The nurse can reassure the patient and family that DIC can be a transient and reversible condition (although serious) in an otherwise healthy individual.[11]

IMPLICATIONS FOR PRACTICE

Early prenatal care is essential for the prevention and early detection of associated conditions that place the pregnant patient at risk for abruptio placentae. These include pregnancy-induced hypertension, chronic hypertension, abdominal trauma, grand multiparity, maternal age over 35, and previous abruption.[27]

Monitoring of prenatal records for existing risks in addition to being alert for developing factors that increase the risk for abruption and/or DIC is necessary. These include intrauterine fetal death, short umbilical cord, rapid/traumatic labor and delivery, intrapartum sepsis, and amniotic fluid embolism.[27] Sorting out normal and pathologic symptoms during labor can be challenging. An example is the normal abdominal tenderness experienced by a laboring woman vs. the pathologic pain and uterine rigidity occurring with abruption.

Recovery room and postpartum nurses must continue vigilant observations. DIC may develop immediately after the emergence of a risk factor or may be delayed. Postpartum hemorrhagic sepsis and amniotic fluid embolus may develop after the immediate recovery period.

The psychosocial aspects must also be addressed. The maternal-infant process should be facilitated as early as is safely possible. Continued support may be needed after this type of pregnancy crisis. Additional support may be needed for a young woman requiring hysterectomy because of the complications of abruptio placentae and DIC, particularly if additional pregnancies were anticipated.

This case report illustrates the rapidity with which a normal pregnancy can become complicated. Severe DIC developed following abruptio placentae in the third trimester of pregnancy. After the onset of contractions in the presence of a size-date discrepancy, the patient had been hospitalized for possible premature labor.

The presenting symptoms of abruption included fetal hypoxia, tetanic contractions, and abdominal pain and tenderness. These were noted after several hours of observation.

The effects of massive intraoperative hemorrhage were confirmed by laboratory studies that showed significant decreases in PT, PTT, fibrinogen, platelet, hemoglobin, and hematocrit levels. FDP were extremely elevated, in keeping with DIC. Efforts to achieve hemostasis of the uterus using oxytocics and massage were unsuccessful. A hysterectomy was performed.

With adequate volume and plasma replacement, DIC was controlled and the patient stabilized. Damage to target organs was averted. In spite of initial low Apgar scores, the neonate did well after the resolution of tachypnea.

REFERENCES

1. Letsky E. Haematological problems associated with the critically ill obstetric patient. In: Baldwin RWM, Hanson GC, eds. *The Critically Ill Obstetric Patient.* Philadelphia, Pa: J.B. Lippincott Co.; 1984:473–500.

2. Sher G, Statland BE. Abruptio placenta with coagulopathy: a rational basis for management. *Clin Obst Gynaecol.* 1985;21(1):15–23.

3. Larcan A, Lambert H, Gerard. *Consumption Coagulopathies.* New York, NY: Masson Publishing USA; 1987.

4. Romero R. The management of acquired hemostatic failure during pregnancy. In: Berkowitz RL, ed. *Critical Care of the Obstetric patient.* New York, NY: Churchill Livingstone; 1983:219–284.

5. Siegrist CW, Jones JA. Disseminated intravascular coagulopathy and nursing implications. *Semin Oncol Nurs.* 1985;1:237–243.

6. Ansell JE. *Handbook of Hemostasis and Thrombosis.* Boston, Mass: Little, Brown & Co.; 1986.

7. Weiner CP. Disseminated intravascular coagulopathy. In: Clark SL, Phelan JP, Cotton DB, eds. *Critical Care Obstetrics.* Oradell, NJ: Medical Economics Books; 1987:152–169.

8. Olds SB, London ML, Ladewig PA. *Maternal-Newborn Nursing: A Family-Centered Approach.* 3rd ed. Menlo Park, Calif: Addison-Wesley Publishing Co., Inc.; 1988.

9. Gilabert J, Aznar J, Parrilla JJ, Reganon E, Vila V, Estelles A. Alterations in the coagulation and fibrinolysis system in pregnancy, labour, and puerperium, with special reference to a possible transitory state of intravascular coagulation during labour. *Thromb Haemost.* 1978;40:387–396.

10. Letsky EA. *Coagulation Problems during Pregnancy.* Edinburgh, Scotland: Churchill Livingstone; 1985.

11. Mayberry LJ, Forte AB. Pregnancy-related disseminated intravascular coagulation (DIC). *MCN.* 1985;10:168–173.

12. Suzuki S, Murakoshi T, Sakamoto W. Studies on the various causal factors related to hypercoagulability in the field of obstetrics—with special reference to the onset of DIC as viewed from the changing of kinin-kallikrein system and fibrinopeptide A. *Adv Exp Med Biol.* 1983;156(pt B):1055–1065.

13. Finley BE. Acute coagulopathy in pregnancy. *Med Clin North Am.* 1989;73:723–743.

14. Naumann RO, Weinstein L. Disseminated intravascular coagulation—the clinician's dilemma. *Obstet Gynecol Surv.* 1985;40:487–492.

15. Gottesfeld KR. Placental abruption. In: Queenan JT, Hobbins JC, eds. *Protocols for High-Risk Pregnancies.* Oradell, NJ: Medical Economics Books; 1982:223–226.

16. Howell RJS. Haemorrhage from the placental site. *Clin Obstet Gynaecol.* 1986;13:633–658.

17. Gilabert J, Estelles A, Aznar J, Galbis M. Abruptio placentae and disseminated intravascular coagulation. *Acta Obstet Gynecol Scand.* 1985;64:35–39.

18. Maki M, Soga K, Gotoh K. The kinin-forming enzyme system in pregnancy and obstetrical DIC. *Bibl Haematol.* 1983;49:239–246.

19. O'Brien WF, Knuppel RA, Saba HI, Angel JL, Benoit R, Bruce A. Platelet inhibitory activity in placentas from normal and abnormal pregnancies. *Obstet Gynecol.* 1987;70:597–600.

20. Krohn M, Voigt L, McKnight B, Daling JR, Starzyk P, Benedetti TJ. Correlates of placental abruption. *Br J Obstet Gynaecol.* 1987;94:333–340.

21. Suzuki S, Sakamoto W. The kinetics of blood coagulability: fibrinolytic and kallikrein-kinin system at the onset and during labor. *Eur J Obstet Gynecol Reprod Biol.* 1984;17(2–3):209–218.

22. Hansson HM. The role of enzymes in disseminated intravascular coagulation: an overview. *JOGN Nurs.* 1974;3(3):27–29.

23. Pauerstein CJ, ed. *Clinical Obstetrics.* New York, NY: John Wiley & Sons, Inc.; 1987.

24. Monteiro AA, Inocencio AC, Jorge CS. Placental abruption with disseminated intravascular coagulopathy in the second trimester of pregnancy with fetal survival: case study. *Br J Obstet Gynaecol.* 1987;94:811–812.

25. Olah KS, Gee H, Needham PG. The management of severe disseminated intravascular coagulopathy complicating placental abruption in the second trimester of pregnancy. *Br J Obstet Gynaecol.* 1988;95:419–420.

26. Metzger DA, Bowie JD, Killam AP. Expectant management of partial placental abruption in previable pregnancies: a report of two cases. *J Reprod Med.* 1987;32:789–792.

27. Yla-Outinen A, Palander M, Heinonen PK. Abruption placentae—risk factors and outcome of the newborn. *Eur J Obstet Gynecol Reprod Biol.* 1987;25(1):23–28.

28. Gilbert ES, Harmon JS. *High-Risk Pregnancy and Delivery: Nursing Perspectives.* St. Louis, Mo: C.V. Mosby Co.; 1986.

29. Boulton FE, Letsky E. Obstetric hemorrhage: causes and management. *Clin Haematol.* 1985;14:683–728.

30. Burke L. Abruptio placentae. In: Friedman EA, ed. *Obstetrical Decision Making.* St. Louis, Mo: C.V. Mosby Co.; 1982:64–65.

31. Weeks LR. Case reports: disseminated intravascular coagulation. *J Natl Med Assoc.* 1985;77:830–835.

32. Cunningham FG, MacDonald PC, Gant NF. *Williams Obstetrics.* (18th ed.) E. Norwalk, Conn: Appleton & Lange; 1989.

33. Balgobin B. Coagulopathy. In: Friedman, EA, ed. *Obstetrical Decision Making.* St. Louis, Mo: C.V. Mosby Co.; 1982:84–85.

34. Maki M, Terao T, Ikenoue T, et al. Clinical evaluation of Antithrombin III concentrate (BI 6.013) for disseminated intravascular coagulation in obstetrics. *Gynecol Obstet Invest.* 1987;23:230–240.

35. Conklin MM. DIC in the pregnant patient. *J Obstet Gynecol Neonatal Nurs.* 1974;3(3):29–32.

36. Stratta P, Canavese C, Colla L, et al. Acute renal failure in obstetric complications. *Biol Res Pregnancy.* 1986;7(3):113–117.

37. Degroot KD, Damato MB, eds. *Critical Care Skills.* E. Norwalk, Conn: Appleton & Lange; 1987.

38. McKay ML, Martin JN, Morrison JC. Disseminated intravascular coagulation, idiopathic thrombocytopenic purpura, and hemoglobinopathies. In: Knuppel RA, Drukker JE, eds. *High Risk Pregnancy: A Team Approach.* Philadelphia, Pa: W.B. Saunders Co.; 1986:440–471.

39. Pernoll ML, Brown RC, eds. *Current Obstetric & Gynecologic Diagnosis & Treatment 1987.* E. Norwalk, Conn: Appleton & Lange; 1987.

Chapter 4

Pregnancy in a Patient on Chronic Renal Dialysis

Mary Ellen Burke

Pregnancy in a patient undergoing hemodialysis for chronic renal failure is a rare event. Information regarding the fetus and maternal uterine activity during dialysis is almost nonexistent. Nurses working with a patient who becomes pregnant while undergoing dialysis will realize that there is a striking lack of information regarding any part of the nursing care of these patients. This chapter provides a review of the literature and a case presentation of a patient who became pregnant and had a successful outcome of pregnancy while undergoing dialysis for the treatment of chronic renal failure.

REVIEW OF THE LITERATURE

A review of the literature revealed 16 cases of women who became pregnant and had successful outcomes while undergoing dialysis.[1-13] Chronic renal failure is associated with amenorrhea[14-17] and abortion, either spontaneous or induced. Many of the induced abortions were performed because of fear that the pregnancy would further endanger the life of the mother. It is impossible to ascertain the number of pregnancies that have actually occurred while a patient is undergoing dialysis. There are few case reports regarding women who conceived but did not continue the pregnancy.[3,17] The successful pregnancies in women on dialysis were followed by a team of physicians and nurses representing renal, perinatal, and neonatal specialty areas. Also, the patients were usually cared for in a tertiary setting.

Renal Function in Pregnancy

A review of renal function during pregnancy is a necessary start to understanding how renal failure affects both the mother and fetus. Any woman who becomes

39

pregnant experiences a tremendous increase in plasma volume. The plasma volume increases 40 to 50%, starting in the first trimester, and achieving the maximal amount at approximately 30 weeks of pregnancy.[2,18–20] This volume is sustained until the immediate postpartum period. The blood pressure is maintained within normal limits by a decrease in peripheral vascular resistance. The healthy renal system works to achieve a normal balance during this period. The glomerular filtration rate (GFR) starts to rise after conception and continues to rise until the end of the first trimester. The GFR usually is at least 40 to 50% higher at this point than in the nonpregnant state. This increase is sustained until delivery, when it rapidly returns to normal.[18] Creatinine clearance increases to 150 to 200 ml/min by the end of the second trimester.[19]

Ultrasound of the kidney during pregnancy in a healthy woman reveals a moderate dilatation of the renal pelvis and ureter. This may lead to some confusion regarding hydronephrosis, but a grade 1 hydronephrosis is normal in the pregnant woman. Dilatation of the renal pelvis, calyces, and ureters is more apparent in the right kidney. This is secondary to hormonal factors and concomitant compression by the uterus. Normally, there is an increase in the need to urinate, as well as a decrease in the bladder capacity, secondary to the growing uterus. The tremendous increase in plasma volume also inversely leads to a decrease in levels of hemoglobin, hematocrit, blood urea nitrogen (BUN), and creatinine and uric acid due to hemodilution. "Normal" levels of these biochemical data are greatly lowered in pregnancy (Table 4-1). Renal tubular reabsorption also changes in pregnancy, leading to a decreased reabsorption of glucose, amino acids, and lactose. Pregnant women are at higher risk for developing ascending urinary tract infections because of dilatation of the ureter. Protein loss is a common occurrence in the pregnant state, although any protein loss of greater than 300 mg in a 24-hour urine sample should be investigated for the development of renal disease and/or preeclampsia.[5] Pregnant women also excrete small amounts of cells and casts in their urine.[2]

Table 4-1 Normal Lab Values

	Nonpregnant	Pregnant
Hemoglobin, g/dl	12–16	10–14
Hematocrit, %	37–47	32–42
BUN, mg/dl	10–16	7.2–10.2
Creatinine, mg/dl	0.5–0.8	0.3–0.6
Creatinine clearance, ml/min	100–180	150–200
Uric acid, mg/dl	2.2–7.5	3.2–3.5

Source: Reprinted from *Taber's Cyclopedic Medical Directory*, ed 16 by D. Coustan, and R. Plotz with permission of F.A. Davis, 1989.

Renal Function in Women with Chronic Renal Disease

Pregnancy in women with chronic renal disease presents an entirely different picture, particularly for those diagnosed with chronic renal failure and treated with renal dialysis. Blood pressure regulation by the kidneys seems to be an important factor in the outcome of pregnancy in these women. Blood pressure regulation is an extremely important function of the kidneys. Hypertension may be secondary to any of the underlying pathophysiologies of renal disease, including renal paren-chymal destruction, renal ischemia, or renal artery stenosis.[5] Hypertension in pregnancy is associated with intrauterine growth retardation, abuptio placentae, an increased incidence of fetal stress or distress with contractions, and intrauterine fetal demise. Superimposed preeclampsia is associated with an increased inci-dence of these morbidity and mortality factors. The majority of women with ad-vanced renal disease requiring chronic dialysis are women who also experience hypertension.

The first and most pervasive question regarding pregnancy in the woman under-going chronic renal dialysis is Can a woman conceive while undergoing renal dialysis for the treatment of chronic renal failure? The obvious answer is Yes. Chronic renal failure is associated with amenorrhea,[3,8,9,10,16,17,19] yet there is defi-nitely a portion of the population who are able to become pregnant. The majority of women who become pregnant on dialysis present in the second or third tri-mester for perinatal care because they had not thought it possible for themselves to become pregnant. Late prenatal care may compound the inherent problems. Case reports of successful pregnancies indicate that the most promising fetal outcome occurs when the BUN levels are controlled to stay below 30 mg/dl,[18] although there are reports of successful pregnancy with a BUN level of 70 to 80 mg/dl.[6,9] Serum creatinine levels are also monitored, and successful outcomes have oc-curred with serum creatinine levels between 3 and 8 mg/dl.[6]

Care of Pregnant Women with Chronic Renal Disease

The nursing and medical care of a patient who becomes pregnant while under-going chronic renal dialysis is fraught with uncertainty. There is no "cookbook" method to follow to increase the incidence of a successful outcome. The majority of patients present for care later than the first trimester because they had been warned that hemodialysis impairs fertility. The nurse caring for the patient is faced with a variety of problems. First of all, the patient has renal disease, and the major-ity have some degree of hypertension. Patients undergoing renal dialysis are prone to anemia and frequently require blood transfusions, as often as 1 to 2 units/week. Add the normal physiologic anemia of pregnancy to this scenario, and it becomes obvious that both mother and fetus will require close monitoring of the maternal hemoglobin (Hgb) and hematocrit (Hct) values during pregnancy. (The suggested guidelines vary with each institution, although an Hct of less than 28% is an indication to transfuse blood.)

In case reports, the frequency of dialysis has been increased for patients undergoing chronic dialysis to decrease the serum BUN and creatinine levels. One problem never identified or dealt with in the case reports is that of dry weight. Patients undergoing dialysis, acute or chronic, are weighed when they enter a dialysis unit. Past medical history, including weight, figures into the "formula" that determines how much fluid to remove during each dialysis treatment. Pregnancy complicates this formula greatly because pregnancy requires a certain amount of weight gain for both the mother and the fetus.

Determining a patient's dry weight becomes a difficult proposition. How many pounds is too much to gain for the pregnant dialysis patient? How much fluid should be removed during each treatment? The removal of too great a quantity of fluid could result in impaired perfusion to the fetus. Leaving too much fluid could cause an increase in the BUN and creatinine, which could be hazardous to the mother and the fetus. There are, unfortunately, no good answers to these questions. Physicians and nurses currently try to utilize formulas for weight gain that are prescribed for the normal pregnant population. Until a study can be performed on this particular deviation from normal pregnancy, this is probably the best answer. However, for the nurses in the dialysis unit, this is an unsatisfactory answer, as they are responsible for determining the patient's dry weight after hemodialysis, based on nonpregnant formulas.

Hemodialysis is accompanied by frequent fluid shifts and often by hypotension. The pregnant patient must be monitored carefully to ensure that hypotension is avoided so that placental perfusion to the fetus will be continuous.

Heparin therapy is a necessary part of hemodialysis and has not been shown to be an impediment to a successful outcome. There are no reports of problems with normal heparin therapy during dialysis, although it becomes a cause of concern for the patient who may deliver after hemodialysis. Concerns over the possibility that heparin therapy during dialysis may contribute to the risk of uteroplacental hemorrhage have not been researched.

One cause for concern that has not been reported in the literature is the use of methylene blue in the intravenous solution administered to patients during hemodialysis. The solution may be utilized by the staff of the hemodialysis unit to show that the machine has been primed with solution (an extremely important point in the care of the dialysis patient, as the dialysis machine can infuse air into the shunt, causing an air embolus). Methylene blue solution is potentially hazardous to the fetus and may cause methemoglobinemia.[20] This solution *should not be* utilized in any pregnant woman undergoing hemodialysis.

A review of the literature did not reveal any formal discussion on the use of electronic fetal monitoring (EFM) during dialysis as a means of assessing fetal well-being. There have been reports of patients experiencing contractions during or immediately after dialysis.[6,10,11,21] EFM was utilized in this case to evaluate fetal status during the period of dialysis. The patient also had biweekly nonstress tests (NSTs) and oxytocin challenge tests (OCTs), as indicated. EFM was instituted at 27 weeks gestation, when the fetus was considered viable.

* * * * *

CASE STUDY

A 32-year-old woman, gravida II, para I, had had one full-term cesarean delivery in 1977 of a healthy male child. The patient had a history of anemia since the first delivery and has been treated with vitamin B_{12}, folate, and transfusions. The patient had an otherwise benign medical history until 1984, when she was hospitalized with a cellulitis in the area of her neck and chest. Routine work-up also revealed that she was severely hypertensive and azotemic. The cause of the azotemia was not discovered despite a thorough work-up. The patient was then started on peritoneal dialysis, but this had to be discontinued as she developed a *Pseudomonas* infection of the peritoneum. The patient decided to obtain a second opinion at that time and underwent a renal biopsy. The biopsy revealed rapidly progressing glomerulonephritis. She was initially treated with steroid therapy, which improved her urinary output; however, she was developing increasing symptoms of azotemia, including nausea, increasing fatigue, and insomnia. Concurrently, her BUN and creatinine levels were rising, reaching levels of 67 and 6 mg/dl, respectively. A 24-hour urine collection revealed a creatinine clearance of 12 ml/min.

The patient was started on renal hemodialysis, hydralazine, and propranolol. Hemodialysis was initially performed twice weekly for 4 hours at a time. The patient started this regime in April 1985.

Medications were discontinued in December 1985 secondary to improvement of the hypertension on dialysis. The patient presented in October 1986 complaining of gastrointestinal problems. A physical examination revealed that the patient was pregnant. The patient had not been utilizing any form of birth control as she had been informed that she could not become pregnant and had had amenorrhea for the past 2 years. Ultrasound examination dated the pregnancy at 12 weeks gestation, a single fetus, intrauterine pregnancy. The patient's dialysis was increased to five times weekly for 3 hours at a time. Bicarbonate dialysis was started, using a bicarbonate bath that the physicians thought would be more homeostatic than an acetate bath. Heparinization was minimized, and a fresh dialyzer was utilized for each dialysis. The calcium/phosphorus level was also increased. The patient's medications were as follows: Oscal 500 mg, 15 tablets per day; Ro-Calcitrol, 1 tablet q.d.; folic acid, 1 mg q.d.; and Neutraphos, 2 tablets q.d. The patient had an initial prenatal visit with her gynecologist, who started her on prenatal vitamins, and her care was transferred to a regional tertiary center.

The patient was seen on her first prenatal visit in November with a blood pressure (BP) of 160/110. She was admitted and started on Aldomet 250 mg, q.i.d. Baseline laboratory values were: Hgb 9.4, Hct 27.6, platelet count 174,000, BUN 46, creatinine 4.7, uric acid 5.1, and serum glutamic oxaloacetic transaminase (SGOT) 14. An initial screen for hepatitis B was negative. The patient's BP was quickly brought under control, and she was discharged home. Her pregnancy continued smoothly, with the BUN being maintained between 40 and 76 mg/dl and the creatinine between 4.2 and 5 mg/dl. The higher values were obtained on the days when she was not dialyzed. The patient had an elevated glucose screen of 144, although a follow-up oral glucose tolerance test (OGTT) was normal. She was readmitted at 31 weeks for a small amount of bright red spotting of unknown origin, and an extensive work-up was normal. The fetus was followed with ultrasonography, which consistently documented normal fetal growth and normal amounts of amniotic fluid. BPs ranged from 112/72 to 140/100. The patient's blood pressure was noted to decrease toward the end of the dialysis session and this was treated with fluid boluses. The patient was maintained in left lateral position during dialysis. Her shunt was in her left arm, so care had to be taken to position her arm to maximize blood flow. The fetus was monitored during dialysis at least once a week starting at 27 weeks gestation. The patient experienced several episodes of contractions while on dialysis, but these were infrequent events. She also experienced occasional late decelerations while on dialysis, although follow-up OCTs were always negative. She received one to two transfusions per week to keep the Hct above 28%. The patient was readmitted at 35 weeks gestation to rule out superimposed preeclampsia.

The patient remained hospitalized and the fetus was followed by NST and OCT until 38 weeks gestation. Fetal monitoring was performed during the dialysis periods. Amniocentesis was performed and a mature L/S ratio of 2.4:1 was noted. The patient had a repeat cesarean section and bilateral tubal ligation. The infant, a 5-lb, 6-oz female, had Apgar scores of 8 and 9 and a cord pH of 7.35.

The patient's dialysis therapy was returned to the prepregnant regimen of two times per week for 4 hours/day. The patient is currently stable and off all hypertensive medications. The infant has been followed closely in the neonatal clinic, and at the age of 1 year is reported to be physically and developmentally normal.

*   *   *   *   *

CASE ANALYSIS

Pregnancy in a woman undergoing renal dialysis for chronic renal failure is rare. The case presented documents that pregnancy is not only possible, but may be associated with a successful outcome. The importance of early diagnosis of the pregnancy, followed by early prenatal care, cannot be overemphasized. A second major factor is close monitoring of the patient and fetus, with appropriate interventions performed as necessary.

The patient had no idea that she was pregnant or that she could become pregnant. She had been informed that pregnancy was not possible in women undergoing renal dialysis. Therefore, she had not utilized any contraceptive methods for 2 years. Patients undergoing dialysis during childbearing years should be informed that, although the incidence of pregnancy is very low, it may occur. Contraceptive counseling is still indicated for these women. This patient discovered that she was pregnant when she suffered from gastrointestinal complaints (nausea and vomiting). She presented to the internist at a very early gestational age and began her prenatal care fairly early for a patient in this situation. The signs and symptoms of pregnancy other than amenorrhea should be discussed with these patients.

The emotional effect of pregnancy in a woman with renal failure is enormous. Shock, disbelief, and tremendous physical fears for herself and the fetus were the initial responses in this patient. As the feelings of shock and disbelief were worked through, fear became the most overwhelming emotion. The spouses and families of these patients were also terrified, especially for the outcome of the mother. Nursing management of this patient included long supportive listening sessions, coordination of social work support, and religious support regarding the decision to have a tubal ligation.

Nursing management of this patient including coordinating care at a community dialysis center and, later, at the tertiary care center. The nurses in these dialysis units were eager to be educated regarding the pregnancy aspects of dialysis and provided a major support system for the patient. These nurses, in turn, provided the perinatal nurses with an education about dialysis, and the two teams investigated how to determine dry weight, the problem of using methylene blue as a primer, and the fetal response to renal dialysis.

The patient presented in this case study had a successful outcome of pregnancy. As more cases are reported in the literature, the knowledge base integral to planning the nursing and medical management of these patients will expand. The team approach to the care of these complex patients, combined with more data and strong team communication, may afford more successful outcomes in the future.

IMPLICATIONS FOR PRACTICE

The major implications for practice are recognizing that women who are undergoing chronic renal dialysis may become pregnant and caring for the pregnant patient on renal dialysis. Recognition and integration of the knowledge that pregnancy is indeed a possibility among this population are necessary beginnings for any health care provider in contact with these women. Birth control is rarely discussed with these patients, since it is taken for granted that ovulation ceases with chronic renal failure and the dialysis process. Obviously, pregnancy is a possibility, and full counseling regarding methods of birth control must be made available to these patients.

A patient who decides to continue her pregnancy is at high risk for developing hypertension, superimposed preeclampsia, intrauterine growth retardation, and premature delivery. A team approach involving perinatal nurses and physicians working closely with renal nurses and physicians is imperative. Neonatal health care givers need to be informed of the pregnancy and to be present at delivery. The fetus should be monitored during dialysis. The perinatal nurse and the renal nurse need to work side by side during each dialysis.

The exact gestational age when EFM should begin is controversial; this patient was started at 27 weeks gestation. This decision was reached by the perinatal team working with the patient and her husband. The risks and benefits of delivering a fetus at gestational ages from 24 weeks up were presented to the couple. The perinatal team was also concerned with obtaining false-positive test outcomes at early gestational ages. The "best" gestational age to begin EFM, serial ultrasonographic studies, or biophysical profile monitoring has not been determined.

Women undergoing chronic renal dialysis can have successful pregnancies and positive outcomes. Health care providers must discuss the possibility of pregnancy with these patients and provide integrated, intensive care to those who become pregnant.

REFERENCES

1. The Registration Committee of the European Dialysis and Transplant Association. Successful pregnancies in women treated by dialysis and kidney transplantation. *Br J Obstet Gynaecol.* 1980;87:839–345.

2. MacCarthy EP, Pollak V. Maternal renal disease: effect on the fetus. *Clin Perinatol.* 1981;8:307–319.

3. Tejani A, Gurumurthy K, Sen D. Accidental pregnancies in teenage children on dialysis. *NY State J Med.* July 1982;1234–1235.

4. Rotellar C, Ferragut A, Borrul J. Pregnancy in a patient on regular hemodialysis. *Nephron.* 1983;35:66–67.

5. Gabert H, Miller J Jr. Renal disease in pregnancy. *Obstet Gynecol Surv.* 1985;40:449–460.

6. Kobayashi H, et al. Successful pregnancy in a patient undergoing chronic hemodialysis. *Obstet Gynecol.* 1981;57:382–386.

7. Marwood R, Ogg C, Coltart T, Klopper A. Plasma oestrogens in a pregnancy associated with chronic renal dialysis. *Br J Obstet Gynaecol.* 1977;84:623–627.

8. Unzelman R, Alderfer G, Chojnacki R. Pregnancy and chronic hemodialysis. *Trans Am Soc Artif Intern Organs.* 1973;19:144–149.

9. Sheriff M, et al. Successful pregnancy in a 44-year-old hemodialysis patient. *Br J Obstet Gynaecol.* 1978;85:386–389.

10. Ackerill P, et al. Successful pregnancy in patient on regular dialysis. *Br Med J.* 1975;2:172–174.

11. Thomson N, Rigby R, Atkins R, Walters W. Successful pregnancy in a patient on recurrent haemodialysis. *Aust Soc Nephrol.* 1978;8:243.

12. Lindley J, Beathard G, Moncrief J. Successful pregnancy in the long-term hemodialysis patient. *Kidney Int.* 1978;14:679.

13. Confortini P, et al. Full term pregnancy and successful delivery in a patient on chronic hemodialysis. *Proc Eur Dial Transplant Assoc.* 1971;8:74–78.

14. Board J, Lee H, Draper D, Hume D. Pregnancy following kidney homotransplantation from a non-twin. *Obstet Gynecol.* 1967;29:318–323.

15. Bailey G. The sick kidney and sex. *N Engl J Med.* 1977;296:1288.

16. Roxe D, McLaughlin M. Reproductive capacity in female patients on chronic hemodialysis. *Int J Artif Organs.* 1984;7:249–250.

17. McGeown M, Houston J. Chronic renal disease. *Clin Obstet Gynecol.* April 1982;9:101–113.

18. Hirsch D, Hayslett J. Renal disease during pregnancy. In: Berkowitz R, ed. *Critical Care of the Obstetric Patient.* New York, NY: Churchill Livingstone; 1983;443–462.

19. Michael J. The management of renal disease in pregnancy. *Clin Obstet Gynecol.* June 1986;13:319–334.

20. Burke ME. Chronic renal disease and pregnancy. *NAACOG Clin Issues Perinatal Women's Health Nurs.* July 1990;1:154–164.

21. Berkowitz R, Coustan D, Mochizuki T. *Handbook for Prescribing Medicines in Pregnancy.* Boston, Mass: Little, Brown & Co.; 1986;194.

ADDITIONAL BIBLIOGRAPHY

Coustan D, Plotz R. The laboratory in diseases associated with pregnancy. In: Mandell H, ed. *Laboratory medicine in Clinical Practice.* Boston, Mass: John Wright; 1983.

Hou S. Pregnancy in women requiring dialysis for renal failure. *Am J Kidney Dis.* April 1987;9:368–373.

Lindheimer M, Katz A. *Kidney Function and Disease in Pregnancy.* Philadelphia, Pa: Lea and Febiger; 1977.

Chapter 5

Multiple Sclerosis and Pregnancy

Meredith Goff

REVIEW OF THE LITERATURE

Multiple sclerosis (MS) is a chronic neurologic disorder that most frequently presents during the childbearing years. It is two to three times more common in females than males;[1] therefore, it is a disease that may be encountered by the practitioner caring for pregnant women. Multiple sclerosis is characterized by scattering areas of damage to the myelin sheath surrounding the nerve fibers of the central nervous system, resulting in delayed or absent impulse conduction.[2] Multiple sclerosis is classified as clinically definite, probable, or possible, based on the certainty of the diagnosis. The diagnosis is made based on the history, neurologic findings, and laboratory tests. The most common presenting symptoms are paresthesias, double or blurred vision, gait difficulties, decreased fine motor coordination, fatigability, weakness, and urinary dysfunction. Laboratory testing may include analysis of cerebrospinal fluid (CSF) for increased levels of immunoglobulin G and evoked response testing. Magnetic resonance imaging (MRI) may confirm the diagnosis of multiple sclerosis by detecting central nervous system (CNS) lesions.

The diagnosis of MS may be confirmed by evidence of two or more widely separated areas of central nervous system involvement, based on history, physical examination, and testing. For the diagnosis to be considered clinically definite, the patient must have symptoms that cause some physical disability in a remitting and relapsing course with at least two episodes 1 or more months apart.[2]

The incidence of the disease varies according to geographic location. Areas with the highest prevalence are all located in the higher latitudes, including the northern United States, Canada, Great Britain, Scandinavia, northern Europe, New Zealand, and Tasmania. In these areas the incidence may be as high as 30 to 80 cases per 100,000 people.[7] This suggests that environmental factors play a role in the development of MS, but what these factors may be is unclear.

The cause of multiple sclerosis is unknown. There are several hypotheses. The first is that the disease is caused by a viral infection, probably first contracted during childhood, which is capable of existing in a dormant form and is subject to episodic activation. The virus directly attacks the myelin sheath. A second theory suggests that MS is caused by an autoimmune disease, which itself is triggered by a childhood infection. Third, MS may be more than one disease with more than one pathogenic mechanism.[8]

Prognosis depends on the course of the disease, which is classified as benign, progressive, chronic relapsing, or exacerbating and remitting. Benign MS is characterized by few mild relapses followed by complete recovery. Approximately 20% of patients with multiple sclerosis will follow this course. Progressive disease is found in 15% of patients and involves gradual deterioration of neurologic function, without well-delineated remissions or relapses. Forty percent of patients will have chronic relapsing MS. These patients have less complete remissions after attacks, and physical disability is cumulative. Exacerbating-remitting MS is characterized by long periods of stability, with some degree of disability. Twenty-five percent of patients are in this category.[9]

Treatment is symptomatic and supportive. There is no cure, nor is there any medication that alters the long-term course of the disease. Adrenocorticotropic hormone (ACTH) and steroids may be used during acute exacerbations to shorten the attack but will not alter the overall course of the disease.[10] Treatment includes physical therapy, proper nutrition, good skin care, and avoidance of heat. This includes avoiding hot baths and sunbathing, which may worsen symptoms. Common relief measures used for constipation may be of help, as well as the maintenance of slightly acidic urine to avoid infection. Family members should be included in the treatment plan when appropriate.

In the United States several hundred pregnancies per year occur in women with the diagnosis of clinically definite or probable multiple sclerosis. Multiple sclerosis has no known effect on fertility. Two studies showed diminished fertility in women with MS but attributed it to physical disability and/or a decision not to have children, often based on advice from physicians.[11] No studies show an effect on biologic fertility.[12] Similarly, studies have shown no increase in the incidence of spontaneous abortion, malformations, or stillbirth in women with multiple sclerosis.[13]

On the basis of the results of retrospective studies, the practitioner may inform the pregnant woman with MS that the results are mixed. Most women with MS enjoy stability or even improvement of their symptoms while pregnant. However, symptoms often worsen during the early postpartum months (Table 5-1). Multiple studies strongly suggest that pregnancy is somewhat protective for women with MS.[14] Some suggest that this action may be due to the presence of α-fetoprotein or high levels of estrogen. Others suggest that the naturally occurring immunosup-

Table 5-1 Effects of Pregnancy on Multiple Sclerosis

Source/Year	Number of Pregnancies after Onset of MS	Number Worse in Pregnancy	Number Worse Postpartum	Conclusions
Tillman (1950)	70	6	22	No effect on MS
Sweeney (1955)	36	3	—	No effect on MS
Millarletal (1950)	170	6	39	Increased incidence of relapse postpartum
Shapira et al. (1966)	86	12	19	Increased incidence of relapse postpartum
Ghezzi & Caputo (1981)	206	34	91	Improved antepartum Worse postpartum No overall adverse effect
Poser & Poser (1983)	158	13	28	Improved antepartum Worse postpartum No overall adverse effect
Korn-Lubetzki et al. (1984)	199	20	65	Improved antepartum Worse postpartum No overall adverse effect

Source: Adapted with permission from K Birk and R Rudick, "Pregnancy and Multiple Sclerosis" in *Archives of Neurology* (1986;43:720), Copyright © 1986, American Medical Association.

---

pression of pregnancy may be responsible.[14] The fetus and placenta produce α-fetoprotein, human chorionic gonadotropin, human placental lactogen, progesterone, and estrogen, which have immunosuppressive activity. In addition, the pregnant woman has a decrease in the number of T-lymphocytes and helper T cells, as well as increased synthesis of adrenal corticosteroids, all of which contribute to the immunosuppressive state.

Multiple sclerosis has no apparent effect on labor or delivery. Labor should be managed based on the individual needs of the laboring woman, and MS should not preclude analgesia as needed.

The rate of postpartum relapse in the woman with MS is between 20 and 40%.[15] The postpartum period may be stressful for any new mother, particularly the woman with multiple sclerosis.[11] It is often a time characterized by little sleep, difficulty in adapting to a role change, uncertainty, and loss of control over daily life events. All of this adds up to increased stress, which (in addition to the sudden decrease of the seemingly protective hormones of pregnancy) may lead to a relapse. The pregnant woman and her family must be counseled regarding necessary preparations for the postpartum period. Family members and friends should be available for assistance when possible.

Breast-feeding should be encouraged, but it, too, requires a strong support system. If symptoms of a relapse are severe and medication is prescribed, the breast-feeding woman should consult her pediatrician or lactation consultant regarding the advisability of continuing breast-feeding. The risk of MS exacerbation decreases after the first 3 months postpartum. Neither pregnancy nor breast-feeding seems to alter the overall long-term course of MS.[12]

Couples considering pregnancy should be aware that there is a slightly increased risk of MS in children born to a parent with the disease. One study found a 3% lifetime risk vs. 0.1% in the general population.[13] The practitioner may wish to refer couples to a genetic counselor.

* * * * *

CASE STUDY

J.B. is a 37-year-old white woman who was first diagnosed with multiple sclerosis at age 26. Her initial symptoms were numbness in her legs and feet. At that time she consulted her family physician, a general practitioner, who strongly suspected multiple sclerosis. He referred her to a neurologist, who confirmed the diagnosis.

Over the ten-year span from diagnosis to conception, her symptoms progressed to increasing numbness over the lower half of her body. Because of this, J.B. found her balance to be increasingly impaired, and walking downhill or downstairs became very difficult. In addition, her fine motor skills diminished, which was especially evident in her handwriting. Also, speech became less clear. She found that she was unable to achieve orgasm, and her peripheral vision diminished. During this time she experienced several acute exacerbations that were treated with corticosteroids.

In spite of the worsening symptoms, J.B. continued in her job as a school teacher, married, and hoped to have a family. In August 1986, she stopped using oral contraceptives, switching to a diaphragm for 5 months. In February 1987, J.B. and her husband began attempting conception. On 15 April 1987, she had her last normal menstrual period. Several days after her missed menses in May she performed a home pregnancy test, which was positive.

J.B. and her husband were very determined to be cared for by certified nurse-midwives during the pregnancy, and during the several months preceding conception had contacted several midwifery services to discuss the pregnancy with them. At approximately 6 weeks gestation from her last menstrual period, J.B. and her husband had their first prenatal visit with a midwifery practice affiliated with a major teaching hospital where her neurologist also practiced. During that visit J.B. and her husband expressed their desire for genetic counseling because of advanced maternal age. Arrangements were made for chorionic villus sampling, which was performed uneventfully at 9 weeks gestation, revealing a normal female fetus.

During the first trimester J.B. experienced the normal discomforts characteristic of this time in pregnancy (nausea, fatigue, etc.). From approximately 12 weeks of gestation until delivery, however, she experienced a marked decrease in her MS symptoms, as well as what she described as "a strong feeling of well-being." She did not require any medication during the pregnancy except a 10-day course of erythromycin for a fever, thought to be due to an upper respiratory infection. During the course of the pregnancy, J.B. gained 35 lb over her prepregnant weight. She continued full-time employment, teaching developmentally disabled children, until 36 weeks gestation.

All laboratory tests during the course of pregnancy were within normal limits except a class II Pap smear. Colposcopic examination of the cervix was performed, and biopsies were taken during the second trimester and postpartum. They were negative for malignant cells.

Labor and delivery were remarkable only for their rapidity and relative ease for an "elderly primip." Bloody show and irregular contractions began at 6:30 A.M. on 13 January 1988, at 39 weeks gestation. A previously scheduled midwifery appointment was kept later that morning, where the cervix was found to be soft and 1 cm dilated, with intact membranes. J.B. and her husband went home to await active labor. Regular contractions began at 10:30 A.M. At 2:45 P.M., J.B. and her husband arrived at the hospital in very active labor. Her cervix at that time was 8 cm dilated, with intact membranes and a reactive fetal heart rate pattern. At 4:37 P.M. a normal spontaneous delivery of a 6-lb 4-oz girl (Apgar scores of 9 and 9) occurred in the birthing room, attended by the nurse-midwife. A first-degree laceration was noted and repaired under local anesthesia.

The third stage was complicated by a retained placenta and bleeding. After 20 minutes of unsuccessful attempts at spontaneous delivery of the placenta, arrangements were made for a manual removal. An intravenous line was started, and under general anesthesia in the delivery room the placenta was manually removed by the consulting obstetrician. J.B. tolerated the procedure well.

The remainder of the hospital stay was uneventful for J.B. Baby D. required 2 days of phototherapy because of ABO incompatibility. Mother and baby were discharged home on the fourth postpartum day.

During the first 6 weeks postpartum, J.B. experienced what she described as "bad depression." During the second and third postpartum months, her MS symptoms worsened. Her gait became increasingly unsteady, often forcing her to use a cane. Her fine motor skills also deteriorated, making caring for her baby more difficult. Her speech also became less clear. In addition, Baby D. was not adequately gaining weight on breast milk alone. At approximately 2 months of age she was started on formula. She is now a thriving infant. J.B.'s depression and motor symptoms have diminished over time. She now ambulates without a cane and finds herself enjoying her role as a mother.

*   *   *   *   *

CASE ANALYSIS

J.B. typifies the patient with multiple sclerosis and the effects of pregnancy on the disease. She has been a lifelong resident of the northern United States. Her initial symptoms were consistent with those most frequently reported. The diagnosis was made by a neurologist based on her progressive symptoms and the findings of physical examination.

J.B. did enjoy a diminution of symptoms during pregnancy, which is true in the majority of women with MS. Unfortunately, she also was one of the 20 to 40% of women who experience a postpartum relapse.[16] Initially she experienced the postpartum depression that many women experience. This was a time of great stress for her. After a 1-week paternity leave, J.B.'s husband returned to work—a demanding job that often required a 12-hour work day.

This left J.B., a very social person, with sole responsibility for child care, in the middle of a cold winter, unable to get out of the house, with no immediate family in the area. Fortunately, she lived in an area with a strong support system available to new mothers. In her neighborhood there was a mothers group that met weekly to discuss the needs of the members and offer support. J.B. was able to connect with this network during the first month postpartum, enabling her to share her concerns and meet with other new mothers. She was able to form new friendships based on new common interests. Members of this network, all neighbors, included midwives, nurses, and a lactation consultant, all of whom were able to provide their own expertise and assistance.

By the time J.B.'s symptoms began to worsen, in the second month postpartum, she was feeling better psychologically and had a strong network willing to assist as necessary. In addition, it was then spring. J.B. found it easier to get outside (in spite of her need for a cane), which gave her a psychologic boost. J.B. is now functioning well, both physically and emotionally.

IMPLICATIONS FOR PRACTICE

Women's health care providers are often the only source of health care for many women, either interconceptionally for family planning advice and well-woman gynecology or during a pregnancy. Since MS is a disease that most often presents during the childbearing years, all providers of women's care should be familiar with the signs and symptoms. Furthermore, women with MS must be provided with accurate information regarding the risks of pregnancy, childbirth, and parenting. In the past, many patients with MS had been advised not to consider pregnancy;[16] clearly, the research findings do not support this recommendation.

In addition to providing accurate information, the provider must also be aware of the psychosocial stages of MS. This allows more effective counseling. The first stage is uncertainty, which lasts from the onset of symptoms to the confirmation of the diagnosis. The second stage is shock and settling in—shock at the diagnosis and working through the denial and anxiety such a diagnosis brings. The third stage is one of self-confrontation, during which the patient begins to deal realistically with the disease. The fourth stage is accepting the need for chronic care. Such care can bring devastating financial and emotional costs, such as unemployment or breakdown of the family. Pregnancy can be an additional stressor during this time. Families must be assisted in setting realistic goals and finding the support necessary to get them through this potentially difficult time.

Fortunately, J.B. was in a very unique environment where neighbors could offer the necessary support; many women are not as fortunate. Families must be offered help to mobilize their resources before symptoms worsen, and health care practitioners must be available to them for assistance as necessary. These women may need to be scheduled for postpartum visits before 6 weeks, with revisits as necessary and telephone contact readily available.

There must also be good contact with the pediatric practitioner for evaluation of the mother/infant dyad. An infant who is failing to thrive may reveal a mother who is also failing to thrive. Intervention should be aimed at promoting a healthy, intact family.

REFERENCES

1. Scheinberg LC. *Multiple Sclerosis: A Guide for Patients and Their Families.* New York, NY: Raven Press; 1983.
2. Scheibel WR, Isensee S. Multiple sclerosis. *J Fam Pract.* 1986;23:543–550.
3. Neurology Service, Department of Medicine and Surgery, Veterans Administration. *Multiple Sclerosis: Guideline for Diagnosis and Management.* Washington, DC; 1980.
4. Ellison GW, et al. Multiple sclerosis. *Ann Intern Med.* 1984;101:514–526.
5. Graves MC. Viruses and demyelinating disease. pp517–520. In: Ellison GW, moderator. *Multiple Sclerosis. Ann Intern Med.* 1984;101:514–526.
6. Paty DW, et al. The challenge of detecting MS. *Patient Care.* 1989;23:62–68.
7. Visscher BR. Evidence for an environmental agent as the course. In: Ellison GW, moderator. *Multiple Sclerosis. Ann Intern Med.* 1984;101:514–526.
8. McFarlin DE, McFarland HF. Multiple sclerosis. *N Engl J Med.* 1982;307:1246–1251.
9. Clark VA, et al. Factors associated with a malignant or benign cause of multiple sclerosis. *J Am Med Assoc.* 1982;248:856–860.
10. Rose AS, et al. Cooperative study in the evaluation of therapy in multiple sclerosis—ACTH vs. placebo: final report. *Neurology.* 1970;20(suppl):1–59.

11. Shapira K, et al. Marriage, pregnancy, and multiple sclerosis. *Brain.* 1966;89:419–428.

12. Poser S, Poser W. Multiple sclerosis and gestation. *Neurology.* 1983;33:1422–1427.

13. Sadovnick AD, Baird PA. Reproductive counselling for multiple sclerosis patients. *Am J Med Genet.* 1985;20:349–354.

14. Birk K, Rudick R. Pregnancy and multiple sclerosis. *Arch Neurol.* 1986;43:719–726.

15. Korn-Lubetzki I, et al. Activity of multiple sclerosis during pregnancy and puerperium. *Ann Neurol.* 1984;16:229–231.

16. Burrow GN, Ferris TF. *Medical Complications during Pregnancy.* Philadelphia, Pa: W.B. Saunders Co.; 1982.

ADDITIONAL BIBLIOGRAPHY

Ferguson JM. Helping an MS patient live a better life. *RN.* December 1987;50:22–27.

Friedman ML, et al. Multiple sclerosis and the family. *Arch Psychiatr Nurs.* February 1987;(1):47–54.

McBride EV, et al. Explaining diagnostic tests for MS. *Nursing 88.* February 1988;18:68–72.

Van der Plaste C. Psychological aspects of multiple sclerosis and MS treatment: toward a biopsychosocial perspective. *Health Psychol.* 1984;3:253–272.

Chapter 6

Morbid Obesity

Ava R. McCarthy Sauer

REVIEW OF THE LITERATURE

Obesity is an endemic disease in the United States, with an estimated 20% incidence. Sociologically, the presence of obesity in Western society is interesting because, unlike many other societies, the incidence decreases as the socioeconomic level increases. In the United States and other Western nations, more poor women are obese than are middle-class and wealthy women.[1]

In many societies, particularly those in the East and the Pacific, feminine obesity has been seen as a positive physical attribute and increased the perceived value of a woman as a mate and bearer of children. "Fattening huts" were used in at least one South Pacific society to house pubescent women, while they were fed the group's most choice dishes, in preparation for childbearing. Logically, when periods of plenty were frequently followed by periods of famine, the individuals with the most ample stores of body fat had the greatest chance for survival, and the perpetuation of the group was directly dependent on women of childbearing age. Obesity became, for them, survival insurance.

Heredity, environmental, and psychologic factors influence the incidence of obesity. In at least one study,[2] obese mothers were observed overfeeding their infants much more frequently than those mothers in the nonobese control group, indicating that increased calorie consumption may be a behavior taught at a very early age.

Definitions of obesity vary greatly, depending upon the source. Nicholson and Santos defined morbid obesity as more than twice the normal predicted weight for height and build.[3] Freedman and his associates stated that, if the weight at delivery is twice the desirable weight, the parturient is "markedly obese" and, if she is more than three times her ideal weight, she is "grotesquely obese."[4] Another method of determination is by computing the body mass index (BMI).

Computing Body Mass Index

$$BMI = \frac{Weight\ (kg)}{Height\ (m^2)}$$
$$BMI > 30 = morbid\ obesity$$
$$25-29 = obesity$$
$$25 = normal$$

Broca's law states that ideal weight in kilograms equals the height in centimeters minus 100.

Both pregnancy and obesity are associated with distinct physiologic alterations that accentuate the other, making management of the gravid, morbidly obese patient both difficult and challenging. Numerous studies have shown that morbid obesity increases the risk in pregnancy of diabetes, macrosomia, and preeclampsia.[2,5–8] Between 1956 and 1973 in Chicago, four of seven maternal deaths occurred in morbidly obese women. In Minnesota between 1963 and 1972, 12% of maternal deaths occurred in women who weighed more than 200 lb even though demographically they represented a far lower percentage of the total.[2] Most deaths were reported to be secondary to embolic phenomena.

System Changes Relative to Obesity

Every major body organ system is affected by pregnancy. The same statement can be applied to obesity, especially morbid obesity, in pregnancy. Cardiac output in a normal intrauterine pregnancy is increased by 35 to 40%; in the obese patient, it increases by 50%. The left ventricular end pressure is increased compared to the normal parturient's, causing an increase in stroke volume. Blood pressure is usually decreased in pregnancy, secondary to decreased systemic vascular resistance (SVR); however, blood pressures are often increased in the morbidly obese, with a normal SVR. Cardiac load and myocardial oxygen consumption are both increased in pregnancy, and excess fat stores increase both oxygen consumption and carbon dioxide production, even at rest. The incidence of aortocaval compression syndrome is increased in the obese parturient.

Hemodynamics are significantly altered in obesity. A higher left ventricular preload and afterload may lead to an increased incidence of edema. The "pickwickian" syndrome (named after fat Joe in the *Pickwick Papers* by Charles Dickens) may be present when the obese patient presents a history of sleepiness during the day, snoring, or waking frequently during the night. Caused by upper airway obstruction, the syndrome can be fatal. Its incidence increases proportionately with the degree of obesity and is characterized by the triad of somnolence, obesity, and hypoventilation. If "obesity hypoventilation," or pickwickian syndrome, is present (as it will be in 10 to 20% of the morbidly obese), high flow and elevated pulmonary resistance lead to pulmonary hypertension. Obesity causes an increase in the cardiac workload.

The exaggerated lumbar lordosis normally present in pregnancy is more pronounced in the obese, who may also have thoracic kyphosis. This mechanical alteration, along with the weight of the chest wall, breasts, and viscera, greatly increase the respiratory workload as well. Chest wall compliance is decreased, respiratory muscles have a diminished ability to respond, and the inspiratory capacity is decreased. The functional residual capacity, normally lower in pregnancy, is more markedly lowered in obesity and is adversely affected by supine, lithotomy, or Trendelenburg positions, leading to a decreased oxygen saturation.

The weight of the chest wall can lead to alveolar compression and even alveolar collapse, especially in the supine or lithotomy position. The pregnant patient usually has a normal or elevated arterial oxygen saturation, but oxygen saturation is markedly decreased in the obese parturient. Additionally, the obese patient may demonstrate a reduced carbon dioxide response, leading to an increased risk of hypoxemia with the administration of drugs that depress respiration, such as narcotics and sedatives.

In the obese parturient, there is an increased incidence of hiatal hernia, secondary to the increased pressure from abdominal wall adipose. While gastric pressures, the volume of gastric contents, and gastric emptying time are all elevated in pregnancy, these become markedly elevated in patients with morbid obesity. For example, a normal parturient has a mean gastric volume of 22 ml, but the obese parturient has a 131-ml volume, with 80% having a pH lower than 2.5, the critical pH for the development of chemical pneumonitis if aspiration occurs. In short, the obese are at much higher risk for aspiration and chemical pneumonitis.

Obstetric Considerations Relative to Obesity

According to Garbaciak et al.[2] the incidence of perinatal mortality in obese patients was about the same as in the nonobese if there were no antenatal problems; however, in the presence of prenatal complications, the mortality was almost double that of the nonobese. (See Table 6-1.)

There is a much higher incidence of primary cesarean section among the obese.[7] This is significant because of both surgical and anesthesia risks, both intraoperatively and postoperatively. These include embolic phenomena, respiratory complications, and wound infection or dehiscence, in addition to an increased risk of aspiration. Additionally, the surgery may be technically difficult because of the size of the panniculus (the pendulous, fatty abdomen).

Assessment for progress of labor can be challenging. Vaginal examinations are mechanically difficult, external fetal monitoring may be impossible, and monitoring of contractions may well be inaccurate.

Table 6-1 Incidence of Obstetric Complications

Complication	Oats et al.[9]		Ruge et al.[10]		Johnson et al.[7]	
	Obesity %	Control %	Obesity %	Control %	Obesity %	Control %
Preeclampsia	32	9.5	24	—	—	—
Hypertension	3.5	0.4	17	—	27.6	3.1
Gestational diabetes	1.9	0.7	4	—	9.9	2.2
Antepartum hemorrhage	4.5	3.7	—	—	—	—
Infection	13.7	4.2	—	—	37.6	10.2
Venous thrombosis	0.7	0.2	—	—	—	—
Shoulder dystocia	—	—	—	—	5.1	0.6
Cesarean section	19.2	11.3	17	—	—	—

The presence of maternal antenatal complications in the obese contributes to a number of fetal complications. The risk of birth trauma is increased secondary to macrosomia and shoulder dystocia. Kliegman and associates reported a threefold increase in macrosomia among obese parturients, but only one-half the incidence of low birth weight found in normal weight women.[8] Additionally, they reported that the prepregnancy weight of the mother is of greater importance to fetal weight than is weight gain during pregnancy.

* * * * *

CASE STUDY

S.M., a 26-year-old white woman, was referred to the Perinatal Treatment Center at University Hospital by her private obstetrician when she became pregnant with her second child. At 374 lb, S.M. was 110 lb heavier than she had been during her first pregnancy (4 years previously), when she had delivered a healthy 4,300-g boy (by cesarean section because of breech presentation). During the course of this pregnancy, a vaginal birth after cesarean (VBAC) was planned.

Pleasant, well-groomed, and articulate, S.M. stated that she had "always" been obese and expressed a high level of interest in participating in good prenatal care. At 14 weeks gestation, the weight gain was 22 lbs over her prepregnancy weight, and she seemed responsive to consultation with the perinatal dietitian. At 63 in. in height, S.M. met all definitions of morbid obesity.

She reported a fairly good exercise tolerance, with the ability to care for her family and home, walk several blocks, and climb stairs without dyspnea or angina. She did, however, report ankle swelling after being on her feet for an extended

period and had difficulty sleeping flat, stating that she preferred "two or three pil-
lows." She had no history of drug, tobacco, or alcohol abuse.

S.M.'s previous pregnancy had been complicated by diet-controlled diabetes
mellitus and mild pregnancy-induced hypertension, both of which had resolved after delivery. She had epidural anesthesia for cesarean section, apparently without
complications, and had an uneventful postoperative course. Referral was based
solely on the increased weight at this time.

Initial physical examination revealed a very obese white woman, in no acute
distress, with a 14-week-size intrauterine pregnancy. Fundal height was determined, with great difficulty, to be consistent with 14 weeks gestation. Lungs were
clear, heart sounds were normal, and the deep tendon reflexes were normal. Blood
pressure, using a large thigh cuff, was 134/84, heart rate was 88, and respiratory
rate was 20. The hemoglobin and hematocrit were 14 g and 42%, respectively;
serum glucose level was 114 mg/dl; and urine was negative for protein and glucose. Initial ultrasound revealed a fetus consistent with 14 to 16 weeks gestation.

The remainder of S.M.'s pregnancy was uneventful, with weekly blood pressure,
urine, and fetal heart checks remaining within normal limits, until the 37th week of
gestation. At this time, she was noted to have a blood pressure of 144/90, a trace of
protein in the urine, and 2+ deep tendon reflexes, with no clonus. Although the
electronic fetal heart tracing was reassuring, the physician elected to hospitalize
S.M. for bed rest and further monitoring. Her weight at this time was 413 lb, representing a 36-lb weight gain since her initial evaluation.

On admission to the obstetric special care unit, S.M. reported "a gush of fluid"
from the vagina, and it was determined that membranes had ruptured. On vaginal
examination, the cervix was 50% effaced and 2 cm dilated, and the presenting part
was floating. Sonography revealed a vertex presentation, and S.M. reported contractions occurring about every 15 minutes.

Blood pressure was 140/90, but when repeated in 15 minutes was 132/84. Because the respiratory rate was 24, a pulse oximeter was used, which showed an
oxygen saturation of 90%. With the head of the bed elevated 45° and 2 liters of
nasal oxygen, O_2 saturation improved to 95%, respirations were 16, and S.M.
stated that she felt more comfortable.

An anesthesia consult was obtained shortly after admission to allow formulation
of an appropriate anesthesia case plan. The nurse anesthetist reviewed the history
and the anesthesia note that had been written earlier during the pregnancy and
again carefully explored with S.M. the risks and benefits of unmedicated labor,
intravenous analgesics, and epidural, spinal, and general anesthesia, including
those associated with vaginal delivery after cesarean section. S.M. stated that she
preferred to have epidural anesthesia for the trial of labor and delivery and seemed
to accept the possibility that placement of the epidural catheter might be difficult
and time consuming because of the increased weight gain since the last epidural
with the previous pregnancy.

Airway evaluation revealed normal dentition in good repair and adequate man-
dibular extension, but the tongue partially obscured the uvula. The trachea was

difficult to palpate because of fat over the neck and, although there was fairly good range of motion, neck extension was decreased because of shoulder fat pads. The anesthetist also explained that she would be drawing an arterial blood sample for baseline analysis and that S.M. would be receiving medication to help empty her stomach, followed by antacid, to be administered at regular intervals throughout labor. The arterial blood gas evaluation showed, on 2 liters of oxygen, a PaO_2 of 104, $PaCO_2$ of 48, and PH of 7.43; her measured oxygen saturation was 96%, which corresponded well to the peripheral monitor.

Because of ruptured membranes, borderline pregnancy-induced hypertension, and increased risks secondary to obesity, the perinatologist requested that the epidural catheter be placed, tested, and made ready for institution of analgesia or anesthesia as it was needed. In the sitting position, with full cooperation, catheter placement was achieved after two attempts. When she complained of increased discomfort, the epidural was injected with good pain relief, and vaginal examination showed the cervix to be 4 to 5 cm dilated and 90% effaced and the station to be −1. At this time, an internal fetal scalp electrode and an intrauterine pressure catheter were placed.

S.M. continued to labor in a semisitting position with left lateral uterine displacement. Her blood pressure, after epidural injection, remained in the 130/84 to 120/78 range, deep tendon reflexes were +1, and urine continued to show a trace of protein. Oxytocin augmentation was begun after 4 hours of labor when no further cervical changes were noted but was discontinued when the fetus showed signs of distress. S.M.'s white blood count remained within normal limits, but the temperature was 100° Fahrenheit. Contractions continued after oxytocin was discontinued, and the fetus showed a decrease in variability, deep variable decelerations, and a slow return to baseline on the fetal monitor. Despite repeated attempts, the perinatologist was unable to obtain a fetal scalp blood sample for analysis, and with full agreement from S.M. and her spouse, scheduled her for immediate cesarean section.

In the operating room, S.M. was positioned on the operating table with uterine displacement and her head and shoulders elevated. Both legs were wrapped with antiembolic wraps, and the anesthesia level was extended with additional epidural catheter injections. Oxygen was given by mask during the entire procedure, and both S.M. and her husband were shortly able to greet their new 5,400-g daughter. The operative procedure was uneventful, and S.M. was transported to the recovery room, where she continued to be monitored closely for 24 hours. The infant required an intravenous line for hypoglycemia, which was discontinued after 6 hours.

Postoperatively, S.M.'s pain was well controlled with epidural morphine, and she walked, with help, after 6 hours. On the second postoperative day her temperature rose to 101° Fahrenheit, and she was noted on physical examination to have decreased breath sounds over the right lung base. Chest x-ray film showed right lower lobe atelectasis, and S.M. was assisted by means of vigorous respiratory toilet. Minidose heparin was continued throughout the postoperative course, and mother and baby were discharged on the seventh day in good condition.

* * * * *

CASE ANALYSIS

Successful management of the pregnant, morbidly obese patient, as with any other high-risk patient, requires teamwork, early intervention, and coordination of efforts to effect a successful outcome. Because S.M. was followed throughout her second and third trimester by the same perinatologist, nurse clinician, and dietitian, they were able to arrange appropriate consultations with anesthesia, pediatric, and labor and delivery personnel before she went into labor. Frank, honest discussions with her about the realities of her health and special needs because of her size allowed her to participate in the planning of care from an informed perspective.

S.M. experienced several of the antenatal, intrapartum, and postpartum complications commonly found in the morbidly obese (mild pregnancy-induced hypertension, hypoxemia during labor, fetal distress, dystocia, macrosomia with fetal hypoglycemia, and postoperative atelectasis), but they were anticipated and were managed aggressively.

Maternal monitoring during labor was limited to the use of an automated blood pressure device and a pulse oximeter. However, if the hypoxia had not improved to near-normal with positioning and oxygen administration, an arterial line would have been appropriate to monitor pressures and serial blood gases. Increasing severity of the pregnancy-induced hypertension may have necessitated magnesium sulfate and antihypertensive therapy, as well as a central line to monitor fluids.

Among some institutions, the management of the laboring woman undergoing VBAC remains controversial. Crawford stated in 1974 that "previous cesarean section is not in itself a contraindication to epidural analgesia,"[11] but some obstetricians and nurse-midwives are reluctant to mask any symptoms that may indicate dehiscence. Communication among the obstetric, nursing, and anesthesia teams is of paramount importance in determining management, as is their immediate presence in the delivery suite to manage possible complications. True segmental lumbar epidurals (those that block only the segments from T10 to L1 or, roughly, from umbilicus to symphysis pubis during first-stage labor) were reported by Uppington, in 1983, to be used safely during vaginal birth following cesarean section.[11]

Careful airway evaluation as early as possible can be life saving. In any high-risk patient, general anesthesia, even in the presence of a functioning epidural, may be required in emergency situations. The obese pregnant patient can be excruciatingly difficult to intubate and ventilate and may require two experienced anesthesiologists or nurse anesthetists. If general anesthesia is required, the obese patient must be preoxygenated for a minimum of 5 minutes before induction; it is for this reason that S.M. was given 100% oxygen by mask during her cesarean section (to anticipate a possible need for conversion from epidural to general anesthesia). Postoperatively, the obese parturient who has had general anesthesia will probably require that the endotracheal tube be left in place, with ventilatory support, for 12 to 24 hours.

Because of the high mortality associated with embolic phenomena and their high incidence, the morbidly obese parturient requires aggressive preventive measures. These include antiembolic leg wraps, heparin administration, and early ambulation.

The use of epidural narcotics can encourage ambulation, since there is usually no central depression from their administration. Drugs commonly used for analgesia via epidural catheter include morphine sulfate, fentanyl, sufentanyl, and butorphanol. Possible side effects include respiratory depression (as much as 12 hours after administration), pruritis, nausea or vomiting, and urinary retention. The most serious possible side effect, respiratory depression, has been reported in 0.9% of cases, with none of these having sudden or delayed (4 hours or more after administration) onset.[12] General guidelines for caring for the patient who has received epidural narcotics include the following:

- Keep the head of the bed elevated 30° to 45° for the first 24 hours.
- Have resuscitative equipment, including an Ambu-bag, O_2, and naloxone, readily available.
- Flag the chart or Kardex that the patient has received epidural narcotics.
- Monitor the respiratory rate every 15 minutes for 1 hour, every 30 minutes for 2 hours, and then every hour for 21 hours.
- If the respiratory rate drops below 10 or if the patient is lethargic or difficult to arouse, give oxygen and call for immediate assistance.
- Assess the patient for nausea and/or pruritus and treat according to orders (usually with metoclopramide or naloxone, respectively).
- Leave the Foley catheter in place for 24 hours.
- Encourage ambulation within 6 to 8 hours.

Epidural anesthesia, while mechanically quite difficult in the obese, is desirable because it can help to avoid general anesthesia and the many complications that can be associated with it. Early placement of the epidural catheter is desirable to obtain full patient cooperation.

IMPLICATIONS FOR PRACTICE

In many ways, managing the physical requirements of the morbidly obese parturient, while not without difficulty, may be more simple than addressing the psychosocial factors of a body habitus which, in our society, is all too frequently met with "repulsion, revulsion, rejection, contempt, ridicule, taunts, discrimination, patronizing aversion, tactless staring, questioning, and devaluing pity."[13] Members of the health care team are as susceptible to these reactions as are members of the general public and must honestly confront their own feelings about obesity; inability to do so may significantly interfere with the ability to give good patient care and may contribute to a decrease in the patient's self-esteem.

Self-concept, which includes an awareness and evaluation of one's self and body image, influences profoundly how one deals with crises, everyday occurrences, and personal expectations; however, according to Brundage and Broadwell, "obese subjects failed to develop an organized, differentiated and inner sense of self and of integrity."[13] This distorted sense of self, frequently accompanied by lowered self-esteem, requires sensitivity, support, and positive feedback from the primary care givers. An encounter with a care giver who communicates that the patient is valued may well empower her in other areas of her life.

Patient teaching is of the utmost importance during all phases of parturition. Dietary counseling, with special emphasis on good, basic nutrition, may actually help to maintain prepregnancy weight without reducing caloric intake, primarily from a marked decrease in "empty calories" from junk food. Pregnancy is never a time for dieting, not only because of the relationship between prematurity and low weight gain, but also because caloric restriction has been implicated in ketonemia, a situation that creates an inability for the fetus to utilize essential nutrients, resulting in decreased brain development.[14] Nutritional counseling, however, can have an additional benefit in that it may ultimately decrease the risk of obesity in the child.

Early intervention may also help with the very real requirements of recovery in a patient who is at high risk for postoperative problems. She will require help with coughing, deep breathing, turning, moving, and ambulating, and full cooperation will result in an optimal recovery.

In summary, a team approach to total patient care, including psychosocial issues, dietary counseling, anesthesia consultation, and recovery regimes can minimize the difficulty of delivering the morbidly obese pregnant women. Anticipation of possible complications, attention to adaptations that may be required to accommodate the large patient, and a commitment to deal honestly with the patient will greatly enhance her opportunity for a positive birth experience.

REFERENCES

1. Brown PJ, Konner M. An anthropological perspective on obesity. *Ann NY Acad Sci.* 1985;499:29–46.
2. Garbaciak JA, Richter M, Miller S, Barton JJ. Maternal weight and pregnancy complications. *Am J Obstet Gynecol.* 1985;152:238–245.

3. Nicholson C, Santos D. *The Practice of Obstetrical Anesthesia: A Review.* Ohio Medical; 1984.

4. Freedman et al. 1972.

5. Boyd, ME, Usher RH, McLean FH. Fetal macrosomia: prediction, risks, proposed management. *Obstet Gynecol.* 1983;61:715–722.

6. Dewan DM. The obese parturient. *Virginia Apgar Seminar Syllabus.* 1988;83–95.

7. Johnson SR, Kolberg BH, Varner MW, Railsback LD. Maternal obesity and pregnancy. *Surg Gynecol Obstet.* 1987;164:431–437.

8. Kliegman R, Gross T, Morton S, Dunnington R. Intrauterine growth and postnatal fasting metabolism in infants of obese mothers. *J Pediatr.* 1984;104:601–607.

9. Oats JN, Abell DA, Andersen HM, Belscher NA. Obesity in pregnancy. *Compr Ther.* 1983;9:51–55.

10. Ruge S, Andersen T. Obstetric risks in obesity: an analysis of the literature. *Obstet Gynecol Surv.* 1985;40:57–60.

11. Palmer SK. Anesthetic management of the obstetric emergency. *ASA Refresher Courses.* 1984;136:1–6.

12. Sauer AM. Complicated obstetrics. *AANA Summaries of Professional Sessions.* 1987;85–89.

13. Brundage DJ, Broadwell DC. Altered body image. In: Phipps WJ, Long BC, Woods NF, eds. *Medical Surgical Nursing Concepts and Clinical Practice.* St. Louis, Mo: C.V. Mosby Co., 1983;544–555.

14. Houde CA. Nutrition in pregnancy. In: Angelini DJ, Knapp CMW, Gibes RM, eds. *Perinatal/ Neonatal Nursing, A Clinical Handbook.* Boston: Blackwell Scientific Publications; 1986:1–18.

ADDITIONAL BIBLIOGRAPHY

Bray GA. Complications of obesity. *Ann Intern Med.* 1985;103:1052–1062.

Cohen SE. Anesthesia for the morbidly obese pregnant patient. In: Snider SM, Levinson G, eds. *Anesthesia for Obstetrics.* Baltimore, Md: Williams & Wilkins, 1987.

Cohen SE. The anesthetic implications of the physiologic changes of pregnancy. *ASA Refresher Courses.* 1986;261:1–6.

Cohen SE, Tan S, Albright GA, Halpern J. Epidural fentanyl/bupivacaine mixtures for obstetric analgesia. *Anesthesiology.* 1987;67:403–407.

Ellis WE. Anesthesia and obesity. *AANA Summaries of Professional Sessions.* 1987;75–76.

Gross T, Solcol RJ, King KC. Obesity in pregnancy: risks and outcome. *Obstet Gynecol.* 1980;56:446–450.

Holmes J, Magiera L. *Maternity Nursing.* New York, NY: Macmillan Publishing Co., Inc.; 1987:671.

Justins DM, Francis D, Houlton PG, Reynolds F. A controlled trial of extradural fentanyl in labour. *Br J Anaesthesia.* 1982;54:409–413.

Kliegman RM, Gross T. Perinatal problems of the obese mother and her infant. *Obstet Gynecol.* 1985;66:299–306.

Long BC, Gorwin CJ, Bushong ME. Surgical intervention. In: Phipps WJ, Long BC, Woods NF, eds. *Medical Surgical Nursing Concepts and Clinical Practice.* St. Louis, Mo: C.V. Mosby Co.; 1983:404–405.

Philipson EH, Kalhan SC, Edelberg SC, Williams TG. Maternal obesity as a risk factor in gestational diabetes. *Am J Perinatol.* 1985;2:268–270.

Rutherford SE, Phelan JP. Deep venous thrombosis and pulmonary embolus. In: Clark SK, Phelan JP, Catton DB, eds. *Critical Care Obstetrics.* Oradell, NJ: Medical Economics Books; 1987:126–151.

Stenseth R, Sellevold O, Breivik H. Epidural morphine for postoperative pain: experience with 1085 patients. *Acta Anesthesiol Scand.* 1985;29:148–156.

Sugerman HJ. Pulmonary function in morbid obesity. *Gastroenterol Clin North Am.* 1987;16:225–237.

Terry BE. Morbid obesity: cardiac evaluation and function. *Gastroenterol Clin North Am.* 1987;16:215–223.

Wasserstrum N, Cotton DB. Volume expansion and antihypertensive therapy in severe pre-eclampsia. In: Clark SL, Phelan JP, Cotton DB, eds. *Critical Care Obstetrics.* Oradell, NJ: Medical Economics Books; 1987.

Chapter 7

Asymptomatic HIV Infection in Pregnancy

Kathleen Sullivan

The expanding epidemic of acquired immunodeficiency syndrome (AIDS)—the focus of intensive medical, social, and political attention in recent years—has slowly but definitively established itself as a problem area for clinical providers of obstetric care. Infection with human immunodeficiency virus (HIV) is steadily increasing in women of reproductive age, and gynecologic and obstetric providers must expect to encounter the HIV-infected woman with increasing regularity.

HIV infection can result in a spectrum of clinical states, ranging from a brief acute viremic illness, to a prolonged period of asymptomatic carrier status, to infection with a series of lymphadenopathy-associated syndromes once identified as AIDS-related complex (ARC), through overt illness with the opportunistic infections associated with "full-blown" AIDS. The unique features of this disease make it most likely that the pregnant woman with HIV infection will present during the asymptomatic phase. Early detection of the illness, then, will depend on clinical providers' familiarity with the epidemiology of the syndrome. This chapter describes a case of asymptomatic HIV infection in a woman identified through screening during pregnancy.

REVIEW OF THE LITERATURE

Epidemiology of HIV Infection

As of June 1990, nearly 140,000 cases of AIDS had been reported to the Centers for Disease Control (CDC) since 1981, with 28% of those reported during the previous year.[1] It is clear, given the lengthy incubation period for the illness—now believed to be up to ten years following infection[2]—that AIDS cases represent only a small proportion of the total HIV-infected population.

Specific risk groups with high HIV prevalence rates have gradually been identified since the epidemic first surfaced. Homosexual and bisexual men, drug injectors, hemophiliacs and other recipients of blood products, immigrants from geographic high-risk areas of sub-Saharan Africa and parts of the Caribbean, and, most recently, sexual partners and children of individuals from known risk groups have been gradually identified by patterns of illness within these groups.

The incidence of HIV infection varies considerably by geographic area (highest for homosexual or bisexual men in California and the northeast, highest for drug injectors around New York City and in Puerto Rico); by sex (higher for men in all groups except drug injectors, where prevalence rates are the same for both sexes), and by race (higher for blacks and Latinos).[3] Intravenous (IV) drug use is currently most prevalent in inner-city urban areas, and these regions have large minority populations; thus, AIDS prevalence rates for minorities are elevated. Even among IV drug injectors, however, blacks and Latinos have higher HIV seropositivity rates than do whites.[3]

HIV Infection in Woman

Women currently represent 9% of all known AIDS cases in the United States.[1] Slightly more than half of these women have a history of drug injection,[1] but heterosexual transmission of HIV is now surfacing as an increasingly important transmission source for women. In 1982, heterosexual contact with men at risk for AIDS was the sole risk factor for only 12% of all women with AIDS; by 1990 this proportion had risen to 33%.[1]

As expected, the highest incidence of AIDS in women occurs in areas with high rates of substance use. Again, racial and ethnic disproportion is seen. In 1990, a majority of women with AIDS were black (52%) or Latina (21%).[1] HIV infection and AIDS are now the leading cause of death in black women aged 15 to 44 in New York and New Jersey.[4]

To date, the number of heterosexually transmitted AIDS cases is small—only 5% of all AIDS cases in the United States[1]—but this represents a significant increase over the 1% proportion reported in 1983,[3] and this is the only transmission category that has significantly increased since surveillance began.[5] A further trend within this transmission category is now evident. During the early surveillance period, the majority of women in this category were from countries where heterosexual transmission is an important source of AIDS (50% of cases in Haiti and Zaire are believed due to heterosexual transmission[6]). By 1988, however, more than three-quarters of the women with heterosexually transmitted AIDS were United States-born,[7] and by 1990 75% of these cases had occurred in minority women.[1]

HIV Infection in Children

Children (under 13 years old) now comprise 1.7% of U.S. AIDS cases.[1] Four-fifths of these cases are assumed to be perinatal in origin, since the children were born to women with AIDS, ARC, HIV infection, or risk factors for HIV infection.[1] The demographics of this disease typically match those of women with HIV infections: 77% of pediatric AIDS cases have occurred in blacks and Latinos.[1] Although pediatric AIDS is associated with maternal drug injection in 41% of cases, heterosexually transmitted HIV infections is increasing as a source category and now accounts for 24% of pediatric AIDS cases.[1]

Prevalence of HIV Infection in Pregnant Women

Two major approaches to the problem of identifying asymptomatic HIV infection in the childbearing population have been developed. The first attempts to identify prevalence through screening of pregnant women for risk factors for HIV infection. Voluntary screening based on individual assessment of risk factors is proving to be of limited effectiveness. Reliable self-reporting of significant risk factors (IV drug use, sexual contact with IV drug users or bisexual men) may be difficult to obtain, partly because these factors carry considerable stigma and partly because women may simply be unaware of a sex partner's true risk status. Studies have repeatedly demonstrated significant numbers of pregnant seropositives who would not have been uncovered by self-assessment for risk.[8-11]

Another approach is to determine the prevalence of unrecognized HIV infection through random or serial testing of cord or newborn blood samples. Predictably, in urban communities where drug use or pediatric AIDS are already identified, seroprevalence rates are rising, especially in some public institutions in the northeast, Florida, and Puerto Rico. However, the Centers for Disease Control emphasize that surveillance of pediatric AIDS cases through 1990 reveals increasing numbers of cases from outside the initially affected urban areas.[12]

The message for obstetric providers is clear. First, HIV infection is epidemic in some parts of the United States and in these regions may be considerably more common than other infections routinely screened for during prenatal care. Second, women without identified risk factors—including geography—do have HIV infection, possibly as a result of unrecognized exposure through sexual activity.

Perinatal Transmission of HIV Infection

Perinatal transmission of HIV is now well documented. The transplacental route has been identified as the most likely transmission mode. Several case studies have established the presence of HIV antigen in fetal tissue from 8 to 28 weeks gestation.[13,14] Although these data establish that transplacental infection may occur quite early in pregnancy, it is unknown at what precise point in gestation the majority of intrauterine infections will occur.

Indeed, some uncertainty exists as to whether intrauterine infection is the only mode of transmission. Since HIV has been isolated in cervical secretions of seropositive women,[15-17] the potential for infection during childbirth (as in the transmission mode for other viruses) has been of concern. Pediatric AIDS has been repeatedly documented in children of HIV-infected mothers delivered by cesarean section, however, and by cesarean without antecedent rupture of membranes,[18] and at present it is considered unlikely that contact with virus present in the birth canal represents a major risk for transmission of the virus.[19] Since it is theoretically possible that contact between a seropositive mother's vaginal secretions and the baby's blood could provide a portal of entry for the virus, it is currently recommended that fetal scalp sampling and scalp electrode application be avoided if possible.[19]

The most basic and pressing question about perinatal HIV transmission—how many babies of HIV-infected mothers will also be infected?—has proved difficult to answer. The earliest studies reported widely discrepant transmission rates: 21% to 65%. Currently a small but growing number of prospective studies seem to indicate that the infection may be transmitted to roughly one child in three.

There are a number of reasons why these data have been slow to develop. Diagnosis of the infection in children is difficult, in part because clinical findings may be nonspecific and unpredictable in onset and in part because currently available technology cannot provide a clear laboratory profile.

Since maternal HIV antibody is passively transmitted in late pregnancy, newborns are uniformly seropositive for HIV. While most will lose this maternal antibody at 9 to 10 months, some will carry the antibody up to 18 months before reconverting.[20,21] Further complicating this picture, some seronegative children may have a false-negative antibody test (and be virus-positive by culture[21]) or be in a "window phase"—before they begin active antibody production of their own—that can last up to 6 months.[22]

Two techniques now available in research centers may provide more reliable means of identifying the truly HIV-infected infant. HIV culture, while expensive and technically difficult, is an accurate way to establish the presence of infection, but a negative HIV culture unfortunately does not confirm the absence of infection, as HIV viremia can present intermittently.[23] Polymerase chain reactor (PCR), a gene amplification technique, has looked more promising as a means of distinguishing the truly infected infant but still needs improvement in both specificity and sensitivity.[24]

A second area of difficulty in establishing precise rates for perinatal HIV transmission involves the population of seropositive women studied. The earliest studies were performed in women identified because they were mothers of children known to have AIDS: their high transmission rates (up to 65% in one much-quoted study[25]) may have been affected by the duration of seropositivity or by the presence of symptomatic infection in the mothers. More recent prospective studies, often of populations identified through screening during pregnancy, have only rarely identified transmission rates over one-third. Indeed, two well-studied U.S.

populations were recently reported as having transmission rates as low as 13% in Atlanta[26] and 19% in Newark.[27] New York researchers report a 29% transmission rate[28]; the large European collaborative study reported a 24% transmission rate in 1988.[29]

There are a number of other puzzling features of perinatal transmission of HIV. Both symptomatic and asymptomatic mothers may transmit the infection.[30,31] A seropositive mother may give birth both to infected and subsequently to noninfected offspring.[25,30] Twins may be discordant for the infection.[31] Current research into the role of potential cofactors of transmission (symptomatic illness, coexistence of other infectious disease) is inconclusive. It is hoped that biologic indices (the duration of seropositivity, the presence of HIV antigenemia, low CD4 (T4 cell counts) levels) or epidemiologic factors (source category for HIV infection) will help predict which women are most likely to transmit the virus to their offspring. One researcher reported preliminary results suggesting that presence or absence of a particular epitope on the HIV antigen may be a predictor of transmissibility.[28]

HIV Transmission and Breast-feeding

The issue of whether HIV may be transmitted through breast-feeding is also quite complex. The first case of pediatric AIDS presumed to be transmitted through breast milk was reported in 1985.[32] HIV was soon thereafter isolated in the breast milk of HIV-infected women,[33] and a small number of case reports— usually of breast-fed infants of mothers who had received infected transfusions in the postpartum period—subsequently confirmed that this is a mode of transmission for HIV infection.

Perinatal HIV transmission rates have not been demonstrated as higher in breast-fed than in bottle-fed infants, however, and it is conceivable that it is the seroconverting (and thus probably antigenemic) mother who is effective at transmitting HIV through breast milk. Since it is not currently possible to state, however, that it is risk-free for certain seropositive women to breast-feed, the CDC have recommended since 1985 that HIV-positive women avoid breast-feeding. The World Health Organization, on the other hand, feels that the clear health risks of formula feeding in developing countries and the known immunologic benefits of breast-feeding, warrant a recommendation that seropositive women be encouraged to breast-feed.[34]

HIV Infection and Pregnancy

HIV Disease in Women

There are significant gaps in our knowledge of the natural history of HIV infection in women. A handful of studies have suggested gender differences in HIV infection. Some have suggested that the disease may be more aggressive in women than in men,[35,36] although the possibility exists that women simply present later in the course of illness or are diagnosed later, and these factors may be a stronger influence on the observed progression of illness than is gender alone.[37] Cervical dysplasia,[38] especially related to human papillomavirus,[39] and vaginal candidiasis[40] may be manifestations of HIV disease in women. Some question also exists as to whether pelvic inflammatory disease may represent a form of opportunistic infection in women.[41] Most observers note that Kaposi's sarcoma occurs less frequently in women but that *Pneumocystis carinii* pneumonia, as in men, is the most common AIDS-defining event.[37]

Effects of Pregnancy on HIV Infection

The effect of pregnancy itself on the health of an HIV-infected woman is poorly understood. Suppression of certain immunologic features noted in normal pregnancy (decreased killer cell activity,[42] decreased T-helper cells[43]) has raised questions of whether pregnancy itself could accelerate the progression of HIV disease. Furthermore, dramatic early case reports of maternal deaths in women with opportunistic infections, previously undiagnosed for HIV infection,[44-47] raised concerns that pregnancy could contribute to a rapid progression of the illness. Follow-up data for women first identified because they were mothers of children with AIDS seemed to suggest both a high rate of illness and possibly a somewhat earlier onset of illness than has been seen in the general adult HIV-infected population.[25,26]

Most subsequent prospective studies concluded that pregnancy does not influence the progression of illness, however.[48,49] Since observation periods have rarely exceeded 3 years, concern still exists that pregnancy may exacerbate immunocompromise. Nationwide research currently in progress may clarify this question. Most of the seropositive pregnant women followed at clinical trial centers in the United States are asymptomatic. The National Institutes of Health reported that, through 1989, only 6% of these women had overt AIDS and only 12% had any HIV-related symptoms.[50]

Immunologic studies also attempted to determine the effect of pregnancy on health status. Pregnancy appears to be associated with a transient decrease in CD4 cell levels, especially at about 7 months[51,52]; one study found that CD4 levels in seropositive women dropped again in the postpartum period, while seronegative women's levels returned to normal.[51] Transient HIV antigenemia has been noted in pregnant seropositive women compared to nonpregnant controls, but without apparent influence on the progression of HIV infection in the postpartum period.[48]

The potential interaction of pregnancy and HIV infection also indirectly but significantly affects both the recognition and the treatment of clinical illness. First, since nonspecific symptoms of HIV infection (fatigue, weight loss, and anorexia) may mimic some pregnancy symptoms, pregnancy could effectively mask HIV symptoms and thus delay diagnosis of this early phase of illness. Furthermore, several common opportunistic infections (toxoplasmosis, herpes, cytomegalovirus [CMV]) also have significant fetal effects, yet medical treatments for these illnesses may require agents whose safety in pregnancy is unclear.[19]

Possibly most importantly, treatment opportunities for HIV infection in women have been limited. Antiviral agents are now increasingly in use for treatment of symptomatic adults and children and for prophylaxis in asymptomatic adults with falling CD4 counts. But concern over potential fetal effects of zidovudine (AZT or ZDV) has until recently prevented its use in pregnant women (and in some instances in any seropositive woman of childbearing age). Now, initial treatment efforts for pregnant women have two goals: preventing progression of the disease in the woman and potentially preventing transmission of the virus to the fetus. While uncertainty exists about the metabolism of zidovudine in pregnancy and about the precise timing of fetal infection, since late 1989 study protocols for the administration of zidovudine (beginning the the third trimester or beginning during labor) have been in use. In 1989, only 29 pregnant women had yet received medication in these trials; no fetal effects have been observed.[50] One case report described the experience of zidovudine use throughout pregnancy in a woman who elected to continue her prepregnancy dosages; her infant was nevertheless infected with HIV.[53]

Effects of HIV Infection on Pregnancy

A final question about the interaction of HIV infection and pregnancy—whether the virus affects the outcome of pregnancy—has also not been simple to answer. Conflicting data exist, possibly because many outcome measures are strongly associated with potentially confounding variables of substance abuse, poor access to care, and low socioeconomic status. Most well-controlled studies are not able to identify HIV serostatus as an independent influence on intrauterine growth retardation, low birth weight, or preterm delivery, although one study noted that premature birth was more common in children later found to be infected with the virus.[28] Similarly, it is as yet unclear whether there is an association between HIV infection and an increased incidence of spontaneous abortion. Premature rupture of membranes, chorioamnionitis, thrombocytopenia, and anemia have each been described in infected patients.[54]

* * * * *

CASE STUDY

A 28-year-old Puerto Rican woman, gravida III, para II, presented for routine prenatal care at 18 weeks of amenorrhea. Her past medical history was unremarkable; she denied prior surgery, transfusion, and sexually transmitted diseases. Her family history was negative. Obstetric history included two full-term vaginal deliveries of healthy 7-lb babies, 3 and 5 years previously, following uncomplicated pregnancies. She lived with her husband, who was unemployed, and her children. She reported no history of drug, alcohol, or tobacco use.

Routine counseling regarding HIV risk assessment and screening was performed at the initial visit. Risk factors for HIV infection were described, testing was offered, and a pamphlet further detailing HIV and hepatitis B risks and screening was supplied. The patient denied risks for HIV infection for herself and her husband, her only sex partner in 9 years.

Three weeks after her initial interview, the patient returned for routine care but opened the encounter stating that she thought she ought to have "the AIDS test" as she suspected that her husband had in the past injected drugs. She described his current health as excellent. She was unable to pinpoint the period when he might have used drugs but reiterated her suspicion and repeated the request for screening.

The HIV screening process was described, and the patient provided written consent for testing. Counseling included a review of risk factors, discussion of the significance of a positive or negative test result, and discussion of risk reduction and measures to prevent transmission of the virus. The implications for pregnancy in the case of a positive test were emphasized. The patient stated that, because of her religious beliefs, she could not under any circumstances consider terminating her pregnancy but that she wanted to know whether she had been infected with the virus. She described her mother and her sisters as potential supports to her in the event of learning that she was infected.

The patient's serum was repeatedly ELISA-positive and confirmed as HIV-positive by Western blot. Results were made available to the provider at 23 weeks gestation. The patient was informed of the results during an interview with her obstetric provider and a clinical social worker.

The patient's initial reaction was of shock and distress. She repeatedly questioned whether the results were accurate. She expressed her sense of horror that her husband's behavior, which she had always feared as dangerous for him, would also have consequences for herself and for the health of their future child. Her responses, interestingly, dealt with her own sense of guilt and responsibility rather than with anger toward her husband. She indicated her intention to delay disclosing her test results to her family until she had had time to think it over.

Supportive counseling was recommended, and follow-up 2 days later for continued discussion was arranged. At this visit, the patient presented with specific requests for information: What effect could her seropositivity have on her fetus? Was there something medically that could be done to prevent the baby from being infected? Was it certain that her husband would also be HIV-infected? At this visit she admitted being fearful that her husband was an active drug user and expressed her shame and anger about this. Again she expressed feelings of guilt that she had failed to heed her own early suspicions about his life-style and her sense that she was therefore responsible for her HIV infection. She expressed a growing reluctance to discuss her test results with her husband or with anyone in her family.

This first postdiagnosis visit was also dedicated to providing medical information, expanding on issues that had first been discussed prior to testing. In addition to counseling about the general implications of HIV seropositivity, the two areas of risk assessment specific to pregnancy were again emphasized: the risk of maternal HIV infection to the fetus and the possibility of risk to the HIV-infected mother of the pregnancy itself. The current state of knowledge about the natural history of HIV infection in both women and children was discussed. Common symptoms of HIV infection were briefly described.

In this case, the patient expressed understanding that the data regarding HIV transmission to the newborn, although alarming, did not allow for a prediction about whether the baby would be infected. This uncertainty was not problematic because she was sure that she would not terminate the pregnancy to avoid delivering an infected child, and she chose to take some comfort from data estimating a probable transmission rate under 50%. (Other women who do consider pregnancy termination an option may need more extensive discussion of the variant transmission rates now being reported.) However, counseling of this patient regarding the theoretical possibility that pregnancy could accelerate progression of her infection raised disturbing questions for her, as she considered for the first time the effect of her own life-threatening illness on her family's future.

Discussion of sexual activity in the context of risk reduction and the prevention of further HIV transmission was extremely difficult for this patient. She did not respond verbally during discussion of "safe sex" practices and indicated her discomfort through body language. Written information was then provided to reinforce counseling, and a supply of condoms was offered, which the patient refused, emphatically stating that she intended to avoid coitus altogether.

The pregnancy was unremarkable obstetrically. Routine pregnancy screens had been performed on registration: VDRL, purified protein derivative, Papanicolaou smear, HBsAg, and cultures for gonorrhea and chlamydia were all negative. Once HIV seropositivity was determined, additional baseline titers for cytomegalovirus, toxoplasmosis, and varicella were performed to aid in the diagnosis of future symptomatic illness, should it occur. (Herpes and Epstein-Barr virus titers, recommended by some practitioners,[55,56] were not performed.)

The complete blood count (CBC) remained normal throughout pregnancy, with the hematocrit ranging from 35 to a low of 29, with a subsequent return to 34. CD4 (or T4) cell counts performed at 23 and 32 weeks gestation were within the normal range. Repeat screening in the third trimester for sexually transmitted disease, tuberculosis, and cervical dysplasia were negative.

Physical assessment included routine evaluation of obstetric parameters, with additional inspection of the skin and oropharynx, palpation of lymph glands, and auscultation of lungs. Fetal growth was adequate by clinical examination and confirmed by second and third trimester ultrasound studies.

The patient had two major physical complaints during pregnancy, fatigue and poor appetite. Weight gain, adequate until the time of diagnosis, was low throughout the second trimester, a period when the patient described herself as very anxious and upset. Frequent nutritional counseling visits and gradual resolution of anxiety were probably jointly responsible for improvement in nutritional status, and by 36 weeks of gestation the patient had gained 22 lb.

Fatigue and weight loss, commonly seen in normal pregnancy, can represent nonspecific symptoms of early HIV illness; maintenance of an adequate hematocrit and optimal nutritional intake will perhaps help differentiate these from pregnancy-related complaints. Dyspnea, likely to increase in the third trimester as a relatively common complaint of pregnancy, might also be a nonspecific symptom of early HIV infection. Other symptoms of infection (prolonged fever, diarrhea, lymphadenopathy, or night sweats) are more likely to be specific for disease progression, however, and should be carefully evaluated.

Although it is important to educate the seropositive woman about signs and symptoms of HIV infection, it can be difficult to describe the vague symptoms without causing undue alarm. In this case, a mild upper respiratory infection at 30 weeks gestation was the occasion for extreme anxiety in this patient, until she could be reassured that the slight fever and mild cough were unlikely to be pathognomic. Clinicians themselves may find it difficult to be reassuring. Indeed, the persistence of even a mild, dry cough or sore throat could represent an early sign of a respiratory manifestation of HIV infection and cannot be dismissed without careful assessment.

This woman's concern over physical symptoms presented an opportunity for the development of supportive and educational responses from health care providers. In this woman's case, frequent visits with her social worker and obstetric provider allowed reinforcement that the painful emotions of distress and depression were natural reactions to the threat offered by HIV infection and that anxiety and depression could both manifest with physical symptoms. Both providers were careful to acknowledge that chronic fatigue and shortness of breath, although likely to be effects of the pregnancy, represented fearful experiences for her.

Emotional complaints were more common in this patient than were physical complaints. For months she struggled intermittently with anxiety and depression as she considered the implications of HIV infection, the possibility that she could die, and feelings of both self-blame and anger toward her husband. She often expressed sadness and frustration that her illness could not be cured and frequently asked for information about progress in treatment possibilities for newborns at risk for HIV infection. Positive expressions of hope did occasionally occur during prenatal visits, when reports of good fetal growth and improved weight gain seemed to validate her efforts to take good care of herself during the pregnancy.

Her most persistent concern was over disclosure of the diagnosis. She was firm in her intention not to notify her husband and family and became concerned that the information might inadvertently become available to them. Her husband's drug use was unknown to her family. The patient felt that the stigma associated with drug use would be overwhelming for her mother and sister, and she feared that they would actively reject her and her children. Furthermore, she became insistent that she could not inform her husband of her diagnosis. She was convinced that he would be angry, possibly violently so, and accusing toward her, rather than supportive.

Her fears clearly left her in a double bind—in need of emotional support, yet unable to disclose her distress to her most likely support network. Although she was initially able to engage with her clinical social worker, who worked with her at first to help contain her anxiety and then to encourage her to seek social support, she nevertheless experienced increasing feelings of shame and self-blame and developed nearly complete isolation from her family.

By 36 weeks of pregnancy she had still been unable to disclose her diagnosis to her husband, despite encouragement from health care providers and the development of a plan for disclosure in conjunction with her social worker. At this point her anxiety and sense of hopelessness may have again increased, and she failed for the first time to attend scheduled prenatal and counseling visits.

The patient's failure to inform her partner, the likely source of her HIV infection, of her seropositive status raised difficult issues for health care providers. This patient had a good understanding of transmission modes, and she understood that prevention of further transmission of HIV infection would involve her husband's learning of his own serostatus. She felt incapable of discussing the issue with him because of the risks to herself and expressed that she would be unable at any rate to discuss his use of drugs, needle-sharing and needle-cleaning habits, or even safe sexual activity, since she felt that even her familiarity with these subjects would be cause for rage in her husband. She expressed despair that health care providers and social workers could understand the extent of her fear of her husband. At the same time, she declined to participate in a newly formed support group for HIV-infected individuals, expressing both her personal sense of privacy and her fear that she would feel culturally isolated in such a group.

The patient presented to the labor and delivery unit at 39 weeks gestation in active labor. Membranes ruptured spontaneously at 6 cm dilatation, and moderate meconium staining of the amniotic fluid was noted. Fetal monitoring was performed by Doppler mode. The quality of external monitoring was adequate, and the tracing was consistently reassuring. The patient progressed rapidly through labor, and a normal spontaneous vaginal delivery of a 3020-g female infant with Apgar scores of 8 and 9 ensued. Oronasopharyngeal suctioning by wall-mounted DeLee suction was performed before delivery of the shoulders.

The neonatal course was uncomplicated, and the mother's early postpartum course was normal. However, this period proved to be extremely difficult emotionally for the patient. She later described a mounting fear, toward the end of pregnancy, that her newborn would be very ill and that she would also become ill and unable to care for her children. She felt mounting pressure to inform her family of her situation and to enlist their help in caring for her children and increasing anxiety over the probability of confrontation with her husband.

Ultimately, circumstances encouraged her to disclose her diagnosis. When family members questioned her as to why she had chosen to bottle-feed her baby, she found it too stressful to search for plausible responses. On the third postpartum day, she tearfully informed her mother and one sister of her HIV status. To her surprise, they both expressed love and concern for her and shared their own longstanding fears about her husband's drug-using behavior. Their emotional support and the relief of finally ending her isolation about this problem enabled her to accomplish what repeated counseling from health care providers had not been able to do. She informed her husband, in a joint interview with him and the social worker, of her HIV status and her fear that he had been exposed through needle sharing.

As she had feared, his reaction was one of fury at his wife and outrage toward the social worker, who suggested that he undergo screening for HIV and take advantage of opportunities for drug treatment. The husband subsequently disappeared. Upon his return a few weeks after the baby's birth, he stated that he would not undergo HIV screening, but he did indicate his intention to enroll in drug treatment.

The entire family attended counseling sessions for discussion of HIV infection, transmission risks, and prevention. Again the patient's fears proved realistic to some extent. One of her sisters was unable to accept the information that casual contact with HIV-infected individuals could not transmit this virus. She forbid her children all contact with the family.

The patient experienced intense emotions during the early postpartum period. The relief of seeing her apparently healthy newborn and of sharing the burden of her diagnosis, together with the stress of the delivery and of the confrontation with her husband, left her exhausted and finally able to grieve. She relied heavily on her sister and mother for physical care of herself and her children and for emotional support as she shared her fears about her own death and about the health of her children. In continuing counseling sessions, she turned toward consideration of the future and established plans for the children's medical care and guardianship. She considered the options of sterilization and marital separation and explored the conflicts these issues raised for her.

Care of this newborn reactivated much of the anxiety she had felt during pregnancy, however. It was difficult for her to accept that diagnosis of HIV infection in the baby could be delayed, and she presented frequently to pediatric providers for reassurance. An early febrile infection requiring the baby's hospitalization for observation clearly represented a crisis for her. Intensive supportive counseling and ventilation of fears about the baby's health proved helpful, but early, spontaneous resolution of the fever provided the most reassurance.

The baby remained well, and serum antibody screening, although positive at 3 and 6 months, was negative for HIV when the baby was tested at 9, 12, and 18 months of age. (Viral culture and PCR were not performed.) Two years after birth, the child continued to be free of signs of illness.

The mother also remained well, with CD4 counts remaining in the normal range. At 2 years postpartum, no signs or symptoms characteristic of illness progression or opportunistic infection had appeared. The father's whereabouts and health status were unknown.

*   *   *   *   *

CASE ANALYSIS

Since this patient never developed a clinical picture suspicious for advancing HIV infection, the focus of her care was on the emotional and psychologic aspects of living with HIV seropositivity and on the public health imperatives of education and prevention of further spread of the disease.

Individual, supportive counseling was a valuable resource for this patient, especially because she was initially unable to seek emotional support from her family. However, she did apparently experience a sense of pressure from both her medical and her social service worker to disclose her seropositivity, and this may have added to her difficulty in coping with the distress caused by her diagnosis.

Indeed, a support group may be most likely to assist HIV-infected patients to deal with their conflicts surrounding disclosure of their diagnosis, as well as to help in coping with the sorrow and fearfulness attendant on living with a chronic, progressive illness of unpredictable course. Although this may be the most valuable resource a health care system might offer, it, like other services, must be designed to be culturally appropriate for the diverse groups now affected by this virus.

For health care providers, care of the HIV-infected pregnant woman is characterized by unusual frustrations and challenges. Since the natural history of the disease is still poorly understood, monitoring for markers of illness progression must be constant, and reassurance for patients may be hard to provide. There is at present no cure for this disease, and yet even promising new therapies aimed at preventing progression of illness or the development of opportunistic infections have been used only rarely in pregnancy. Prevention of further transmission of the virus is still the strategy most likely to yield results. Prevention efforts, however, are based on attempts to effect change in areas of behavior that are both the most intimate—in specific sexual practices and in reproductive choices—and the most socially charged—illicit drug use and monitoring of an asymptomatic sexually transmitted disease.

This patient's failure to inform her partner, the likely source of her HIV infection, of her seropositivity highlights one of the most frustrating issues for health care providers. Under current federal and most state laws, HIV infection, although a communicable and probably ultimately fatal illness, is not reportable to public health authorities. Contact tracing systems are rare, and confidentiality provisions of medical codes prohibit providers from disclosing medical information without the patient's consent. Lively debate over this issue has existed since the illness was first described, and the continuing spread of HIV infection is likely to intensify discussion of the competing interests of confidentiality, patient rights, and public health.

IMPLICATIONS FOR PRACTICE

This case of asymptomatic HIV infection in a pregnant woman has underscored a number of the psychosocial issues caregivers will need to become skilled at dealing with in clinical practice in maternal and child health. Health care providers working with women of childbearing age are in a unique position to develop and demonstrate familiarity with the epidemiology and science of this disease, commitment to prevention of further spread of the epidemic, and sensitivity in identification and care of the HIV-infected individual and family.

Counseling and education are a central focus. While routine counseling about HIV infection was provided as part of early pregnancy care, this patient's heterosexually transmitted HIV infection was not confirmed until more than halfway through her pregnancy. This clearly underscores the need for routine counseling of all women, regardless of perceived risk status, before the planning or conception of a pregnancy.

Counseling regarding HIV infection may then be reinforced, rather than introduced, in early pregnancy, with emphasis on pregnancy-related risks. One-to-one counseling, supplemented with appropriate written material and review of risks at the follow-up visit, may provide the most effective way of providing information about the infection and its importance to women's health. Providers need to develop interview techniques that will encourage patients to disclose sensitive historical information. However, requiring a patient to self-identify for socially stigmatized behaviors may often be counterproductive to the overall goal of prevention of perinatal AIDS. Carefully describing the risk behaviors, acknowledging the difficulty that many women have in accurately assessing their risk status, and simply offering a woman screening for the infection, without attempting to label her risk, may be the most effective approach.

When a patient elects to be screened for HIV infection, pre- and post-test counseling sessions—with adequate time for discussion with a consistent provider—should be offered, focusing on the implications of a positive or negative screening test. Early follow-up should be planned for the HIV-seropositive woman to help her begin to cope with the effect of the diagnosis and to help her understand specifically what is and what is not currently known about HIV infection and pregnancy and about pediatric care and prognosis. Prevention of further transmission of the infection also needs emphasis, with provision of explicit, culturally appropriate information on sexual practices and needle use.

Providers should acknowledge the special burden of decision-making for a pregnant woman who may be learning of her seropositivity early in pregnancy and must suddenly confront the potential for illness in herself, in her child, and also possibly in her partner. Reproductive decision-making, complex at best, becomes even more difficult, and the timetable imposed by feasibility of termination of pregnancy may cause additional stresses. Data indicate that few women choose termination on the basis of their seropositivity.[57] These decisions may be in conflict with the values of medical personnel, even those who have supported traditions of nondirective counseling for genetic illnesses with similar potential for transmission and devastating outcome. Early referral to social service and mental health workers is indicated to help the patient with these concerns.

Indeed, support for the psychosocial effects of this disease is the next and ultimately the primary focus in care of the seropositive pregnant woman. Social workers and other mental health care providers may anticipate the shock, denial, and grief experienced by the newly diagnosed seropositive woman and, in the context of ongoing therapy, may assist her in coping with the isolation, guilt, and difficulty in relationships that are demonstrated in this case study. Supportive therapy may also provide anticipatory guidance of both family and community responses, perhaps facilitating support of the patient by family, friends, and even community agencies. Even with support, however, as we saw in the case study, the social stigma attendant on this disease is so strong that a woman may have considerable difficulty with disclosure of her diagnosis.

Monitoring for signs and symptoms of advancing HIV disease and screening for the development of associated infections do not at present imply major modifications in obstetric care. It may soon be true that early diagnosis of HIV infection in pregnancy will open doors for treatment as new medical knowledge develops. At present, however, the diagnosis establishes a mandate for excellent health maintenance efforts. Routine recommendations for self-care in nutrition, rest, exercise, and avoidance of potentially damaging substances are doubly important, of course, to the HIV-infected pregnant woman, since they not only promote fetal well-being but offer the opportunity to teach health practices that may be crucial to future immune function.

The magnitude of the AIDS crisis is slowly being appreciated by the general public, but the epidemic for women and children is only beginning to unfold. Daily contact with affected families should gradually improve our abilities to respond with compassion to the emotional crisis that this disease represents. Vigorous research efforts should improve our ability to respond effectively to the medical challenge of caring for families affected by this chronic, unpredictable illness.

REFERENCES

1. Centers for Disease Control. *HIV/AIDS Weekly Surveillance.* US Department of Health and Human Services; July 1990.

2. Chin J. Current and future dimensions of the HIV/AIDS pandemic in women and children. *Lancet.* 1990;2:221–224.

3. Centers for Disease Control. HIV infection in the US: a review of current knowledge. *MMWR.* 1987;36(S-6):14.

4. Chu S, Buehler J, Berkelman R. Impact of HIV epidemic on mortality among women 15–44 years of age, US. *Proceedings of the Sixth International Conference on AIDS*, San Francisco, June 1990. 1:311. Abstract.

5. Guinan ME, Hardy A. Epidemiology of AIDS in women in the United States: 1981 through 1986. *JAMA.* 1987;257:2039–2042.

6. Quinn TC, Mann JM, Curran JW, et al. AIDS in Africa: an epidemiologic paradigm. *Science.* 1986;234:955–963.

7. Centers for Disease Control. *AIDS Weekly Surveillance Report.* US AIDS Program 1988; October 24.

8. Landesman S, Minkoff H, Holman S, et al. Serosurvey of human immunodeficiency virus infection in parturients. *JAMA.* 1987;258:2701–2703.

9. Donegan SP, Edelin KC, Craven DE. Prevalence of antibodies to human immunodeficiency virus in fetal cord blood at a municipal hospital. *Proceedings of the 4th International Conference on AIDS, Stockholm, June 1988.* Abstract.

10. Krasinski K, Borkowski W, Bebenroth D, Moore T. Failure of voluntary testing for HIV to identify infected parturient women in a high-risk population (letter). *N Engl J Med.* 1988;318:185.

11. Kelen GB, Fritz S, Qaqish B, et al. Unrecognized human immunodeficiency virus infection in emergency department patients. *N Engl J Med.* 1988;318:1645–1650.

12. Caldwell B, Fleming P, Oxtoby M. National surveillance for pediatric AIDS in US. *Proceedings of the 6th International Conference on AIDS, San Francisco, June 1990.* 1:300. Abstract.

13. Sprecher S, Soumenkoff G, Puissant F, Degueldre M. Vertical transmission of HIV in 15-week fetus. *Lancet.* 1986;2:288–289.

14. Lewis S, Reynolds-Kohler C, Fox H, Nelson J. HIV-1 in trophoblastic and villous Hofbauer cells, and haemotological precursors in 8-week fetuses. *Lancet.* 1990;2:565–568.

15. Vogt MW, Craven DE, Crawford DF, et al. Isolation of HTLV-III/LAV from cervical secretions of women at risk for AIDS. *Lancet.* 1986;1:525–527.

16. Donegan S, dela Monte S, Stegar K, et al. HIV-1 infection of the lower female genital tract. *Proceedings of the 6th International Conference on AIDS, San Francisco, June 1990.* 2:268. Abstract.

17. Henin Y, Porrot F, Montagnier L, Henrior R. Prevalence of HIV in the cervicovaginal secretions of women seropositive for HIV: correlation with the clinical status and implications for heterosexual transmission. *Proceedings of the 6th International Conference on AIDS, San Francisco, June 1990.* 1:263. Abstract.

18. Minkoff H, Nanda D, Menez R, Fikrig S. Pregnancies resulting in infants with acquired immunodeficiency syndrome or AIDS-related complex. *Obstet Gynecol.* 1987;69:285–287.

19. Minkoff HL. Care of pregnant women infected with human immunodeficiency virus. *JAMA.* 1987;258:2714–2717.

20. Johnson JP, Nair P. Early diagnosis of HIV infection in the neonate. *N Engl J Med.* 1987;316:273–274.

21. Mok JQ, Rossi AD, Ades AE, et al. Infants born to mothers seropositive for human immunodeficiency virus: preliminary findings from a multicentre European study. *Lancet.* 1987;1:1164–1167.

22. Tovo PA, Gabiano C, Riva C, et al. Specific antibody and virus antigen expression in congenital HIV infection. *Lancet.* 1987;1:1201–1202.

23. Settlage R. AIDS in obstetrics: diagnosis, course and prognosis. *Clin Obstet Gynecol.* 1989;32:437–444.

24. Williams P, Simmonds P, Yap P, et al. The polymerase chain reactor in the diagnosis of vertically transmitted HIV infection. *AIDS.* 1990;4:393–398.

25. Scott GB, Fischl MA, Klimas N, et al. Mothers of infants with the acquired immunodeficiency syndrome: evidence for both symptomatic and asymptomatic carriers. *JAMA.* 1985;253:363–366.

26. Nesheim S, Lindsay M, Sawyer M, Jones D. Perinatal transmission of HIV to infants of seropositive mothers identified by prenatal screening. *Proceedings of the Sixth International Conference on AIDS, San Francisco, June 1990.* 1:276. Abstract.

27. Oleske J, Oxtoby M, Denny T, et al. Perinatal infection with HIV-1 in New Jersey. *Proceedings of the Sixth International Conference on AIDS, San Francisco, June 1990.* 1:276. Abstract.

28. Goedert J, Mende H, Drummond J, et al. Mother-to-infant transmission of HIV type 1: association with prematurity or low anti-gp120. *Lancet.* 1989;2:1351–1354.

29. The European Collaborative Study. Mother-to-child transmission of HIV infection. *Lancet.* 1988;2:1039–1043.

30. Minkoff H, Nanda D, Menez R, Fikrig S. Pregnancies resulting in infants with acquired immuno-deficiency syndrome or AIDS-related complex: follow-up of mothers, children and subsequently born siblings. *Obstet Gynecol.* 1987;69:288–291.

31. Miller G, Martin K, Katz BZ, Andiman WA. AIDS and antibodies to human immunodeficiency virus (HIV) in children and their families: clinical experience at Yale-New Haven Hospital. *Yale J Biol Med.* 1987;60:527–535.

32. Ziegler JB, Cooper DA, Johnson RO, Gold J. Postnatal transmission of AIDS-associated retrovirus from mother to infant. *Lancet.* 1985;1:896–897.

33. Thiry L, Spencer-Goldberger S, Jonckheur T. Isolation of AIDS virus from cell-free breast milk of 3 healthy virus carriers. *Lancet.* 1985;2:891–892.

34. Nicoll A, Killewo J, Mgone C. HIV and infant feeding practices: epidemiologic implications for sub-Saharan countries. *AIDS.* 1990;4:661–665.

35. Kloser P, Grigoriu A, Kapila R. Women with AIDS: a continuing study. *Proceedings of the 4th International Conference on AIDS, Stockholm, June 1988.* a:4605. Abstract.

36. Desmond-Hellmann S, Mbidde E, Kizito A, Hellmann N. The epidemiology and clinical findings of Kaposi's sarcoma in African women with HIV infection. *Proceedings of the Sixth International Conference on AIDS, San Francisco, June 1990.* 3:213. Abstract.

37. Young M, Pierce P. Natural history of HIV disease in an urban cohort of women. *Proceedings of the Sixth International Conference on AIDS, San Francisco, June 1990.* 2:186. Abstract.

38. Marte C, Cohen M, Fruchter R, Kelly P. Pap test and STD findings in HIV positive women at ambulatory care sites. *Proceedings of the Sixth International Conference on AIDS, San Francisco, June 1990.* 2:211. Abstract.

39. Schafer A, Friedmann W, Mieke M, et al. Increased frequency of cervical dysplasia/neoplasia in HIV-infected women. *Proceedings of the Sixth International Conference on AIDS, San Francisco, June 1990.* 3:215. Abstract.

40. Rhoads JL, Wright DC, Redfield RR, Burke DS. Chronic vaginal candidiasis in women with human immunodeficiency virus infection. *JAMA.* 1987;257:3105–3107.

41. Safrin S, Ng V, McGrath M, et al. HTLV-I/II infection in women with acute pelvic inflammatory disease (letter). *JAMA.* 1990;263:2181.

42. Okamura K, Furukawa K, Nakakuki M, et al. Natural killer cell activity during pregnancy. *Am J Obstet Gynecol.* 1984;149:396–399.

43. Sridama V, Pacini F, Yang S-L, et al. Decreased levels of helper T-cells: a possible cause of immunodeficiency in pregnancy. *N Engl J Med* 1982;307:352–356.

44. Wetli CV, Roldan EO, Fojaco RM. Listeriosis as a cause of maternal death: an obstetric complication of the acquired immunodeficiency syndrome (AIDS). *Am J Obstet Gynecol.* 1983;147:7–9.

45. Rawlinson KF, Zubrow AB, Harris MA, Jackson K. Disseminated Kaposi's sarcoma in pregnancy: a manifestation of acquired immunodeficiency syndrome. *Obstet Gynecol.* 1984;63:2S–6S.

46. Jensen LP, O'Sullivan MJ, Gomez-del-Rio M, et al. Acquired immunodeficiency syndrome (AIDS) in pregnancy. *Am J Obstet Gynecol.* 1984;148:1145–1146.

47. Minkoff H, deRegt RH, Landesman S, Schwarz R. Pneumocystis carinii pneumonia associated with acquired immunodeficiency syndrome in pregnancy: a report of three maternal deaths. *Obstet Gynecol.* 1986;67:284–287.

48. Berrebi A, Puel J, Tricoire J, Herne H. Influence of gestation of HIV infection. *Proceedings of the Sixth International Conference on AIDS, San Francisco, June 1990.* 1:287. Abstract.

49. Bledsoe K, Olopoenia L, Barnes S, et al. Effect of pregnancy on progression of HIV infection. *Proceedings of the Sixth International Conference on AIDS, San Francisco, June 1990.* 1:288. Abstract.

50. Stratton P, Mofenson L, Willoughby A. HIV infection in pregnant women under care at clinical trial centers in the US. *Proceedings of the Sixth International Conference on AIDS, San Francisco, June 1990.* 2:192. Abstract.

51. Biggar R, Pahwa S, Minkoff H, et al. Immunosuppression in pregnant women infected with HIV. *Am J Obstet Gynecol.* 1989;161:1239–1244.

52. Lutz R, Hiller K, Stauber M, et al. Effect of lymphocyte depletion during pregnancy on clinical complications, birth weight and HIV-infection of the newborn. *Proceedings of the Sixth International Conference on AIDS, San Francisco, June 1990.* 2:189. Abstract.

53. Cromblehome W, Wara D, Gambertoglio J, et al. Perinatal HIV transmission despite maternal/infant AZT therapy. *Proceedings of the Sixth International Conference on AIDS, San Francisco, June 1990.* 1:276. Abstract.

54. Feinkind L, Minkoff HL. HIV in pregnancy. *Clin Perinatol.* 1988;15:189–120.

55. Minkoff H, Feinkind L. Management of pregnancies of HIV-infected women. *Clin Obstet Gynecol.* 1989;32:467–476.

56. Fekety SE. Managing the HIV-positive patient and her newborn in a CNM service. *J Nurs-Midwif.* 1989;34:253–258.

57. Kurth A, Hutchinson M. A context for HIV testing in pregnancy. *J Nurs-Midwif.* 1989;34:259–266.

Chapter 8

Narcotic Addiction in Pregnancy

Susan Givens

In the United States, at least 5000 babies are born each year to narcotic-dependent women.[1] These babies are more likely to suffer from prematurity, low birth weight, cognitive and motor delays, and sudden infant death syndrome than are nonaddicted infants.[1-12] Many will experience neonatal abstinence syndrome (NAS), a potentially life-threatening syndrome characterized by central nervous system (CNS) hyperirritability, gastrointestinal (GI) dysfunction, respiratory distress, and generalized autonomic symptoms. Many of the health and developmental difficulties suffered by passively addicted babies can be diminished when their mothers are cared for in a comprehensive program of prenatal methadone maintenance, medical care, and intensive psychologic and social support.[1,5,10,11,13-15]

Methadone maintenance programs lower infant morbidity and mortality in several ways. Women enrolled in such programs are less likely to experience narcotic withdrawal; withdrawal during pregnancy can lead to preterm labor, fetal anoxia, and intrauterine death. Equally important, methadone maintenance programs act as a lure to draw women into prenatal care. Participants are removed from a dangerous social milieu where they are often forced into a life of theft and prostitution to support their drug habit. They are less likely to use illicit drugs and more likely to use available medical, psychologic, and social support systems to provide a safer environment for themselves and their unborn infants.

REVIEW OF THE LITERATURE

Heroin is derived from the juice of the opium poppy plant. To produce a euphoric high, the user smokes, inhales, or injects it subcutaneously or intravenously. As tolerance develops, larger doses of heroin are needed to produce the euphoric effects and avoid withdrawal symptoms.

Descriptions of neonatal narcotic withdrawal have appeared in the medical literature since the late 19th century. As recently as three decades ago, most infants born to drug-dependent women did not survive.[16] In the 1960s, research focused upon the treatment of NAS but, by the 1970s, attention had shifted from treatment to prevention of neonatal withdrawal. Prevention efforts led to the development of methadone maintenance programs for pregnant heroin users. Early on, the Food and Drug Administration recommended that methadone withdrawal be initiated 21 days after acceptance into a treatment program, but the disastrous consequences of rapid maternal narcotic withdrawal were soon realized.[17] There is now general agreement that methadone maintenance throughout pregnancy, using the minimal dose required to prevent withdrawal symptoms, is preferable to complete drug withdrawal.[18]

Current research efforts are aimed toward examination of the short- and long-term developmental effects of prenatal methadone exposure. Although evidence is inconclusive, several researchers suggest that the adverse developmental effects seen in children of methadone-dependent women are not caused by the direct toxic effect of methadone but by the disrupted, chaotic life-styles of their opiate-addicted mothers.[6-9]

Antenatal Management

Pregnancy complications from maternal heroin use include an increased risk of placental abruption, preeclampsia, placental insufficiency, breech presentation, premature rupture of the membranes, and premature labor. Maternal complications can also be caused by additives used to "cut" heroin before use and sale and by unsterile paraphernalia used to inject the drug.[19]

The goals of antepartum management for narcotic-dependent women are (1) prevention of maternal/fetal withdrawal through methadone maintenance, (2) prevention of polydrug use, (3) high-risk pregnancy monitoring, (4) psychosocial counseling and support, and (5) prenatal education with emphasis on nutrition, preparation for labor and delivery, and encouragement of appropriate parenting skills.

Most narcotic-dependent women enter prenatal care late in pregnancy. Menstrual irregularities and anovulation are common in heroin users; many are not aware of the pregnancy until the second trimester.[12] Furthermore, early signs of pregnancy such as nausea, vomiting, and fatigue are sometimes mistaken for drug withdrawal. Some women seek prenatal care only when their resources for obtaining drugs are exhausted.

Drug use may not be readily apparent when a woman presents for prenatal care. A nonjudgmental assessment of substance abuse should be a component of every prenatal history. More information may be revealed if the woman is allowed to complete a written questionnaire before drug use is discussed. Clues to intravenous drug abuse can include missed appointments, a history of hepatitis or endocarditis, needle marks or red needle tracks on the arms, edema over superficial veins, and difficult venipuncture.

When narcotic dependence is identified, hospital admission at an institution designed to care for substance-abusing pregnant women is recommended so that the mother and fetus can be stabilized and evaluated.[12,20] After a drug history is completed, a supervised urine specimen is obtained for toxicology screening. Most narcotic-dependent women use multiple drugs, even during methadone maintenance. It has been estimated that 88% of women maintained on methadone will use additional drugs including heroin, cocaine, alcohol, marijuana, and Valium.[1] For this reason, urine toxicology screening throughout pregnancy is indicated.

The objective of prenatal methadone maintenance is not to detoxify every patient but to adjust the drug dosage to the smallest amount needed to prevent withdrawal symptoms. Signs and symptoms of withdrawal can include increased fetal activity, abdominal cramping, nausea, diarrhea, perspiration, uterine irritability, hypotension, rhinorrhea, yawning, sleep disturbances, and dilated pupils. The peak period of discomfort is 48 to 72 hours after the last drug dose. If a pregnant woman is uncomfortable because the methadone dosage is too low, she will invariably resort to street drugs. Erratic exposure to street drugs of unknown quantity and quality is more damaging to the fetus than methadone maintenance. Therefore, the woman should be questioned often about whether she feels tempted to return to street drugs, and the methadone dosage should be adjusted accordingly.

The initial methadone dose will depend on the woman's drug history. A suggested dosage regimen is 10 mg of methadone with increases of 5 mg every 4 to 6 hours as long as withdrawal symptoms persist. Methadone peaks in plasma 2 to 6 hours after ingestion. The total amount given in 24 hours will constitute the maintenance dose unless withdrawal symptoms occur. Most women can be maintained on a daily dose of 20 to 35 mg.[12] After adjusting the maintenance dose, methadone is given in one daily dose rather than in divided dosages.

Once the patient is stabilized, she must decide if she will try to decrease her dose by very gradual increments (1 to 2 mg/week). Newborns are less likely to suffer withdrawal symptoms if their mothers can be maintained on 20 mg or less of methadone per day.[21] Detoxification, however, should be approached cautiously. Some women try very hard to detoxify themselves rapidly without a good understanding of the fetal consequences. Detoxification should not be attempted before 14 weeks gestation due to the risk of spontaneous abortion or after 32 weeks because it may induce preterm labor.[12]

The life-style of a narcotic addict is characterized by factors that put her at risk for infectious disease such as inadequate nutrition and housing, prostitution, and needle sharing. Screening for sexually transmitted diseases including hepatitis and (with consent) human immunodeficiency virus (HIV) is an important component of care.

Drug-dependent women are likely to suffer from anemia and folic acid deficiency.[22] In addition to nutritional counseling and vitamin and mineral supplementation, the pregnant user will probably need help accessing food assistance programs.

Serial ultrasound tests are performed throughout the pregnancy to assess fetal growth and well-being. The incidence of growth retardation is not expected to be higher than in the general population.[22] As with other high-risk patients, nonstress tests, contraction stress tests, and biophysical profiles may be indicated.

Critical components of antenatal care are psychosocial assessment and support. Frequently, the drug-dependent mother must cope with a myriad of problems including single parenthood, social isolation, poor housing, lack of education, financial problems, and fear for physical safety. Quite often, there are depression and isolation along with a deep sense of guilt, inadequacy, low stress tolerance, and an inability to cope.[23,24] This woman is often a victim of physical and sexual abuse that began in childhood. In one prenatal methadone program, 70% of the women had been beaten as adults.[24] Illicit drug use may begin as a means to cope with violent abuse.

Most researchers agree that the extent to which the child of a narcotic-dependent woman is able to recover from a hostile intrauterine environment depends on how well the mother is able to parent the child.[6,10,11] Frequently deprived of nurturance in her own childhood, however, the pregnant heroin user may not know how to parent. Without resolution of feelings of depression, guilt, helplessness, anger, and fear, the continuum of neglect and abuse is likely to prevail.

Fortunately, pregnancy can be the event that motivates the drug-dependent woman to change her life-style for the better. This opportunity is enhanced when the care system is sensitive and responsive to her needs, particularly the need to cope with problems of daily living in a chaotic environment. A woman who feels like a partner in her own care will be more involved in decision-making and come to understand the important role she plays in her child's well-being.[25,26]

Prenatal education, another component of care, is most effective when it is adapted to individual needs and learning styles. The woman may have experienced difficulty in formal learning situations in the past and may therefore be more responsive to an informal teaching format.[27] Group sessions promote active participation, particularly when group members share similar needs and concerns. The pregnant drug user's concerns will likely focus on pain management during delivery. Anticipatory guidance regarding newborn characteristics, behaviors of narcotic-exposed infants, and techniques for consoling can help such women develop realistic expectations of their infants.

Intrapartum Care

The course of labor and the incidence of cesarean section are similar to those of nonaddicted women.[20,28] However, the incidence of breech delivery, forceps delivery, chorioamnionitis, and preeclampsia is slightly higher.[20] Narcotic withdrawal during labor should be avoided. Even mild withdrawal increases both maternal and fetal oxygen consumption and further stresses the fetus. The woman is maintained on the regular dose of methadone throughout labor and delivery, and signs and symptoms of withdrawal are promptly treated with additional doses of methadone.

One of the most difficult labor management issues is pain control.[29] Many narcotic-dependent women medicate themselves before coming to the hospital because they mistake signs of labor for withdrawal or because they fear that analgesia will be denied. Labor preparation and reassurance that analgesia will be available when she becomes uncomfortable may help to discourage this practice. Urine toxicology screening upon admission can help to identify when self-medication has occurred.

Use of narcotic analgesics such as Demerol is appropriate and may improve neonatal outcome if the laboring woman is particularly anxious.[20] However, butorphanol (Stadol) and other narcotic analgesics with mixed agonist-antagonist effects should be avoided because they may provoke withdrawal.[12] Epidural anesthesia can limit the need for narcotic analgesia as well.

Care of the Newborn

Infants of methadone-maintained women usually adapt well to extrauterine life and are admitted to the normal nursery. Apgar scores are generally not affected by maternal methadone maintenance, nor is methadone associated with any specific congenital malformations.[3,10,14,30] Infants born to methadone-maintained mothers weigh less than drug-free controls but outweigh infants born to heroin-abusing mothers. Although lighter in weight, methadone-exposed infants are usually not small for gestational age.[3,4,11,13,19,28]

At least 60% of infants whose mothers are maintained on methadone during pregnancy will experience moderate to severe NAS at birth or during the early days of life.[1,5,11] Factors that influence the onset and severity of NAS include maternal drug dosage, labor analgesia, and the condition of the infant at birth. Usually some manifestations of NAS occur within 72 hours of delivery, although symptoms may be delayed up to 2 weeks. The trend toward early postpartum discharge means that some drug-exposed infants will not be identified during the neonatal period. The usual duration of symptoms is 6 days to 8 weeks, but some subtle symptoms may persist up to 6 months.[31]

NAS is characterized by CNS irritability, G.I. dysfunction, respiratory distress, and generalized autonomic symptoms that can include sneezing, yawning, mottling, and fever.[32] One of the earliest symptoms is tremulousness. Skin on the knees, toes, and elbows can become abraded from constant activity. Other early symptoms of NAS include frantic fist sucking, irritability, and a shrill, high-pitched cry. The infant may experience mild nasal stuffiness or more severe respiratory symptoms, which can include cyanosis, retractions, tachypnea, and apnea. The incidence of sudden infant death syndrome (SIDS) is also thought to be increased in babies of opiate-addicted mothers.[33]

Not all babies withdrawing from opiate addiction require pharmacotherapy. Thirty to 50% can be managed with careful observation and supportive care.[31] The decision to treat NAS with drugs is based on the severity of symptoms. Indications for pharmacologic therapy include excessive weight loss, dehydration, inability to sleep, fever unrelated to infections, and seizures.[31] Scoring systems, such as Finnegan's Neonatal Abstinence Scoring System, permit an objective clinical estimate of the onset, progress, severity, and diminution of the symptoms of NAS during the neonatal period.[32]

Symptoms of NAS can often be minimized with supportive nursing care such as moving the newborn to a quiet, dimly lit area of the nursery. Crying and fist sucking are sometimes mistaken for hunger when they are in fact symptoms of irritability. Firm swaddling and the opportunity to suck on a pacifier or fist can help the infant achieve a more organized behavioral state.

Infants experiencing NAS often have disrupted sleep cycles. When possible, feedings should be on a demand schedule so that sleep is interrupted as little as possible. Frequent small feedings of hypercaloric formula may be required if the infant has vomiting and diarrhea or if he or she is excessively active.[31]

When pharmacologic treatment is required, paregoric is most often the drug of choice. If NAS symptoms are not controlled by paregoric in the methadone-exposed infant, maternal polydrug use should be suspected. Phenobarbital and Valium have both been used to control NAS in infants with multiple drug exposures.[33]

The growth and development of methadone-exposed infants is a subject of considerable research interest. Infants who experience withdrawal are generally more difficult to care for and may continue to experience irregular sleep patterns, loose stools, and irritability for up to 6 months. These are fussy babies who are not easily consoled. They seem to lack the ability to engage their caretakers. This is a characteristic reported both by opiate-addicted mothers and by foster mothers.[15] Inability to respond to the mother's invitations to interact can have disastrous consequences, particularly if the mother has difficulty coping with anger and frustration. The postpartum period affords an opportunity for women to learn techniques for helping their infants to maintain central nervous system control, thereby encouraging mutually satisfying interactions between mother and infant.[34]

It is encouraging, however, that most of these infants do well in the long term, particularly if they are placed in an adequate home environment that is sensitive to their needs.[6,10,11] No intellectual impairments are specifically associated with maternal methadone use, although heightened activity, energy, impulsivity, and a shortened attention span have been noted by caregivers.[3,6] Before the mother leaves the hospital, medical and social service support should be in place. The mother should have a good understanding of the infant's behaviors and have the names and telephone numbers of alternative caretakers.

* * * * *

CASE STUDY

M.M., an unmarried, 25-year-old heroin user, was referred to a tertiary obstetrical center by the women's prison where she was incarcerated. She was a gravida III, para 0 with a pregnancy history of two elective therapeutic abortions. She admitted to being a 10-year intravenous heroin user, and her forearms were covered with oozing needle tract marks. She had been placed on a 30-mg maintenance dose of methadone by a local drug treatment program. She admitted to Dilaudid and marijuana use during pregnancy and was a one-pack-a-day cigarette smoker. Her medical and family history were otherwise unremarkable.

She was unsure of the date of her last menstrual period. Fundal height measurement was 24 cm, and ultrasound examination revealed a single live intrauterine pregnancy with estimated gestational age of 25.5 weeks. No fetal anomalies were noted, and amniotic fluid volume was within normal limits.

Laboratory tests revealed evidence of a previous hepatitis infection, but findings were otherwise normal. Specifically, blood group and type were B positive, indirect Coombs test was negative, and she was rubella immune. A complete blood count and differential count were within normal limits, as was a 28-week screen for carbohydrate intolerance. Urine, gonorrhea, and group B ß-hemolytic streptococcus cultures were negative, as was a chlamydia screen. She did not report previous herpes infection, and the cervix and vagina were free of lesions. She was counseled regarding transmission of HIV virus and consented to an ELISA test, which was negative. Hepatitis B panel was negative for surface antigen, positive for antibody, and weakly positive for core antibody.

A social history was difficult to elicit because the patient was reluctant to speak openly in front of prison guards, who accompanied her at all times. Two days before the initial prenatal visit, she had been arrested for narcotics possession and placed in a county jail. As soon as the pregnancy and drug dependency were uncovered, she was transferred to a state facility located 150 miles from her home. M.M. suddenly found herself in prison, pregnant, withdrawing from narcotics, and far away from the limited social support that existed for her.

Each day, M.M. was taken from the prison to a drug treatment program for methadone. There she developed rapport with a counselor in whom she trusted and confided. Her blood pressure and fetal heart tones were checked daily in the prison hospital. Weekly prenatal visits took place at a university-affiliated high-risk clinic. At each prenatal visit she was attended by a physician, nurse, nutritionist, social worker, and childbirth educator.

The prenatal course was essentially normal except for one episode of preterm labor that occurred at 32 weeks when an attempt was made to decrease her methadone dose by 1 mg/day. She was admitted to the labor and delivery unit after she complained of diarrhea and abdominal cramps. Her cervix was found to be 1 to 2 cm dilated and 60% effaced. The fetal station was high. She complained of feeling weak and nervous and was quite sure she was in narcotic withdrawal. External fetal monitoring revealed irregular contractions and fetal premature atrial contractions (PACs). No periodic changes were present, and the baseline remained normal. Ultrasound examination did not reveal any cardiac anomalies, nor was there any evidence of hydrops or fetal distress.

M.M. was observed in the hospital for 24 hours, during which time she received intravenous fluids. Her cervix remained unchanged, and withdrawal symptoms diminished. Methadone dosage was increased back to 30 mg/day for the duration of the pregnancy. She was discharged with instructions to increase rest periods and to report any symptoms of preterm labor or drug withdrawal.

Fundal height growth, weight gain, and blood pressure remained normal until 35 weeks of gestation. At that time blood pressure increased from 118/60 (initial value) to 146/94. She complained of headaches and scotoma and had slight pedal edema. Urine was negative for protein. Uric acid and partial thromboplastin time (PTT) were within normal limits. After resting on the left side for 30 minutes, the blood pressure decreased to 130/84, and she returned to the prison hospital on bed rest. On her next prenatal visit 4 days later, her blood pressure was 110/70.

Weekly nonstress tests were performed after the fetal cardiac arrythmia was identified. The nonstress tests were reactive; however, PACs continued until 39 weeks of gestation, when they spontaneously resolved.

Initially, M.M.'s conversations centered on whether or not she would remain on methadone and when she would be released from prison. As trusting relationships developed with her caregivers, she eventually revealed her guilt, fears, and sense of hopelessness. She confided that she believed the pregnancy was the product of a rape that she never reported for fear of retribution.

During the prenatal course, M.M. attended weekly group prenatal classes in the prison and each week at the clinic she practiced breathing and relaxation exercises with the childbirth educator. Because she was concerned about her inability to cope with pain during labor, considerable time was spent building confidence in her ability to manage the discomfort of contractions. M.M. was reassured that she could request an epidural if needed during labor. A tour of the labor and delivery suites and the newborn and intensive care nurseries was arranged.

As the weeks passed, M.M. expressed increasing concern for the baby's well-being. She wanted to know the likelihood that the baby would be "addicted" and spoke often of the baby's activity. Sentencing had not yet taken place, and M.M. was uncertain how long she would be in prison. She verbalized concerns about who would care for the baby but was unwilling to talk about her own parenting role. With support from a counselor at the drug treatment program, a decision was made to give her mother temporary custody of the baby. The county social services worker was notified, and a visit was made to the grandmother's home.

At 41 weeks gestation, M.M. went into labor. When she arrived at the hospital, she was 4 cm dilated, 100% effaced, and at 0 station. Membranes were artificially ruptured, and 5 hours later the cervix was dilated 10 cm. M.M. was uncomfortable with contractions but managed them well with breathing and relaxation techniques as long as a labor coach stayed by her side. She was given her usual daily dose of methadone and in addition received 50 mg of Demerol twice during labor. At 6 cm of dilatation she requested and received epidural anesthesia. Due to a prolonged second stage of labor and the appearance of variable decelerations with decreasing beat-to-beat variability, low forceps were used to aid delivery. A 7-lb baby girl was delivered with Apgar scores of 8 at 1 minute and 9 at 5 minutes.

M.M. was joyous and immediately cuddled and admired the infant. She kept the baby close by her side throughout the hospital stay. The infant demonstrated few signs of neonatal withdrawal during the next 7 days. On the first day of life, the developmental psychologist performed a Brazelton Newborn Behavioral Assessment for evaluation and to demonstrate to M.M. the infant's behavioral characteristics. The baby was somewhat jittery and irritable but was readily consoled when wrapped securely in a blanket. When alert, the baby oriented well to stimulation but was easily aroused from a sleep state, indicating some sleep disturbance. M.M. was intensely interested in the examination and was pleased to learn that the baby responded to the sound of her voice.

Immediately postpartum M.M. was placed on a regimen of rapid methadone detoxification. Methadone was decreased by 5 mg/day from a maintenance dose of 30 mg/day. This was in lieu of complete drug withdrawal, which is the usual procedure for prison inmates. The only withdrawal symptoms she complained of were cramping and diarrhea.

M.M. received positive reinforcement regarding how she handled the labor and delivery experience and for her attention to the infant. She chose rooming-in and spent as much time with the baby as possible. She was receptive to suggestions about baby care and exhibited a great deal of concern and sensitivity to the baby's needs. She spoke of the future when she would be out of prison. "Now I have a reason to clean up my life," she reported over and over again.

On postpartum day 7, M.M.'s mother came to pick up the baby. The child developmental specialist spent time with both the mother and grandmother discussing how problems of wakefulness and irritability would be handled. The baby and grandmother would be followed by a county social service agent and a public health infant-tracking nurse.

On the eighth postpartum day, M.M. requested to return to prison. She was now feeling symptoms of drug withdrawal and acutely grieving the loss of her baby. She felt that other prisoners would offer support. Although sadness and depression were apparent, the sense of hopelessness that dominated her during the antenatal period had diminished. She took with her pictures of the baby, and a follow-up contact was made by the antenatal nurse.

* * * * *

CASE ANALYSIS

The pregnancy, labor, and delivery of M.M. are typical for a methadone-maintained patient. She did not enter prenatal care until late in the second trimester, yet her antenatal and intrapartum course was remarkably free from medical complications. Her prenatal course was complicated only by a transient, benign fetal arrhythmia, an episode of hypertension, and symptoms of preterm labor precipitated by a decreased methadone dosage. Preterm labor is a known consequence of rapid maternal narcotic withdrawal, and after this episode no further attempts were made to decrease the methadone.

The infant had Apgar scores of 8 and 9 and a birth weight of 3175 g. She exhibited only mild symptoms of NAS throughout the hospitalization. The most striking abnormal behavior was tremors of the arms and legs. The baby was relatively easy to console and responded readily to swaddling and soothing. Contributing to this infant's excellent birth outcome, perhaps, was the fact that the mother was not a polydrug user during the last half of her pregnancy. The majority of research on methadone-exposed infants has been conducted on mothers who, in addition to methadone, are likely to use alcohol, marijuana, cocaine, and other drugs.

M.M.'s recovery from heroin abuse was complicated by her incarceration. Generally, the correctional setting does not provide an environment conducive to long-term recovery from alcohol and substance abuse, particularly for pregnant women.[35] Only when life-style changes occur can the substance-abusing woman hope to remain drug free. Such life-style changes usually require intensive, long-term treatment in residential and transitional facilities equipped to provide extensive support and counseling.

Ideally, all narcotic-dependent pregnant women should be cared for in a comprehensive prenatal methadone maintenance program staffed by professionals experienced in the nuances of caring for this special population. Methadone maintenance decreases the likelihood of polydrug use and maternal withdrawal, and providers are able to marshal and direct needed psychosocial support for the pregnant woman, the partner, and the infant.

In reality all pregnant heroin-dependent women do not reside in cities in which such treatment programs are available. The heroin user who does seek prenatal care may find herself at a university-affiliated high-risk clinic, but one that does not have specific services for perinatal drug addiction. This situation can create stress both for staff members who are inexperienced in dealing with drug addiction and for the woman who is in need of medical and psychosocial support.

Such problems become more manageable if the narcotic-dependent client is able to build a trusting relationship with at least one professional who she feels will be her advocate and who is able to assist her in coping with day-to-day problems. Each time M.M. visited the prenatal clinic, she was interviewed by a host of unfamiliar doctors, nurses, and other professionals. Recognizing this patient's need to develop trusting relationships, one nurse volunteered to be M.M.'s care coordinator and advocate. The nurse coordinator accompanied M.M. during each prenatal visit and was there to answer questions, to provide information and support, and to serve as a liaison among patient, drug treatment center, prison, physicians, and a number of community service agencies.

Helping M.M. to build confidence in the ability to handle labor and delivery through instruction and practice in relaxation techniques was relatively easy. The greater challenge was helping to promote attachment when it was certain that M.M. would, at least temporarily, be separated from her infant. The odds of her developing attachment to the baby when she was released from prison were thought to be much greater if she could conceptualize the infant as a person with real needs rather than just an object that was being taken away from her. Encouraging her to talk about the infant's activity (she performed daily fetal kick counts), letting her listen to the heartbeat, and pointing out behavioral characteristics during ultrasound examinations were strategies used to facilitate attachment before the infant was born.

M.M. did not elect to breast-feed her infant. Although heroin, methadone, and other narcotics are transferred to breast milk, breast-feeding by motivated mothers in well-supervised methadone treatment can be considered to encourage bonding.[19]

Some members of the health care team initially had problems accepting a mother who "willingly abused her baby before it was born." M.M.'s painful and guilty feelings were sometimes acted out in hostility and anger, and she was acutely sensitive to resulting anger and mistrust. M.M.'s drug treatment counselor was invaluable in helping staff members understand the reasons for her behavior. Case conferences provided a forum in which staff members could discuss their frustration and anger. The care team eventually recognized that supportive care and attitudes of concern, acceptance, and hope for rehabilitation could indeed influence the short- and long-term outcome for both mother and infant.

IMPLICATIONS FOR PRACTICE

Caring for heroin-dependent pregnant women, particularly those who are incarcerated, presents a special challenge for perinatal nurses. With methadone maintenance, comprehensive medical and psychosocial care that is flexible, respectful, and supportive, and appropriate treatment of neonatal withdrawal, the risk of infant death and disability can be reduced.

REFERENCES

1. Edelin KC, Gurganious L, Golar K, et al. Methadone maintenance in pregnancy: consequences to care and outcome. *Obstet Gynecol.* 1988;71:399–404.

2. Chasnoff IJ. Prenatal cocaine exposure is associated with respiratory pattern abnormalities. *Am J Dis Child.* 1989;143:583–587.

3. Little BB, Snell LM, Klein VR, et al: Maternal and fetal effects of heroin addiction during pregnancy. *J Reprod Med.* 1990;35(2):158–162.

4. Chasnoff IJ, Hatcher R, Burns WJ. Polydrug- and methadone-addicted newborns: a continuum of impairment? *Pediatrics.* 1982;72:210–213.

5. Rosen TS, Johnson HL. Children of methadone-maintained mothers: follow-up to 18 months of age. *J Pediatr.* 1982;101:192–196.

6. Kaltenbach K, Finnegan LP. Developmental outcome of children born to methadone-maintained women: a review of longitudinal studies. *Neurobehav Toxicol Teratol.* 1984;6:271–275.

7. Marcus J, Hans S, Jeremy RJ. A longitudinal study of offspring born to methadone-maintained women, III: effects of multiple risk factors on development at 4, 8, and 12 months. *Am J Drug Alcohol Abuse.* 1984;10:195–207.

8. Bernstein V, Jeremy RJ, Hans SL, Marcus J. A longitudinal study of offspring born to methadone-maintained women, II: didactic interaction and infant behavior at 4 months. *Am J Drug Alcohol Abuse.* 1984;10:161–193.

9. Marcus J, Hans SL, Patterson CB, Morris AJ. A longitudinal study of offspring born to methadone-maintained women, I: design, methodology, and description of women's resources for functioning. *Am J Drug Alcohol Abuse.* 1984;10:135–160.

10. Lifschitz MH, Wilson GS, Smith EO, Desmond MM. Factors affecting head growth and intellectual function in children of drug addicts. *Pediatrics.* 1985;75:269–274.

11. Kaltenbach K, Finnegan LP. Perinatal and developmental outcome of infants exposed to methadone in utero. *Neurobehav Toxicol Teratol.* 1987;9:311–313.

12. Ronkin S, FitzSimmons J, Wapner R, Finnegan L. Protecting mother and fetus from narcotic abuse. *Contemp OB/GYN.* 1988;31:178–187.

13. Kandall SR, Albin S, Lowinson J, et al. Differential effects of maternal heroin and methadone use of birthweight. *Pediatrics.* 1976;58:681–685.

14. Connaughton JF, Reeser D, Schut J, Finnegan LP. Perinatal addiction: outcome and management. *Am J Obstet Gynecol.* 1977;129:679–686.

15. Wilson GS, Desmond MM, Wait RB. Follow-up of methadone-treated and untreated narcotic-dependent women and their infants: health, development and social implications. *J Pediatr.* 1981;98:716–722.

16. Finnegan LP. Substance abuse implications for the newborn. *Perinat-Neonat.* 1982;6(4):17–23.

17. Zuspan FP, Gumpel JA, Mejia-Zelaya A, et al. Fetal stress from methadone withdrawal. *Am J Obstet Gynecol.* 1975;122:43–46.

18. Rogers BD, Lee RV. Drug abuse in pregnancy. In: Burrow GN, Ferris TF, eds. *Medical Complications during Pregnancy*. Philadelphia, Pa: W.B. Saunders Co. 1988:570–579.

19. Cook PS, Peterson RC, Moore DT. *Alcohol, Tobacco and Other Drugs May Harm the Unborn*. Washington, D.C.: Office of Substance Abuse Prevention, U.S. Department of Health and Human Services; 1990.

20. Silver H, Wapner R, Lortiz-Vega M, Finnegan LP. Addiction in pregnancy: high risk intrapartum management and outcome. *J Pediatr*. 1987;7:178–184.

21. Madden JD, Chappel JN, Zuspan F, et al. Observation and treatment of neonatal withdrawal. *Am J Obstet Gynecol*. 1977;127:199–201.

22. Zuspan FP, Rayburn WF. Drug abuse during pregnancy. In: *Drug Therapy in Obstetrics and Gynecology*. E. Norwalk, Conn: Appleton & Lange; 1986:37–51.

23. Fiks K, Johnson HL, Rosen TS. Methadone maintained mothers: 3 years follow-up of parental functioning. *Int J Addict*. 1985;20:651–660.

24. Regan DO, Ehrlich SM, Finnegan LP. Infants of drug addicts: at risk for child abuse, neglect, and placement in foster care. *Neurotoxicol Teratol*. 1987;9:315–319.

25. Davis RC. Psychosocial care of the pregnant narcotic addict. *J Reprod Med*. 1978;20:316–332.

26. Williams A. When the client is pregnant: information for counselors. *J Subst Abuse Treat*. 1985;2:27–34.

27. Fogel CI, Harris BG. Expecting in prison: preparing for birth under conditions of stress. *J Obstet Gynecol Neonatal Nurs*. 1986;15:454–458.

28. Rosner MA, Keith L, Chasnoff L. The Northwestern University drug dependence program: the impact of intensive prenatal care on labor and delivery outcomes. *Am J Obstet Gynecol*. 1982;144:23.

29. Kroll D. Heroin addiction in pregnancy. *Midwifes Chronicle*. July 1986;153–156.

30. Ostrea EM, Chavez CJ. Perinatal problems (excluding neonatal withdrawal) in maternal drug addiction: a study of 830 cases. *J Pediatr*. 1979;94:242.

31. Committee on Drugs. Neonatal drug withdrawal. *Pediatrics*. 1983;72:895–902.

32. Finnegan P. Neonatal abstinence. In: Nelson, ed. *Current Therapy in Neonatal-Perinatal Medicine*. St. Louis, Mo: C.V. Mosby Co.; 1985:262–270.

33. Chasnoff IJ. Newborn infants with drug withdrawal symptoms. *Pediatr Rev*. 1988;9:273–277.

34. Griffith DR. The effect of perinatal exposure of cocaine on the infant and the early maternal-infant interaction. In: Chasnoff IJ (ed). *Drugs, Alcohol, Pregnancy and Parenting*. MTP Press.

35. Barry EM: Pregnant, addicted, and sentenced. *Criminal Justice*. Winter 1991:23–27.

Chapter 9

Pregnancy-Induced Hypertension and HELLP Syndrome in Pregnancy

Dana Jolly

Pregnancy-induced hypertension (PIH) complicates approximately 7% of the pregnancies in the United States.[1,2] Higher incidences are common among primigravidas, particularly those under the age of 17 and over the age of 35.[3] The disease is also common among multiparous women over the age of 35.[3] Complications of pregnancy that increase the likelihood of PIH include diabetes, multiple gestation, and persistent hypertension.[4]

The clinical onset of PIH is often insidious, and thus subjective complaints may not be present. Maternal mortality related to the disease is prevalent around the world.[1,3] Fetal mortality and morbidity is also high. Higher incidences of stillbirth and fetal growth retardation are apparent.[2] Pregnancy-induced hypertension is most likely the leading cause of premature birth.[1,3] Prevention of these dire consequences is dependent upon the recognition by health care professionals of the early signs and symptoms of the disease.

REVIEW OF THE LITERATURE

Pregnancy-induced hypertension includes preeclampsia, which is the occurrence of hypertension, proteinuria, and edema, and eclampsia, which is the progressive worsening of preeclampsia resulting in seizures. The signs and symptoms of PIH and preeclampsia are classified as mild, moderate, or severe. Mild preeclampsia objectively presents with mild hypertension of about 140/90 or an increase of 30 mm Hg systolic and 15 mm Hg diastolic over baseline blood pressure. Edema of mild PIH is differentiated from normal dependent edema of pregnancy by weight gain of greater than 2 lb per week. Urine protein is in the range of 1+ or 2+.

Severe preeclampsia or PIH is differentiated by the appearance of subjective complaints of headaches, visual disturbances, and epigastric or right upper quadrant abdominal pain. Blood pressures are often in excess of 160/110 or exhibit rises of greater than 60 mm Hg systolic and 300 mm Hg diastolic over baseline. Proteinuria is 3+ to 4+ on random sample or greater than 5 g in a 24-hour period. Edema is often pitting, and weight gain in excess of 10 lb per week can be observed. Oliguria of less than 400 ml in 24 hours is also diagnostic.

Weinstein suggested the addition of HELLP syndrome to the list of diagnostic criteria for severe preeclampsia.[5] This syndrome consists of hemolysis, elevated liver enzymes, and a low platelet count. In Weinstein's study sample of 29, all gravidas had subjective complaints of nausea and right upper quadrant tenderness on palpation.[5] All exhibited elevated levels of serum glutamic-oxaloacetic transaminase (SGOT) and/or serum glutamic-pyruvic transaminase (SGPT). All of the blood samples except one demonstrated abnormal peripheral blood smears showing schistocytes. The appearance of schistocytes is consistent with microangiopathic hemolytic anemia. Thrombocytopenia was demonstrated by platelet counts of less than 100,000/cu mm in all subjects. Seventy-eight percent of the multiparous women and 30% of the primigravid women exhibited admission blood pressures of greater than 160/110 mm Hg.

Killam et al. reported five case histories of women with pregnancy-induced hypertension complicated by liver disease and disseminated intravascular coagulation (DIC).[6] Epigastric pain, low platelet counts, and abnormal blood smears and liver function tests were noted in each of these cases. Likewise, Goodlin et al. reported similar findings in a group of 11 gravidas with severe PIH.[7] Right upper quadrant pain, elevated serum uric acid, decreased creatinine clearance, and thrombocytopenia were reported.

The pathophysiology of pregnancy-induced hypertension and HELLP syndrome is systemic vasospasm. The etiology of the vasospasm is as yet unclear. Etiologic theories have included immunologic causes, genetic predispositions, and nutritional factors.[3] More recently, research efforts have focused on the role of prostacyclin, a vasodilator found in increased concentrations in later pregnancy.[8] Goodman et al. reported decreased excretion of prostacyclin metabolites in those gravidas whose pregnancies were complicated by preeclampsia when compared to gravidas experiencing normal pregnancies.[9] Prostacyclin has also been shown to be an inhibitor of platelet aggregation. Decreases in prostacyclin in late pregnancy could result in platelet adhesion and platelet consumption.[10]

Vasospasm is the underlying cause for the development of the symptoms of PIH. With arterial vasoconstriction, increased systemic vascular resistance occurs, leading to measurable hypertension. Decreased renal blood flow produces oliguria and elevations in serum blood urea nitrogen, uric acid, and creatinine levels. Swelling of the glomerular endothelial cells and deposits of fibrin materials result from vasospasm. Proteinuria is thought to result from such lesions.

Generalized vasospasm produces shifts in fluid from the intravascular to the extravascular spaces. As a result, excessive weight gain and pitting edema are objectively identified. Cerebral edema and central nervous system irritability are also evident. Such irritability is responsible for the symptoms of headache and visual disturbances as well as hyperreflexia.

The degree of hepatic involvement seen with the HELLP syndrome is thought to vary with the extent of edema and damage to the endothelium of the liver capsule.[11] Clients complain of epigastric pain and right upper quadrant tenderness on palpation. The liver may be enlarged and elevations in SGOT and/or SGPT can be demonstrated.

A second common finding of the HELLP syndrome is microangiopathic hemolytic anemia demonstrated on peripheral blood smears by the appearance of small, irregularly shaped red blood cell fragments known as schistocytes.[5] Thrombocytopenia is thought to develop from the consumption of platelets utilized to repair damaged vascular endothelium. Platelet values in women with HELLP are often less than 100,000/cu mm.[5]

The disease process of PIH can also adversely affect the fetus. With systemic vasospasm and decreased peripheral blood flow to the uterus and placenta, uteroplacental insufficiency develops. Consequences of uteroplacental insufficiency include intrauterine growth retardation and fetal death.

Medical management of pregnancies with pregnancy-induced hypertension complicated by HELLP is conflicting. Weinstein reported one maternal death (N = 29) and an overall perinatal mortality rate of 9.4%.[5] Ten neonates suffered from varying degrees of respiratory distress syndrome related to preterm delivery. He urged aggressive treatment with delivery to avoid the negative maternal and fetal consequences.[5]

Another study of women with HELLP syndrome (N = 112) reported two maternal deaths, two clients with ruptured liver hematomas, and nine with acute renal failure.[12] Thirty-eight percent developed DIC, and 20% evidenced abruptio placentae. A total of 22 stillbirths and 16 neonatal deaths were reported, for a perinatal mortality rate of 367/1000.

In contrast, MacKenna et al. reported findings of 27 clients who evidenced HELLP syndrome from a total of 223 preeclamptic and eclamptic clients.[13] Management of clients was more conservative. Fetal lung profiles to determine maturity guided the timing of delivery. No maternal death was reported. Two fetal deaths were reported in women experiencing abruptio placentae. One neonatal death was due to sepsis and intraventricular hemorrhage. It has been suggested that HELLP is not an entity separate from PIH but a group of signs diagnostic of the disease.[13]

* * * * *

CASE STUDY

A 15-year-old Hispanic primigravida was admitted to labor and delivery at 38 weeks of pregnancy with the following diagnoses: intrauterine growth retardation, preterm labor arrested, polyhydramnios, and pregnancy-induced hypertension. She had been followed since 15 weeks of pregnancy for 22 prenatal visits. The client had three hospital admissions for preterm labor. At 35 weeks gestational age, blood pressure elevations were noted from a second trimester baseline of 112/68. No significant proteinuria or edema was noted at that time. She was followed with frequent visits, nonstress tests, and serial sonograms until 38 weeks, when blood pressures were found to be elevated to 140/104. There was no proteinuria or significant edema. The cervical examination at that time showed 1 to 2 cm of dilatation and 50% effacement, with −1 vertex. The decision was made to admit the client for induction.

On admission to labor and delivery, her blood pressure was 140/70. No proteinuria was noted on clean catch specimen. Physical examination showed 1+ pretibial edema and normal deep tendon reflexes (DTRs). The client denied any headache, visual disturbances, or epigastric distress. She was placed on a fetal monitor and a dose of prostaglandin gel was applied to the cervix. Prostaglandin gel was used to induce a more favorable Bishop score, making the likelihood of a pitocin induction more successful, should that have become necessary. Within 20 hours she was contracting. A vaginal examination 4 hours later revealed a cervix that was 3 cm/100%/−1. An amniotomy was performed, and clear fluid was noted. She progressed normally in labor with blood pressures remaining in the 130/70 to 140/90 range. Nine hours after entering the active phase of labor, the client delivered a female infant by forceps with Apgar scores of 6 and 8.

Within 8 hours following delivery, her blood pressure became elevated to 170/100 and hyperreflexia was demonstrated with DTRs at 4+ without ankle clonus. Increased edema of the face and hands was noted, along with decreased urinary output. Laboratory results showed the following abnormal values: a hematocrit of 46.6%, uric acid of 10.4, blood urea nitrogen (BUN) of 15, creatinine of 1.3, SGOT of 537, and platelets of 164,000 cu mm. A diagnosis of severe PIH and HELLP syndrome was made, and the client was started on a magnesium sulfate infusion. Four hours after the MgSO$_4$ infusion was begun, laboratory tests were redone. Platelets remained stable at 164,000/cu mm. The hematocrit remained stable at 47%, BUN was elevated to 19, creatinine 1.3, uric acid 10.4, total bilirubin of 1.1, and SGOT of 537. Nine hours later repeat tests showed the following: platelets 170,000/cu mm, BUN 15, creatinine 1.3, total bilirubin 0.7, and SGOT 390. Over the next 24 hours, the patient's blood pressures and laboratory values stabilized. The MgSO$_4$ was discontinued by the end of the second day postpartum, and the client was discharged home on Day 3.

* * * * *

CASE ANALYSIS

The goals of nursing care in monitoring for pregnancy-induced hypertension and HELLP syndrome during the antenatal period include early and frequent assessments of risk factors and clinical signs and symptoms indicative of the disease. It is likely that the disease process begins long before the appearance of any subjective symptoms or objective signs.[14] Knowledge of the predisposing risk factors is important. The case study illustrated several risk factors for the development of PIH. The woman was a 15-year-old primigravida. Women must be instructed to report any of the PIH warning signs, such as headaches, visual disturbances, epigastric pain, nausea/vomiting, edema, and sudden weight gain.

Access to care becomes a critical issue.[15] This includes early prenatal care as well as the availability of that care to high-risk women. Early prenatal care allows the establishment of first trimester blood pressure to determine a baseline by which elevations can be evaluated. Blood pressure characteristically falls during the second trimester as peripheral vascular resistance decreases and the placenta, a low resistance organ, grows.[16] The woman in the case study presented for prenatal care during the second trimester. The establishment of a baseline blood pressure is more difficult at this time because the drop in blood pressure secondary to the physiologic changes of pregnancy may have occurred.

Pregnancy-induced hypertension can occur at any time during pregnancy. The occurrence of symptoms before 24 weeks of gestation is often associated with other complications such as hydatidiform mole, multiple gestation, and chronic hypertension.[14] The earlier the disease appears in pregnancy, the poorer the prognosis. The only cure for PIH is delivery.

Once the diagnosis of PIH is made, nurses working with these women must focus on assessments made at each prenatal visit. Oftentimes women are seen biweekly. The history of subjective symptoms is ascertained at each visit. Weight is checked, and a clean catch urine specimen is tested for protein. Blood pressure should be taken with an appropriately sized cuff. Other components of the physical examination are examinations for hyperreflexia and pitting edema.

If the woman is to be managed at home with frequent visits, education becomes imperative. Bed rest in the left lateral recumbent position relieves pressure from the uterus on the aorta, thus increasing renal perfusion and improving circulation to the placenta. The home situation and available social support must be assessed to identify avenues for help with household chores and other children.[17] Fetal well-being can be evaluated by instructing the client in fetal movement charting. Education regarding the rationale and compliance necessary for sonograms, nonstress tests, or contraction stress tests is imperative. Smoking should be discouraged. Time should be made available for questions and exploration of concerns related to the disease process. Often women have to stop work earlier than anticipated. Worry about self and fetus, as well as loss of income, can be a source of stress.

Laboratory testing includes hematocrit, renal and liver function tests, and blood coagulation studies. Twenty-four-hour urine collections for total protein and creatinine clearance are commonly evaluated. Increased hematocrit signifies decreased intravascular volume secondary to shifting of fluid to extravascular spaces. In the case of HELLP syndrome, hematocrit may be decreased because of red blood cell destruction. Renal function tests include serum BUN, uric acid, and creatinine. During pregnancy, increased renal clearance of these substances results in decreased serum values. It is important to recognize this, as a BUN of 12 reported on a lab slip may be within normal limits for the nonpregnant state but is clearly abnormal in pregnancy. Ferris suggested the upper limits of normal for BUN in pregnancy as 10 mg/100 mg of serum, creatinine of 1 mg/100 ml, and uric acid of <4.5 mg/100 ml.[2] Liver function tests include SGOT and SGPT. Normal values for SGOT are 4 to 20 IU/liter and for SGPT are 3 to 21 IU/liter.[16] These normal ranges do not change in pregnancy. Platelets below 100,000/cu mm are considered abnormal and diagnostic of thrombocytopenia.[5] (See Table 9-1.)

When PIH is suspected, it is often beneficial for baseline measurements of these previously mentioned parameters to have been recorded. If the woman's condition worsens, follow-up measurements should be compared to indicate when changes in status occur. The woman in the case study demonstrated a stable hematocrit. All parameters of renal function were abnormal, as was the SGOT. The client did not evidence any thrombocytopenia, as the platelet level remained at 164,000/cu mm. Prenatal baseline measurements may have demonstrated that 164,000/cu mm, although normal, was actually a decreased value.

Upon admission to labor and delivery, nursing care of the woman with PIH begins again with assessment. Close and frequent monitoring of subjective and objective parameters is warranted. Continuous fetal monitoring is indicated for women with PIH as the possibility of fetal distress exists. A private, quiet room eliminating extraneous stimuli is beneficial to those clients demonstrating a hyperreflexic state. Magnesium sulfate is the drug of choice for the prevention of seizures. The drug acts at the neuromuscular junction to slow transmission of electrical impulses. Magnesium sulfate blocks acetylcholine release and action, preventing seizures.[16] Plasma levels of 4 to 7.5 mEq/liter are effective in preventing seizures, and depressed DTRs are often noted at these levels.[17] Loss of deep tendon reflexes is a sign of magnesium sulfate toxicity. Levels above 15 mEq/liter are associated with respiratory paralysis, whereas levels above 25 mEq/liter are as-

Table 9-1 Normal Lab Values Pregnant State

BUN	< 10mg/100 ml
creatinine	< 1 mg/100 ml
uric acid	< 4.5 mg/100 ml
SGOT	4–20 IU/L
SGPT	3–21 IU/L
platelets	>100,000 cu/mm

Source: Data from Medical Complications During Pregnancy (pp 1–35) by G Burrow and T Ferris (eds), WB Saunders Company, © 1982.

sociated with cardiac arrest. The antidote for $MgSO_4$ is calcium gluconate and should be readily available. Frequent observations of DTRs, respiratory rate, and serum magnesium levels should be monitored. Because $MgSO_4$ is excreted by the kidneys, hourly urine outputs should be assessed. Outputs of less than 30 ml/hr should be reported.

If diastolic blood pressures are greater than 110 mm Hg, other hypertensive drugs such as hydralazine (Apresoline) are used. Hydralazine is often the drug of choice as it causes arteriolar relaxation and decreases blood pressure while stimulating cardiac output and increasing renal and cerebral blood flow.[11] Five milligrams given by slow intravenous bolus are ordered every 15 to 20 minutes to maintain diastolic pressures of 90 to 100 mm Hg.[18]

Because a diagnosis of severe PIH signifies a risk for the development of eclampsia and seizures, seizure precautions should be instituted. Oxygen and suction equipment should be available at the bedside. In many institutions, eclamptic trays are available at the beside; they contain padded tongue blades, airways, syringes/needles, a tourniquet, and various pharmacologic agents, including magnesium sulfate, Valium, hydralazine, and calcium gluconate.

Nursing surveillance should continue for 24 to 48 hours postpartum. Seizures may occur early after delivery in about 25% of all cases.[14] Nursing assessment should continue to include subjective symptoms, vital signs, reflexes, and urinary output. Gilbert and Harmon reported that, as normal postpartum diuresis takes place, increased amounts of magnesium are lost, leading to below-therapeutic levels in the serum and thereby placing the woman at increased risk for seizures.[17]

As evidenced in the case study, the client did not develop clinical signs of severe PIH and HELLP until after delivery. The onset of the clinical presentation was dramatic. Special nursing considerations in the delivery of care to women with HELLP specifically suggest identification of a tendency for excessive bleeding because of thrombocytopenia. Continued bleeding from venipuncture sites and incisions, heavy lochial flow with a firm, correctly positioned uterus, and bruising at the placement site of the blood pressure cuff are early signs of disseminated intravascular coagulation disease and should be reported.

IMPLICATIONS FOR PRACTICE

Nursing judgment will determine the amount of environmental restriction necessary postpartum, especially if the client continues to be hyperreflexic. In addition, the neonate may be at risk because of prematurity or intrauterine growth retardation.[11] Infants born full term may lack the alertness typical of the immediate neonatal period because of the sedative effects of magnesium sulfate. Nurses can communicate to the parents that this is a transient problem and does not indicate any kind of permanent neurologic damage.[11]

Stabilization and resolution of the disease are evidenced by decreasing blood pressures, increasing urine output, and decreased edema and proteinuria. Blood pressure should return to the prepregnancy baseline within the first few weeks postpartum. Failure of blood pressure to return to normal should be reported, and the patient should be monitored for potential chronic hypertension.

REFERENCES

1. Zuspan FP. Hypertension in pregnancy. In: Guilligan EJ, Kretchmer N, eds. *Fetal and Maternal Medicine*. New York, NY: John Wiley & Sons, Inc.; 1980:547–567.

2. Ferris T. Toxemia and hypertension. In: Burrow G, Ferris T, eds. *Medical Complications during Pregnancy*. Philadelphia, Pa: W.B. Saunders Co.; 1982:1–35.

3. Chesley LC. *Hypertensive Disorders in Pregnancy*. New York, NY: Appleton & Lange; 1978.

4. Chesley LC. Hypertensive disorders of pregnancy. *J Nurse-Midwifery*. 1985;30(2):99–104.

5. Weinstein L. Syndrome of hemolysis, elevated liver enzymes, and low platelet count: a severe consequence of hypertension in pregnancy. *Am J Obstet Gynecol*. 1982;142(2):159–167.

6. Killam A, Dillard S, Patton R, Pederson P. Pregnancy-induced hypertension complicated by acute liver disease and disseminated intravascular coagulation. *Am J Obstet Gynecol*. 1975;123:823–828.

7. Goodlin R, Cotton D, Haesslein H. Severe edema-proteinuria-hypertension gestosis. *Am J Obstet Gynecol*. 1978;132:595–598.

8. Lewis P, Boylan P, Friedman L, Hensby C, Downing I. Prostacyclin in pregnancy. *Br Med J*. 1980;1581–1582.

9. Goodman R, Killam A, Brash A, Branch R. Prostacyclin production during pregnancy: comparison of production during normal pregnancy and pregnancy complicated by hypertension. *Am J Obstet Gynecol*. 1982;123:823–828.

10. Thiagarajah S, Bourgeois F, Harbert G, Caudle M. Thrombocytopenia in preeclampsia: associated abnormalities and management principles. *Am J Obstet Gynecol*. 1984;150:1–7.

11. Koniak-Griffin D, Dodgson J. Severe pregnancy-induced hypertension: postpartum care of the critically ill patient. *Heart Lung*. 1987;16:661–669.

12. Sibai B, Taslimi M, El-Nazer A, Amon E, Mabie B, Ryan G. Maternal-perinatal outcome associated with the syndrome of hemolysis, elevated liver enzymes, and low platelets in severe preeclamsia-eclampsia. *Am J Obstet Gynecol*. 1986;155:501–509.

13. MacKenna J, Dover N, Brame R. Preeclampsia associated with hemolysis, elevated liver enzymes and low platelets—an obstetric emergency? *Obstet Gynecol*. 1983;62:751–745.

14. Ouimette J. Potential for maternal/fetal injury from pregnancy-induced hypertension. In: Ouimette J, ed. *Perinatal Nursing: Care of the High-Risk Mother and Infant*. Boston, Mass: Jones and Bartlett Publishers, Inc.; 1986:116–136.

15. Angelini D. Pregnancy-induced hypertension. In: Angelini D, Knapp C, Gibes R, eds. *Perinatal/Neonatal Nursing: A Clinical Handbook*. Boston, Mass: Blackwell Scientific Publications; 1986:191–202.

16. Whittaker A, Hull B, Clochesy J. Hemolysis, elevated liver enzymes, and low platelet count syndrome: nursing care of the critically ill obstetric patient. *Heart Lung*. 1986:15:402–410.

17. Gilbert E, Harmon J. *High-Risk Pregnancy and Delivery: Nursing Perspectives.* St. Louis, Mo: C.V. Mosby Co.; 1986.

18. Brengman SL, Burns MK. Hypertensive crisis in L & D. *Am J Nurs.* March 1988;325–328.

ADDITIONAL BIBLIOGRAPHY

Shannon D. HELLP syndrome: a severe consequence of pregnancy-induced hypertension. *J Obstet Gynecol Neonatal Nurs.* 1987;16:395–403.

Chapter 10

Eisenmenger's Syndrome and Pregnancy

Cheryl Kirkland

Advances in diagnostic and surgical technology have allowed increasing numbers of women with congenital heart disease to reach childbearing age. These women currently account for approximately 25% of all cases of heart disease during pregnancy.[1,2] Maternal and fetal morbidity and mortality vary greatly depending on the specific lesion involved and clinical status. The literature consistently cites Eisenmenger's syndrome as a type of heart disease having maternal and fetal risks significant enough to contraindicate pregnancy.[1–4] The woman with Eisenmenger's syndrome who chooses to continue a pregnancy poses complex nursing challenges.

REVIEW OF THE LITERATURE

Eisenmenger's syndrome is defined as severe pulmonary hypertension with right-to-left shunting which develops in the presence of any congenital cardiac defect allowing communication between the right and left sides of the heart.[1,4,5] Normally, venous blood enters the right side of the heart and is pumped via the pulmonary artery to the lungs. After being oxygenated, arterial blood returns to the left side of the heart before being pumped into systemic circulation. The right and left sides of the heart are normally two separate entities. The right side is a low pressure system of deoxygenated blood associated with the pulmonary circuit and the left side is a high pressure system of oxygenated blood associated with the systemic circuit.

About a dozen congenital defects allow communication between the right and left sides of the heart. Familiar examples include atrial septal defect, ventricular septal defect, and patent ductus arteriosis. When one of these defects exists, the higher pressure in the left side of the heart initially causes some of the oxygenated blood to shunt from the left to the right side of the heart during systole. The right

111

side of the heart is thus chronically exposed to greater volumes of blood under higher pressures. Some patients will develop the complication of Eisenmenger's syndrome where progressive, irreversible changes in the pulmonary microvasculature cause increased pulmonary vascular resistance and fixed pulmonary hypertension. Right ventricular hypertrophy then develops as the ventricle must pump blood to the lungs against resistance.[4] As pressure in the pulmonary artery and right ventricle increases, flow of blood across the abnormal communication channel is affected. Blood under pressure flows from higher to lower pressure along the path of least resistance. As right heart pressures rise to the level of left heart pressures, the shunt flow becomes bidirectional and then predominantly right to left.

With right-to-left shunting, some of the deoxygenated blood bypasses the lungs and enters the aorta. Mixed arterial and venous blood in the systemic circulation gives rise to lower oxygen levels and a state of chronic hypoxia. Characteristics associated with Eisenmenger's syndrome reflect this state and include peripheral cyanosis, especially noticeable in the fingers, toes, and lips; clubbing (a widening, thickening, and flattening of the distal fingers and toes); fatigue; exercise intolerance; poor physical growth; and polycythemia, where the body compensates by producing more red blood cells to increase the oxygen-carrying capacity, thus increasing the circulating oxygen to tissues.

Eisenmenger's syndrome can be prevented by early diagnosis and surgical correction of the congenital defect before the development of pulmonary hypertension. However, once the irreversible pulmonary hypertension has developed, surgery is contraindicated. Although unable to tolerate strenuous exercise, most patients with Eisenmenger's syndrome are able to lead fairly normal lives into the third decade. Life expectancy is limited to an average of 35 to 40 years.[2,5,6] Many patients die a sudden death. Serious medical illnesses, accidents, and surgical procedures all pose threats to the patient with Eisenmenger's syndrome.

Pregnancy also carries significant risk for both mother and fetus. The maternal mortality risk ranges from 30 to 50% and is high during delivery but highest during the first week postpartum.[1,7–9] The incidence of preeclampsia is 18%, compared to 5 to 7% in the general population.[8] Spontaneous abortion occurs in 39 to 50% of patients and seems to be related to the degree of pulmonary hypertension and cyanosis.[5,10] Perfusion of the uteroplacental unit with poorly oxygenated blood results in most infants being small for gestational age, and 30% are classified as suffering intrauterine growth retardation (IUGR).[6] The 28% perinatal mortality risk is closely related to the incidences of IUGR and of premature delivery, which occurs in 55 to 65%.[4,8] The fetus also has a 4 to 15% risk of a congenital heart defect.[10,11] Interpretation of studies of Eisenmenger's syndrome during pregnancy is limited by small numbers of patients, lack of controlled studies, and the tendency of researchers to combine similar cardiac lesions into categories for analysis.

Normal Physiologic Adaptation during Pregnancy

An understanding of normal physiologic adaptation to pregnancy is required to appreciate the dynamics of pregnancy with Eisenmenger's syndrome superimposed. Total blood volume increases an average of 50%.[3,12,13] The increase in blood volume occurs steadily, peaking at approximately 28 weeks gestation.[1] Although both plasma and red cell mass increase, plasma volume increases proportionately more, resulting in a hemodilutional effect and the so-called "physiologic anemia of pregnancy."[9,13] Uterine blood flow increases dramatically as pregnancy advances from 50 ml/min at 10 weeks gestation to 500 ml/min at term.[9]

Cardiac output also increases during pregnancy, peaking at 28 to 32 weeks and then decreasing slightly as term approaches.[1,3,9] Increased stroke volume accounts for most of the 30 to 50% increase in cardiac output, although a 10 to 15-beat per minute increase in heart rate also occurs.[1,5,12]

Vena caval compression by the gravid uterus has dramatic effects. Close to 100% occlusion of the inferior vena cava occurs at term in the supine position, forcing venous blood into the collateral circulation.[3,6] Some degree of venacaval compression occurs during the third trimester regardless of maternal position. The gravid uterus acts as a roadblock, decreasing venous return and thus stroke volume and cardiac output. Reduced cerebral blood flow gives rise to lightheadedness and syncope, while reduced uteroplacental blood flow gives rise to limited fetal growth and reserve. Venous pressure in the lower extremities increases, forcing extravasation of plasma into tissues, resulting in edema. Blood flow through the lower extremities is slowed by the venacaval compression.

Systemic vascular resistance (SVR) and pulmonary vascular resistance (PVR) both decline slightly under hormonally induced vasodilatation, causing a slight decrease in blood pressure (diastolic greater than systolic) during the second trimester.[1] Oxygen consumption increases 10 to 20% to supply the needs of both the fetus and the mother.[9,13] Fibronogen and clotting factors also increase, giving rise to a chronic hypercoagulable state during pregnancy.[13] Aside from third trimester dyspnea, fatigue, and lower extremity edema, most healthy pregnant women readily adapt to the physiologic changes of pregnancy.

Physiologic Changes with Eisenmenger's Syndrome

The normal physiologic changes of pregnancy superimposed on this abnormal cardiopulmonary system with a limited ability to compensate creates the following conditions. As blood volume increases, the already enlarged right ventricle must work harder to pump an increased amount of blood through resistant pulmonary vessels. The increased pressure thus generated increases the amount of deoxygenated blood shunted from the right to the left side of the heart. The slight decline in SVR may also contribute to increasing the right-to-left shunt, since PVR does not decrease with fixed pulmonary hypertension.[2] Aortocaval compression further affects the systemic circulation of deoxygenated blood by decreasing venous return and cardiac output, affecting myocardial, brain, and uterine perfusion. The maternal cardiac oxygen requirement increases in proportion to the increased work of the right and left ventricles; with more deoxygenated blood being shunted, however, less oxygen is available.[2] Finally, the already hypercoagulable state of pregnancy is exaggerated by the increased viscosity of polycythemic blood and stagnant blood in the lower extremities from aortocaval compression.

Prenatal anxiety, fear, stress, and discomfort increase cardiac demand. In addition to the concerns of most pregnant women about the health of their infant, the course of their delivery, and assumption of the maternal role, the patient with Eisenmenger's syndrome also has the additional burden of the very real threat to her own health. The goals of medical care during the prenatal period focus on the prevention and early detection and treatment of maternal or fetal complications. The third trimester is the most physically stressful period for the cardiopulmonary system. Blood volume and cardiac output peak, aortocaval compression increases, fetal needs rise, and the mother's psychologic stress may be high. If one considers the cardiac capacity of the patient with Eisenmenger's syndrome as a limited commodity that must be budgeted, then nonessential cardiac expenditures must be eliminated or reduced to accommodate the demands of pregnancy itself. This concept of reducing cardiac demand is the cornerstone for many of the medical interventions for the pregnancy complicated by Eisenmenger's syndrome.

The activity level of the patient must be evaluated and the patient can be assisted to organize her life to reduce unnecessary activity, especially in the third trimester. With the third trimester comes increasing discomfort, restrictions, and focus on the risks of delivery. Anxiety and stress are another source of cardiac demand, but eliminating these factors is a challenge. A relationship of trust and rapport between patient and caregiver is essential, with the caregiver's approach being one of cautious optimism and honesty. The patient should be assisted to explore and utilize whatever relaxation techniques (i.e., music, massage, breathing exercises, progressive muscle relaxation, yoga, meditation, etc.) benefit her. Identification of stressors and their modification whenever possible should be encouraged. Supportive persons or groups may provide a source of strength for the patient. Additional cardiac demand occurs with infection, excessive weight gain, temperature extremes, humidity, poor air quality, and constipation. The "normal" discomforts of late pregnancy such as backache, sciatica, heartburn, difficulty sleeping, and edematous feet may also stress the patient. Such factors should be moderated to the maximal degree possible.

Concerns during the Prenatal Period

Monitoring in the prenatal period includes periodic measurements of blood pressure, pulse, respirations, and peripheral oxygen saturation at rest, after activity, and with/without oxygen supplementation. The degree of cyanosis, fatigue, dyspnea, palpitations, or syncope must be assessed. Restrictions must be individualized and hospitalizations may be necessary to limit activity, provide supplemental oxygen, and allow close monitoring of mother and fetus.

The already hypercoagulable state of pregnancy is augmented in Eisenmenger's syndrome by increased blood viscosity from polycythemia, activity restrictions, and the effects of vena caval compression on blood flow in the lower extremities. Measures to prevent thromboembolic events include encouraging lateral rather than supine positioning, using elastic stockings and sequential compression devices, initiating leg exercises if on complete bed rest, monitoring the degree of polycythemia, and educating the patient to the signs and symptoms of thrombophlebitis.

Hypertension, increased systemic vascular resistance, and intravascular fluid volume depletion make preeclampsia a dangerous complication. The usual monitoring of blood pressure, proteinuria, edema, and laboratory values must be performed regularly.

Chronic maternal hypoxia reduces the oxygen available for fetal growth and development. Maximization of blood flow to the uterus and optimization of maternal oxygenation may diminish untoward effects. Again, decreasing cardiac demand and vena caval compression are important measures. Fetal status and growth are monitored by serial ultrasonography and periodic nonstress testing with a biophysical profile performed as necessary. The risk of the fetus having a congenital heart defect is significant. Risks of other anomalies may be related to maternal age or teratogenic effects of medications. Ultrasound may be utilized to assess the structural normalcy of the fetus.

In general, the prenatal period is better tolerated by patients with Eisenmenger's syndrome than is the labor and delivery. This may be related to the gradual nature of the hemodynamic changes of pregnancy, the better toleration of increases (vs. decreases) in volumes and central pressures, and the control that exists over other cardiac demands. The majority of complications occur during delivery or in the early postpartum period. An understanding of the hemodynamics of labor and delivery is important to appreciate why this is the time of greatest risk for these patients.

Concerns during Labor and Delivery

Oxygen consumption increases 100% above prepregnant levels.[13] Cardiac output also increases; the magnitude of this increase corresponds with the intensity of contractions, peaking at 60 to 80% above prepregnant levels.[1,3] Each contraction forces 300 to 500 ml of blood out of the uterus and its venous plexus into the maternal circulation, thereby suddenly increasing venous return. Arterial blood pressure increases during contractions, which elicits a reflex fall in heart rate. Cardiac output is increased by the effects of catecholamines secreted in response to pain and anxiety.

Two factors profoundly affect the swings in cardiac output during labor. First, vena caval compression is associated with decreased venous return, causing cardiac output to be 15 to 20% lower in the supine position during the time between contractions when the mother and fetus need maximal oxygenation for recovery.[3] During contractions, cardiac output in the supine position increases by a greater magnitude to a level that approximates that of cardiac output in the lateral position.[9,12] Second, regional anesthesia has the ability to considerably blunt the swings in cardiac output that are related to the influence of pain on the release of catecholamines.[3,9]

In the second stage of labor, bearing down efforts produce dramatic hemodynamic changes. The Valsalva maneuver causes increased intrathoracic pressure, decreased venous return, and a rebound of venous return when pushing stops. Delivery is associated with multiple hemodynamic events occurring simultaneously: blood loss of 500 to 1000 ml, autotransfusion of 500 to 800 ml of blood into the systemic circulation from the uterine vasculature, loss of the uteroplacental shunt, sudden release of venacaval compression allowing mobilization of blood from the lower extremities, and catecholamine release related to emotional factors.[12,13]

The patient with Eisenmenger's syndrome may not be able to adjust rapidly to the extreme hemodynamic changes associated with labor and delivery. Increases in cardiac output may increase right-to-left shunting, thereby lowering the oxygen content of the blood at a time when oxygen consumption is highest.[2] Myocardial compromise with ischemia, dysrhythmias, or cardiac failure may occur if the heart does not receive adequate oxygenation. Maternal hypoxia and acidosis may increase pulmonary vascular resistance, which contributes to more right-to-left shunting.[2] Decreases in systemic vascular resistance induced by hypotension from blood loss, anesthetics, and medications will cause the amount of shunting to increase.[2] Sudden decreases in venous return limit the ability of the right ventricle to perfuse the lungs because high central blood volumes are necessary for the right ventricle to overcome the resistance in the pulmonary artery and pump blood to the lungs.[2,9] The fetus with limited reserve may not tolerate lower oxygen levels in the face of the stress of labor. The supine position adds to the cardiac demand and may contribute to increased shunting. The careful administration of regional anesthesia decreases cardiac demand by minimizing pain. Also, in an effort to limit the hemodynamic roller coaster, the Valsalva maneuver is contraindicated and can be avoided by performing a forceps delivery after the vertex has descended.

The optimal route of delivery is a controversial subject; however, the need for a planned, controlled delivery with the appropriate personnel present is not. In determining whether to allow labor or to perform a cesarean section, one must consider the fetal status, obstetrical status, and cardiac status. The hemodynamic changes associated with contractions must be weighed against the effects of surgical manipulation and the risks of abdominal surgery. These risks include greater blood loss, infection, damage to bowels or bladder, ileus, thrombophlebitis, increased postpartum pain, and a longer recovery period. The risks of unsuccessful induction, fetal intolerance of labor, and cephalopelvic disproportion must also be considered. Regardless of the route of delivery, blood loss, autotransfusion, and release of aortocaval compression occur. A net decrease in blood volume is poorly tolerated by the patient with Eisenmenger's syndrome, and therefore excessive blood loss is to be avoided.[2]

The goals of care at delivery center around prevention and control of hemodynamic changes that might threaten the balance of shunt flow and thus maternal or fetal well-being. Reduction of cardiac demand is accomplished by a positive relationship between patient and caregiver, allowing the presence of supportive persons or objects, encouraging the use of relaxation techniques, and the liberal use of sedatives. Elimination of pain by an effective epidural anesthetic is of paramount importance. Prevention of infection by use of strict aseptic technique and antibiotic prophylaxis is necessary.

An increased amount of blood shunted from the right to the left side of the heart is associated with increased hypoxemia and is to be avoided. Its prevention centers around controlled hydration, avoidance of hypotension and venacaval compression, administration of supplemental oxygen, minimization of blood loss, and avoidance of the Valsalva maneuver. A pulse oximeter allows constant assessment of oxygen saturation and pulse, while an arterial line allows constant assessment of blood pressure and easy access to arterial blood for blood gas analysis. A central venous pressure line or a pulmonary artery catheter for assessment of trends in central pressures and volumes may also be useful.

Minimizing blood loss is accomplished by prompt delivery of the placenta, fundal massage, and the slow infusion of oxytocin. Ergotrate should be avoided because of its hypertensive effects. The risks of myocardial compromise are minimized with reduction of cardiac demand and with measures to maintain the balance of shunt flow. Continuous cardiac monitoring is necessary to detect arrhythmias. Supplemental high-flow oxygen may optimize oxygenation.

Thromboembolism is prevented by avoiding the supine position and wearing elastic stockings. Air embolus is a risk due to the presence of an opening between the right and left sides of the heart and mandates careful placement and maintenance of invasive monitoring lines as well as the use of air filters on tubing. Fetal status is monitored via continuous electronic fetal monitoring.

Concerns during the Postpartum Period

Normal hemodynamic changes and physiologic adaptations in the postpartum period are not as well defined as those in pregnancy, labor, and delivery. It is generally agreed that all parameters have returned to prepregnant baselines by 6 to 8 weeks postpartum.[12,14] Major fluid shifts take place during the first week postpartum, when reabsorption and excretion of extravascular fluid manifests itself with diuresis. The hemodynamic effects of lactation are unclear.

In patients with Eisenmenger's syndrome, twice as many deaths occur during the first week after delivery as during the delivery itself.[8] One study found that deaths correlated with blood loss, thromboemboli, and preeclampsia.[8] Another study postulated that a spontaneous rise in pulmonary artery pressure causes increased shunting and hemodynamic collapse.[4] Sudden death may be preceded by increasing cyanosis and syncope.[7,15] On autopsy, as many as 44% of patients had evidence of pulmonary thromboemboli.[8] However, the use of heparin prophylaxis is of questionable benefit.[16] The care plan for the patient in the postpartum period follows principles similar to those of labor in terms of reducing cardiac demand, preventing increased right-to-left shunting, preventing myocardial compromise, and preventing thromboembolic events. Observation in intensive care is indicated. Once the patient is stable, attention must be focused on promoting maternal/infant attachment and meeting the mother's educational needs regarding infant care.

* * * * *

CASE STUDY

L.M., a 35-year-old gravida III, para 0, therapeutic abortion II, was born with a complete atrioventricular (AV) canal, a complex lesion where a large opening in the center of the heart allows all four chambers of the heart to communicate and where the pulmonary artery and aorta arise from the same space. At age 12, cardiac catheterization revealed severe pulmonary hypertension and right ventricular hypertrophy. Despite counseling to avoid pregnancy, she became pregnant twice and elected therapeutic abortion on medical advice. These two abortions were accompanied by intense emotional trauma associated with suicidal feelings and required long-term psychotherapy.

With this pregnancy, L.M. presented initially at 10 weeks gestation, adamant to continue this pregnancy despite full knowledge and understanding of the risks to herself and her fetus. On initial examination, she was 5 ft 3 in. and weighed 96 lb.

Her blood pressure was 90/60. Electrocardiography (EKG) showed normal sinus rhythm (NSR) at a rate of 85 with evidence of right ventricular hypertrophy. The initial hematocrit was 56.9%. Cardiac catheterization 2 years prior had revealed systemic pressures equal to pulmonary pressures. Physical examination was remarkable for cyanotic nailbeds and marked clubbing. She was able to climb one flight of stairs without dyspnea. Socially, she was separated from her alcoholic and emotionally abusive husband of 7 years and had been involved for a short period with a man from Canada who was the father of the baby. She owned and operated her own bookkeeping business on a small island, 3 1/2 hours from the nearest major medical center. She was an articulate women who was very knowledgeable about her condition. She practiced meditation on a regular basis, ate a vegetarian diet, and was involved in a supportive Al-Anon group.

She was able to maintain her usual activities until 30 weeks gestation, when she decreased working hours due to fatigue. At 34 weeks, minimal activity resulted in a decreased peripheral oxygen saturation to 83 to 84%, which quickly returned to the baseline of 87 to 88% after rest (normal = 97 to 99%). At that point she stopped working and moved to a friend's home to be closer to the medical center. Her activity was limited to short periods within the house and occasional dining out. Dyspnea and fatigue increased with the summer heat and humidity and as the pregnancy progressed. Baseline oxygen saturation levels decreased to 84 to 85%.

Although initially she had no support from friends or family in her decision to continue the pregnancy, they became more supportive as the pregnancy advanced. She experienced multiple stressors. Her estranged husband harassed her, was uncooperative with divorce proceedings, and threatened to claim paternity. The department of immigration wanted the father of the baby to return to Canada as his visa had expired. L.M. had to draw up a will arranging for the disposition of her business as well as for custody of the baby. Moving from her home at 34 weeks was very traumatic as her support systems were removed.

Amniocentesis at 16 weeks had revealed a chromosomally normal fetus. Ultrasound revealed a structurally normal fetus. During the course of the third trimester declining growth was noted, falling from the 50th percentile to the 20th percentile. Nonstress testing and biophysical profiles were consistently reassuring, however.

An interdisciplinary care conference was held to plan L.M.'s intrapartum and postpartum care with input from nursing, obstetrics, cardiology, anesthesia, and social services. The patient and the father of the baby as well as the medical and nursing staffs of both the obstetrical and cardiac units were well prepared and knowledgeable about the patient and the plan of care.

Labor was electively induced at 38 weeks. On the morning of the scheduled induction, L.M. was spontaneously experiencing mild uterine contractions, with cervical findings of 1–2/20%/0, vertex presentation. The fetal heart baseline was 130, and the nonstress test (NST) was reactive. After sedation with Valium, morphine, and Benadryl, a large-bore intravenous line, an arterial line, a central venous pressure line, and an epidural line were placed. A Foley catheter was inserted, oxygen was given by face mask at 10 liters/min, and peripheral oxygen saturation was monitored. Initial assessment data were as follows: blood pressure

(BP) 120/70, central venous pressure (CVP) 11 to 15, oxygen saturation in room air = 71%, with 10 liters oxygen = 82%, negative proteinuria, hematocrit = 48%. After these preparations were complete, membranes were ruptured artificially for clear fluid. Oxytocin was initiated.

After 7 hours of induction, the cervix had dilated to 5 cm. The fetal heart baseline was 130 with minimal variability via internal monitor with no evidence of decelerations or accelerations. At that point, the patient exhibited the following symptoms: BP 165/95, urine output 22 ml over the previous hour, 3+ proteinuria, and upper extremity hyper-reflexia. Magnesium sulfate was started.

Three hours later she was delivered by midforceps of a 4-lb, 12-oz, vigorous female infant with Apgar scores of 8 and 9. Other than the acute development of preeclampsia, the patient tolerated labor well. Peripheral oxygen saturations with high flow oxygen ranged from 84 to 90%. CVP ranged from 10 to 17. After magnesium sulfate was started, BP dropped to 140/90 and urine output increased to more than 30 ml/hr. Within 10 minutes of delivery the patient experienced an episode of severe hypotension (systolic BP = 80, CVP = 1, no change in oxygen saturation), which responded to albumin, ephedrine, and Neosynephrine. This episode repeated itself 20 minutes later, at which time a Neosynephrine drip was started. The patient was transferred to the cardiac intensive care unit and, over the next 24 hours, experienced labile BP and low peripheral oxygen saturation (80 to 82%) despite continuous high-flow oxygen and vasopressors. Initial postpartum hematocrit was 27%.

By postpartum day 2, blood pressure and CVP were consistently back to the patient's baseline. However, despite 100% oxygen and transfusion of 3 units of red blood cells, peripheral oxygen saturation slowly decreased over the ensuring days to a low of 65 to 70% at rest (corresponding to an arterial Po_2 of 40). The patient was asymptomatic throughout and did not experience syncope, dyspnea, or increased cyanosis. On postpartum day 5, peripheral oxygen saturation began to improve, and the patient was transferred to an intermediate care unit on the following day. She was discharged with her baby on postpartum day 10, planning a tubal ligation 6 months postpartum.

*   *   *   *   *

CASE ANALYSIS

Many of the known features of pregnancy complicated by Eisenmenger's syndrome were present in this case. During the third trimester the patient exhibited signs of increased shunting and impaired fetal growth. With activity limitations, stress reduction, lateral rest, and monitoring of maternal/fetal status, the patient was able to reach term pregnancy. During labor, the patient's hemodynamic status was well controlled with appropriate anesthesia, positioning, oxygen supplementation, and hydration. The development of preeclampsia was anticipated given maternal age, parity, and Eisenmenger's syndrome and was quickly treated. Consistent with the literature, this patient presented with a stormy postpartum course. The hypotension in the immediate postpartum period could not be explained by the volume of blood loss or the influence of medication. Prompt attention to the maintenance of venous return and pulmonary perfusion prevented total shunt reversal and hemodynamic collapse from inadequate oxygenation.

Increasing hypoxemia, as evidenced by decreasing peripheral oxygen saturation, was extremely distressing given the maximal medical interventions that were already in place. The pathophysiology of this phenomenon remains unclear. The patient's condition improved spontaneously with continued medical and nursing support and an optimistic attitude on the part of the patient.

This case is an example of a positive outcome that was achieved with interdisciplinary collaboration, intensive prenatal, intrapartum, and postpartum care, and a high level of cooperation by the patient.

IMPLICATIONS FOR PRACTICE

The complexity of the physiology and hemodynamics of Eisenmenger's syndrome and pregnancy coupled with the high risk of maternal and fetal morbidity and mortality present a significant challenge for all members of the health care team. Nursing, with its biopsychosocial focus, has an essential role in caring for these patients during the prenatal, intrapartum, and postpartum periods.

During pregnancy, intensive nursing intervention is required to educate the patient, reinforce and provide rationale for the medical care plan, assist the patient to cope, allow verbalization of concerns and fears, provide anticipatory guidance, and offer emotional support and caring. The patient in this case was highly motivated to comply with medical advice and actively sought information that would assist her to understand her condition, recognize problems, and prepare herself for delivery. Given the complicated social situation, she required much emotional attention, assistance with anticipatory planning in the event of her death, and encouragement in the use of strengths and supports for coping with the stressors she faced. Minimization of cardiac demand produced by stress was a challenge for the patient, the social worker, and the nurse but was accomplished successfully. The patient, her labor coach, and the father of the baby were fully prepared for the labor experience, which was to take place in an operating room with intensive hemodynamic monitoring. A tour of the labor area and the cardiac intensive care unit was provided, complete with introduction to the nurses and viewing the machines and equipment to be used. The patient's requests for the presence of significant others, a stuffed animal good luck charm, and relaxing music during labor were honored in an effort to reduce her anxiety. During labor, nursing actions focused on monitoring maternal and fetal status, administering oxytocin, and providing support.

In the postpartum period, intensive nursing observation was required to allow medical interventions to be implemented quickly in response to threatening hemodynamic changes. The patient's family required continual support during this time. Once the patient was stabilized, collaboration between cardiac and obstetrical nurses was aimed at promoting maternal/infant attachment and providing infant care education within the context of efforts to reduce cardiac demand and monitor hemodynamic status.

Continuity of nursing care was achieved with the involvement of the perinatal clinical nurse specialist, who provided direct nursing care in the prenatal and intrapartum periods, participated in interdisciplinary care planning, provided patient-focused educational programs for staff nurses, and consulted with primary nurses both in labor and delivery and in the cardiac unit to develop nursing care plans.

Nurses who care for obstetrical patients with cardiac disease must have an understanding of the cardiac physiology, the effects of pregnancy on the cardiac condition, and the effects of the cardiac condition on the pregnancy and fetus. Only then can nursing positively influence perinatal outcome by integrating this understanding with the individual needs of the patient.

REFERENCES

1. Ueland K. Cardiovascular diseases complicating pregnancy. *Clin Obstet Gynecol.* 1978;21:429–441.

2. Mangano DT. Anesthesia for the pregnant cardiac patient. In Shnider SM, Levinson G, eds. *Anesthesia for Obstetrics.* Baltimore, Md: Williams & Wilkins Co.; 1979.

3. Ueland K. Pregnancy and cardiovascular disease. *Med Clin North Am.* 1977;61(1):17–39.

4. Berkowitz RL. *Critical Care of the Obstetric Patient.* New York, NY: Churchill Livingstone; 1983.

5. Johnson MD, Holcombe J. Anesthesiologist's view. In: Datta S, Ostheimer G, eds. *Common Problems in Obstetrical Anesthesia.* Chicago, Ill: Yearbook Medical Publishers; 1987.

6. Metcalfe J, McAnulty J, Ueland K. *Heart Disease and Pregnancy: Physiology and Management.* Boston, Mass: Little, Brown & Co.; 1986.

7. Jones AM, Howitt G. Eisenmenger's syndrome in pregnancy. *Br Med J.* 1965;2:1627–1631.

8. Gleicher R, Midwall J, Huchberger D, et al. Eisenmenger's syndrome and pregnancy. *Obstet Gynecol Surv.* 1979;34:721.

9. McAnulty J, Metcalfe J, Ueland K. Cardiovascular diseases. In: Burrow GN, Ferris TF, eds. *Medical Complications during Pregnancy.* Philadelphia, Pa: W.B. Saunders Co.; 1982.

10. Whittemore R, Hobbins JC, Engle MA. Pregnancy and its outcome in women with and without surgical treatment of congenital heart disease. *Am J Cardiol.* 1982;50:641–650.

11. Nora JJ, Nora AH. *Genetics and Counseling in Cardiovascular Disease.* Springfield, Ill: Charles C Thomas, Pub.; 1978.

12. Perloff JK. Pregnancy and cardiovascular disease. In Braunwald E, ed. *Heart Disease.* Philadelphia, Pa: W.B. Saunders Co.; 1980.
13. McMorland GH. Cardiovascular and respiratory changes in late pregnancy. In: Datta S, Ostheimer G, eds. *Common Problems in Obstetrical Anesthesia.* Chicago, Ill: Yearbook Medical Publishers; 1987.
14. Walters WW, Lim YL. Blood volume and haemodynamics in pregnancy. *Clin Obstet Gynecol.* 1975;2:301–317.
15. Nielson G, Galea E, Blunt A. Eisenmenger's syndrome and pregnancy. *Med J Aust.* 1971;1:431–434.
16. Pitts JA, Crosby WM, Basta LL: Eisenmenger's syndrome in pregnancy—does heparin prophylaxis improve the maternal mortality rate? *Am Heart J.* 1977;93:321–326.

ADDITIONAL BIBLIOGRAPHY

Brammell HL, Vogel JH, Pryor R, Bount SG. The Eisenmenger syndrome. *Am J Cardiol.* 1971;28:679–692.

Cobb T, Gleicher N, Elkayamu U. Congenital heart disease in pregnancy. In: Elkayam U, ed. *Cardiac Disease in Pregnancy.* New York, NY: Alan R. Liss; 1982.

Miller LD. Eisenmenger's syndrome and the pregnant patient. *J Obstet Gynecol Neonatol Nurs.* 1983;12(3):175–180.

Neilson G, Galea EG, Blunt A. Congenital heart disease and pregnancy. *Med J Aust.* 1970;1:1086–1088.

Shime J, Mocarski EJ, Hastings D, Webb GD, McLaughlin PR. Congenital heart disease in pregnancy: short and long term implications. *J Obstet Gynecol.* 1987;156:313–322.

Sullivan JM, Ramanthan KB. Management of medical problems in pregnancy—severe cardiac disease. *N Engl J Med.* 1985;313(5):304–309.

Chapter 11

Shoulder Dystocia

Sandra Friedman

The misfortune of being unable to accomplish timely delivery of an infant's shoulders after delivery of the head is an obstetrical nightmare. It is a problem that occurs infrequently and quite unexpectedly. However, it is one that must be solved within a few minutes if severe injury or death of the infant is to be avoided. Health care providers working with obstetrical patients need to be prepared to handle this obstetric emergency. It is necessary for the delivery team to have an awareness of the risk factors associated with shoulder dystocia and to have a plan of action committed to memory. Accurate knowledge of standard maneuvers needed to facilitate an expeditious delivery is imperative. This case study will provide a review of the literature and a case presentation of a patient experiencing shoulder dystocia.

REVIEW OF THE LITERATURE

A definition of shoulder dystocia states that the presentation is always cephalic, the head has been born, but the shoulders cannot be delivered by the usual methods. The head is usually delivered very slowly and retracts back tightly against the perineum. The shoulders are impacted in the maternal pelvis. Spontaneous external rotation of the head usually does not occur. The reported incidence of shoulder dystocia is 0.15% to 0.38% of all deliveries.[1-3]

Impaction of the shoulder has been recognized for at least two centuries.[3] The first known documentation of shoulder dystocia in the literature was by Smellie in 1730, who wrote, "a sudden call to a gentlewoman in labor. The child's head delivered for a long time—but even with hard pulling from the midwife, the remarkably large shoulders prevented delivery. I have been called to many cases of this kind, in which the child is frequently lost."[3] Spiegelberg, in his text of 1878, also gave recognition to the problem of shoulder dystocia and recommended attempted rotation as a method of management.[3]

Seigworth reported in a review of 51 cases of shoulder dystocia that 39 (77%) of the infants weighed greater than 4000 g and 25 (49%) were delivered by midforceps operations.[4] Seigworth also noted the importance of recognizing the pelvic type that may predispose to shoulder dystocia: an anterior projection of the sacrum and coccyx and a platypelloid or android pelvis. Schwartz reviewed the obstetrical experience with shoulder dystocia at Johns Hopkins Hospital from 1950 through 1957.[3] Of 20,599 infants weighing 2500 g or more, shoulder dystocia was recognized in 31 instances, or 0.15% of term deliveries. Twenty-four cases occurred in the 1,409 births of infants weighing 4000 g or more, roughly an incidence of 1.7% in this weight group. In 9,864 deliveries at Los Angeles County-USC Medical Center that were reviewed retrospectively, 90% delivered vaginally and 4.89% had a prolonged second stage with midpelvic delivery.[5] In this study, shoulder dystocia occurred in 0.37% of all vertex vaginal deliveries. Without a prolonged second stage and midpelvic delivery, the incidence of shoulder dystocia was 0.16%. With a prolonged second stage and midpelvic delivery, the incidence was 4.57% ($P < 0.01$). When birth weight exceeded 4000 g associated with a prolonged second stage and midpelvic delivery, the incidence of shoulder dystocia was 23%.

Modanlou and colleagues reported that infants having shoulder dystocia had greater shoulder-to-head and chest-to-head proportions than had macrosomic infants without shoulder dystocia.[6] Also, infants of diabetic mothers showed greater shoulder-to-head and chest-to-head size differences than infants of the same weight of nondiabetic mothers. Modanlou et al. reported that a 1.6 cm chest-to-head circumference difference indicates the possibility of a shoulder dystocia.[6]

If this measurement could be detected antenatally by ultrasound, a cesarean section would be done to avoid shoulder dystocia. William and coworkers reported that cesarean section would be advisable if the ultrasound measurement of the abdominal diameter was 1.5 cm greater than the biparietal diameter.[7]

To understand the maneuvers involved in the management of shoulder dystocia, one must review the normal mechanism of delivery of the shoulders. In general, in a spontaneous delivery, the bisacromial diameter of the shoulders enters the inlet in the oblique diameter. That is, the anterior shoulder tends to emerge beneath the symphysis just off the midline. By this mechanism, the anterior shoulder can usually be delivered with ease.

Shoulder dystocia usually occurs when the bisacromial diameter enters the inlet in the anteroposterior diameter instead of presenting in one of the oblique diameters.[8] The posterior shoulder extends below the sacral promontory and the anterior shoulder becomes impinged behind the symphysis pubis. Over-rotation (either spontaneous or operative) toward the anteroposterior diameter, before the adequate descent of the shoulder in the oblique diameter, may be a predisposition to shoulder dystocia.

Conditions that mimic shoulder dystocia and may cause difficulty in completing the delivery after the birth of the head are listed in Table 11-1. Maternal complications can be life threatening. Hematomas, excessive blood loss secondary to uterine rupture, and lacerations of the vagina are maternal complications of shoulder dystocia. Benedetti and Gabbe reported that 68% of patients in their study had an estimated blood loss of greater than 1000 ml at the time of delivery and a vaginal laceration rate of 37%.[5] Khan analyzed the maternal complication rate in 29 patients and found 3 with vaginal lacerations, 3 with cervical lacerations, and 4 with suburethral midline tears; the remaining patients had no maternal complications.[9]

The two most common fetal complications of shoulder dystocia are death and trauma to the infant. Fetal complications are listed in Table 11-2. The immediate danger to the infant is asphyxia. If the delivery is not accomplished within a few minutes after delivery of the head, the infant will die. If the infant has been compromised by a difficult labor, the infant may have evidence of brain damage. Infant mortality ranges from 21 to 290/1000 deliveries.[4]

Brachial plexus palsy is divided into palsies that involve the fifth and sixth cervical segment (Erb's or Duchenne's palsy) and those that involve the eighth cervical segment and the first thoracic segment (Klumpke's palsy). Klumpke's palsy has an incidence of 2 to 3% and has a prognosis of 40% recovery at 1 year, compared to a 72 to 92% recovery with Erb's palsy.[10] The C_5, C_6, and C_7 upper plexus is most easily injured when there has been forceful downward traction on the head to deliver the shoulders. Forceful traction on the manually extracted posterior arm may cause lower plexus injury. Fractures of the clavicle and/or humerus may be complications at delivery. These fractured bones may also puncture the infant's lung, causing a pneumothorax.

There are basic principles to manage shoulder dystocia safely. First, the nurse and primary care provider must review the maternal history and physical examination to identify risk factors for shoulder dystocia. Recognition of shoulder dystocia first occurs when the fetal head retracts at the perineum and restitution does not take place.

Table 11-1 Conditions That Mimic Shoulder Dystocia

Uterine contraction ring
Meningocele
Tumors of the neck and thorax
Enlargement of the abdomen due to tumors of the kidneys, liver, spleen, or gonads
Bladder distension or ascites
Double monsters
Conjoined or locked twins
Short umbilical cord

Table 11-2 Fetal Complications of Shoulder Dystocia

Brachial plexus injury (Erb's or Klumpke's palsy)
Long-term mental retardation and speech defects
Diaphragmatic paralysis
Fracture of clavicle and/or humerus, punctured lung
Death from asphyxia

At this point, assistance should be called for. The physician backup, the anesthesia team, and the pediatric/neonatal team should be in attendance if the shoulder dystocia is anticipated. Technicians to perform umbilical cord gases should be present. Immediate action is necessary to handle this emergency.

The patient must be taken out of stirrups and placed in the left lateral Sims' position or exaggerated lithotomy (McRobert's maneuver). An intravenous solution of 1 liter of normal saline is used in preparation for the possible complications of postpartum hemorrhage, uterine rupture, or maternal vaginal laceration. Most authors recommend that the episiotomy be extended through the rectum.[2,3,11,12] At this point a hand should be placed posteriorly into the vagina as far within the birth canal as possible to rule out the rare complications that mimic shoulder dystocia.[9]

The placement of the shoulders should be checked. Are the shoulders impacted in the anterioposterior diameter? Is there a nuchal cord? Are there any fetal tumors? If the shoulder dystocia was anticipated, catheterization of the bladder is performed before delivery of the head. Utilizing maternal effort, slight rotation of the fetal shoulders to the oblique diameter and firm downward traction on the anterior shoulder should be attempted to dislodge the shoulder from behind the symphysis. This attempt to rotate the shoulders to the oblique may be combined with suprapubic pressure. Fundal pressure should not be utilized as it further impinges the anterior shoulder behind the symphysis. If the rotation fails, delivery may be attempted by the Screw maneuver of Woods.[12] Woods advocates releasing the anterior shoulder by progressively rotating the posterior shoulder 180° in a corkscrew fashion. The posterior shoulder then assumes an anterior position and can be delivered with downward traction under the symphysis. If delivery is not accomplished, move to the next step. Try to insert the hand deep into the vagina behind the infant's posterior shoulders. Apply pressure to the anticubital fossa of the posterior arm and sweep the infant's arm across the chest to extract the shoulder and arm.[13] If all else fails, the bisacromial diameter of the shoulders can be reduced by breaking the clavicle. McCall stated that intentional cleidotomy is accomplished by inserting the tip of the index finger into the supraclavicular fossa and snapping the clavicle outward.[1]

* * * * *

CASE STUDY

L.B., a 28-year-old gravida IV para I abortus II, was admitted to the labor and delivery unit at 41 1/2 weeks in the latent phase of labor. She had had an uneventful labor and delivery of her first infant, a female weighing 8 lb 2 oz. With the first pregnancy, she had no history of macrosomia, diabetes mellitus, or shoulder dystocia. During the second pregnancy, the antenatal fetal weight was estimated at 8 lb 8 oz. She stood 5 ft 2 in. tall and had a total weight gain of 42 lb (an initial weight of 120 lb progressing to 162 lb at 41 1/2 weeks). The patient had a normal gynecoid pelvis by clinical pelvimetry on initial prenatal examination and upon initial vaginal examination in labor. The cervix was 1 cm dilated and 30% effaced with a vertex at –2 station on the initial vaginal exam.

The first stage of labor lasted 9 hours, and the second stage lasted 1 hour and 55 minutes. In the delivery room, the vertex delivered spontaneously in the occipitoanterior position followed by a tight retraction of the vertex against the perineum, suggesting a shoulder dystocia. A tight nuchal cord had been clamped and reduced before the delivery of the head. When gentle downward traction and suprapubic pressure failed to deliver the anterior shoulder, the Screw maneuver of Woods was attempted. This maneuver also failed. The patient's legs were then removed from the stirrups and sharply flexed against her abdomen (exaggerated lithotomy or McRobert's position). Again, traction was used to free the impacted shoulder—to no avail. An episiotomy had not been performed, nor had any regional anesthesia been given at this time. The patient's perineum had spontaneously torn with a second degree laceration. With the patient still in exaggerated lithotomy, the nurse-midwife intentionally broke the clavicle of the posterior shoulder (cleidotomy) and delivered the posterior arm. Thus, with downward traction, the anterior shoulder was successfully delivered. Delivery of the infant was accomplished approximately 1 1/2 to 2 minutes after delivery of the head.

The infant weighed 9 lb 2 oz, and had Apgar score of 6 at 1 minute and 9 at 5 minutes. After delivery, the broken clavicle was documented by x-ray film. The infant's clavicle was left to heal spontaneously. Upon neurologic examination, the infant had no deficits, and no physical therapy was needed. The mother was visited daily during her postpartum stay. The delivery was reviewed and psychologic support was given. Both mother and infant were discharged without complications on the second postpartum day.

* * * * *

CASE ANALYSIS

There are many risk factors associated with shoulder dystocia (Table 11-3). During the antepartum period, risk factors may be categorized as those that are preventable antenatally and the known, identifiable factors that are already

Table 11-3 Etiologic Factors Associated with Shoulder Dystocia

---

Macrosomia—infant weighing more than 4000 g
Multiparity
Contracted pelvis by clinical pelvimetry
Prolonged second stage of labor
Operative midpelvic delivery
Previous history of shoulder dystocia
History of previous delivery of fetus of more than 4000 g
Maternal diabetes mellitus
Maternal obesity

---

present. The antenatal, preventable factors are an excessive weight gain and a post-term pregnancy.[14] The known risk factors for shoulder dystocia are a contracted pelvis by clinical pelvimetry, a previous history of shoulder dystocia, maternal obesity and soft tissue dystocia, maternal diabetes mellitus or a history of gestational diabetes, a history of a macrosomic infant weighting more than 4000 g, and multiparity.[14]

Intrapartum risk factors may also be divided into those that are preventable and those that are known. A preventable intrapartum factor is operative midforceps delivery. Known intrapartum risk factors are present when there is a prolonged second stage.

In analyzing this case study, one sees that there were several antenatal risk factors that were preventable. The weight gain of 42 lb was excessive and may have been prevented by a prenatal nutritional consult and biweekly prenatal visits to review dietary intake. A total weight gain of 25 to 30 lb is a more acceptable range.[14] The gestational age of 41 1/2 weeks approached post-term dates and should have been a signal that the patient was at risk for shoulder dystocia. The identifiable antenatal risk factor that this patient had for shoulder dystocia was multiparity.

The known intrapartum risk factors were a slow descent of the vertex with a prolonged second stage. With a nurse-midwife aware of these specific risk factors—excessive weight gain, a gestational age approaching postdates, multiparity, and slow descent of the vertex with a prolonged second stage, the management plan for shoulder dystocia was reviewed with the support staff. Anticipation and preparedness in the management of shoulder dystocia are key factors. The pediatric neonatal team could have been called to attend the delivery to handle resuscitative efforts. An episiotomy should have been cut before delivery of the vertex, and an intentional fourth degree extension should have been performed once the head had retracted tightly against the perineum. Upon retrospective examination, the manipulation of the mother's position to the exaggerated lithotomy could have been attempted before the maneuver of Woods was attempted. Delivery of the posterior arm alone was attempted and failed. Since all maneuvers to dislodge the shoulders failed, it was appropriate to utilize the more traumatic technique of breaking the clavicle and delivering the posterior arm.

IMPLICATIONS FOR PRACTICE

Awareness of the prenatal and intrapartum risk factors for shoulder dystocia allows the nurse to anticipate this obstetric emergency. The staff should commit the above maneuvers to memory and review them monthly in mock drills on the labor and delivery floor (Table 11-4). Likewise, the staff should utilize the same criteria in defining shoulder dystocia and have a defined code of documentation of all of the events.[14] Accurate documentation is crucial for medicolegal reasons. Clear, concise documentation describing the exact sequence of events in the delivery room is the responsibility of all care providers. The timing of maneuvers and the maneuvers attempted, maternal positions, the general appearance of the infant, Apgar scores, resuscitative efforts attempted, hand and arm movements of the infant, and the names and titles of all staff involved should be well documented.

Antenatal management is vital in preventing shoulder dystocia. Glucose screening of all pregnancies and tight glucose control of diabetic pregnancies would contribute to reducing macrosomia and shoulder dystocia. In considering the macrosomic infant approaching post-term, induction of patients with a ripe cervix is crucial to prevent further intrauterine growth of the infant. Since shoulder dystocia is difficult to predict accurately, cesarean section is recommended over midpelvic delivery for the macrosomic infant with a prolonged second stage of labor.[2,3,9] More widespread use of ultrasound and computed tomography in the prediction of macrosomia should be pursued. More importantly, the primary care provider and nurse need a well-calculated, predetermined plan of management in the event of unexpected shoulder dystocia. The patient at risk should be moved

---

Table 11-4 Action Plan for Managing Shoulder Dystocia

Call for assistance
Examine vagina to rule out conditions that mimic shoulder dystocia
Enlarge episiotomy
Perform McRobert's maneuver or place in left lateral Sims' position (exaggerated lithotomy)
Apply suprapubic pressure; attempt to rotate shoulder to oblique position
If this fails, attempt screw maneuver of Woods
If this fails, attempt delivery of posterior arm
If this fails, perform cleidotomy and deliver posterior arm

into the delivery room and taken out of the stirrups in preparation for this complication. A parenteral solution of normal saline should be started in anticipation of postpartum hemorrhage or hematoma. The pediatric resuscitation team and anesthesia should be readily available.

Since the parents of an infant with shoulder dystocia are at risk for emotional upheaval, nursing follow-up should provide psychologic support of the process.[14] The labor and delivery events need to be reviewed and explained to the family, with the opportunity for discussion. Nurses have a vital role in coordinating the long-term follow-up of the affected infant. Follow-up of a brachial plexus injury may include physical therapy appointments, passive range of motion exercises, x-ray films of the fractured clavicle or humerus, and evaluation by a neurologist.

In summary, it is evident that shoulder dystocia should always be anticipated in the delivery room. A nursing staff with a well-coordinated, rehearsed approach can assist in managing shoulder dystocia effectively. Accurate documentation is imperative, and coordination of long-term follow-up is essential.

REFERENCES

1. McCall JO Jr. Shoulder dystocia: a study of aftereffects. *Am J Obstet Gynecol.* 1962;83:1486.
2. Resnik R. Management of shoulder girdle dystocia. *Clin Obstet Gynecol.* 1980;23:559.
3. Swartz DP. Shoulder girdle dystocia in vertex delivery. *Obstet Gynecol.* 1960;15:194.
4. Seigworth GR. Shoulder dystocia: review of 5 years' experience. *Obstet Gynecol.* 1966;28:764.
5. Benedetti T, Gabbe S. Shoulder dystocia: a complication of fetal macrosomia and prolonged second stage of labor with midpelvic delivery. *Obstet Gynecol.* 1978;52:526.
6. Modanlou H, Dorchester W, et al. Macrosomia—maternal, fetal and neonatal implications. *Obstet Gynecol.* 1980;55:420.
7. Williams J, Kirz DS, Worthen J, Oakes GK. Ultrasound prediction of shoulder dystocia. *Proceedings of the Fifth Annual Meeting of the Society of Perinatal Obstetricians.* Las Vegas, Nev: Society of Perinatal Obstetricians; 1985:133. Abstract.
8. Oxorn H. *Human Labor and Birth.* 5th ed. New York, NY: Appleton & Lange; 1986.
9. Khan PK. Dystocia of the fetal shoulder. *Int Surg.* 1966;45:137.
10. Gordon M. The immediate and long-term outcome of obstetric birth trauma. *Am J Obstet Gynecol.* 1973;1:117.
11. Lee CY. Shoulder dystocia. *Clin Obstet Gynecol.* 1987;30:1.
12. Woods CE. A principle of physics as applicable to shoulder dystocia. *Am J Obstet Gynecol.* 1943;45:796.
13. Liiamaa R. Shoulder dystocia. In: Angelini D, Knapp C, Gibes R, eds. *Perinatal/Neonatal Nursing: A Clinical Handbook.* Boston, Mass: Blackwell Scientific Publications; 1986.
14. Mashburn J. Identification and management of shoulder dystocia. *J Nurse-Midwifery.* 1988;33:225.

ADDITIONAL BIBLIOGRAPHY

Dignam WJ. Difficulties in delivery, including shoulder dystocia and malpresentation of the fetus. *Clin Obstet Gynecol.* 1976;19:577.

Sack RA. The large infant. *Am J Obstet Gynecol.* 1969;104:195.

Chapter 12

The Pregnant Spinal Cord Injury Patient

Carol J. Harvey

The spinal column surrounds and encases the spinal cord, nerve roots, and cauda equina. The spinal cord is made of vertebral bodies, disks, joints, and ligaments and is the center for the transmission of impulses that monitor and control major physiologic activities. War injuries, automobile accidents, work-related accidents, and sports injuries are common ways that this center may be injured, resulting in lifelong paralysis and loss of sensation, collectively known as spinal cord injury.[1]

Over 200,000 Americans are victims of spinal cord accidents, with an additional 10,000 new injuries occurring each year. The majority of these individuals are young adults, between the ages of 16 and 25.[2] The cost for care is dependent upon the level of the lesion and the resulting incapacitation of the victim. Initial hospitalization costs are reported to range from $51,752 for low paraplegics to $170,055 for respirator-dependent high quadriplegics. Annual follow-up expenses range from $7,699 to $63,663 and are related to the level of the spinal lesion.[3] Overall the federal government states that the lifetime cost of caring for one victim can exceed $200,000, and the total cost to the nation is in excess of two billion dollars a year.[1] More devastating than the financial burden, however, are the emotional and social costs of these injuries to the young adult who is beginning to live independently and establish a career and family.

Approximately 20% of young spinal cord injury (SCI) patients are women who may desire to initiate or continue childbearing after initial treatment of the injury or who may already be pregnant at the time of spinal trauma. Because injury to the spinal cord does not affect fertility, many of these women seek perinatal health care providers to guide them through pregnancy with the goals of minimal complications, avoidance of life-threatening complications, and delivery of a healthy offspring.

REVIEW OF THE LITERATURE

The spinal cord may be injured by the forces of flexion, extension, rotation, vertical compression, or a combination of any of these. The vertebral level of C5-C6 is most vulnerable to flexion injuries. Supraspinous and interspinous ligaments are injured and, when the force is severe, the capsular and posterior longitudinal ligaments may be torn. Hyperextension, common in rear-end collisions, can damage the area of C4-C5. Severe extensions can result in a tear of the anterior longitudinal ligament and the muscles of the anterior neck area. Rotation injuries can produce locked facets that, when they occur as bilateral pairs, are often associated with severe spinal cord injury. Compression fractures, such as those acquired in diving or falls, may cause burst fractures where bone or disk fragments may enter the spinal canal.[2]

The history of the injury may be helpful in the diagnosis of force to the spinal cord. The goals of management with all lesions are stabilization, immobilization, and decompression with fusion.[2] Usually the spinal cord is not severed in an accident, but crushed or bruised. It is during the first few hours following injury (the acute stage) that the cord becomes irreversibly damaged.[1]

Initial injury to the spinal cord initially causes an increase in mean arterial pressure that will last approximately 2 to 3 minutes and will be accompanied by decreased cardiac output, decreased heart rate, decreased peripheral resistance, and decreased right atrial filling pressure. The drop in mean arterial pressure is followed by a prolonged postinjury hypotensive episode that further deprives the injured cord of oxygen.[4] During the acute phase the spinal cord swells. Epinephrine and norepinephrine levels increase, and local blood pressure decreases in the injured area. Hemorrhaging begins in the center of the cord and spreads outward. The nerve cells die, producing a gap in the cord that will eventually scar.[1,2]

Studies are currently under way to evaluate methods to prevent hypoxic damage to the injured cord. Investigational efforts include the effects of high-dose steroids to reduce inflammation, the use of the controversial drug dimethyl sulfoxide (DMSO), and endorphin blockers that may increase local circulation and perfusion to the cord. Although promising, no confirming data on the efficacy and effectiveness of these drugs have yet been published.

Of vital importance to the nurse is the knowledge of functional level and prognosis with a spinal cord injury. Patients with an injury above the level of C5 are totally dependent and may require permanent ventilatory assistance. Injuries from C5 to C7 increase the potential for greater independence. C7 is the level at which patients can rehabilitate to independent living with extensive therapy and architectural changes of their environment.[5] The lower the lesion, the more independent the potential of the patient.

In the initial treatment of the SCI patient, awareness of complications in this time period includes cardiovascular instability with resultant hypotension and bradycardia. Autonomic dysreflexia, referred to as autonomic hyper-reflexia, is also a complication of SCI resulting from an uncontrolled, sympathetic reflex that causes elevated blood pressure, bradycardia, hyperhydrosis, facial flushing, and headache. It occurs with distension of a hollow viscus or contraction of the uterus. Adrenal glands are likewise massively stimulated. If untreated, hypertensive crisis, encephalopathy, or cerebrovascular accident may occur in the patient. Other complications include an impaired pulmonary response, deep vein thrombosis, bowel and bladder dysfunction, skin complications, musculoskeletal complications such as heterotropic ossification, and spasticity.[5] Additional complications that have been reported in the nursing literature include ineffective breathing patterns, impaired physical mobility, alteration in thermal regulation, alteration in sleep patterns, feelings of powerlessness, and ineffective coping strategies.[6]

Long-term management of the spinal cord injury victim includes the diagnosis and subsequent prognostic outcome of the exact level of the injury. Intensive occupational and physical rehabilitation centers on this functional level and has as its objective to restore the individual to the highest level of independence possible. Complications in the long term include skin and tissue breakdown from decreased perfusion and prolonged immobility below the level of the lesion. Normal capillary pressures of circulation are 30 mm Hg; circulation and subsequent oxygenation to tissue will be disrupted at higher pressures. Typically, gravity and body mass place pressures in excess of 70 mm Hg over most bony prominences, producing anoxic damage to tissue in as little as 2 hours if circulation is not restored. Pressure sores and tissue breakdown may necessitate the amputation of the lower extremities if infection and gangrene threaten the health of the patient.[7]

Spasticity, resulting from exaggerated somatic reflexes, is due to lack of modulation of the intact reflex arc and may occur in patients with motor neuron injuries. Although the immediate benefits of spasticity may include increased circulation to the muscle group, the long-term problems may include chronic muscle contractures that prohibit proper positioning for independent activities. Muscle relaxants may be prescribed, and diazepam is also frequently used.[7]

Thrombophlebitis due to stasis of venous blood and clot formation is another complication of the SCI patient's immobility. Treatment includes elevation of the affected limb, compression, and anticoagulation. Application of heat is contraindicated in the SCI individual because of the lack of temperature sensation and the possibility of burns. In approximately 20 to 25% of quadriplegic patients, para-articular heterotropic ossification occurs about the hip and knee joints. Initial symptoms include heat, redness, and swelling of the thigh, followed by gradual limitation of the mobility of the hip. Treatment includes maintaining active range of motion of the hip to break up the deposits of new bone. If ossification continues to impair function, surgery may be done to remove the ossification area.[7]

Osteoporosis of the long bones begins after injury, but it is usually at least one year after the accident that bone degradation is sufficient enough to cause pathologic complications such as fractures. The most common fracture is the spiral fracture of the supracondylar area of the femur, and the majority of fractures will heal without operative treatment.[7]

Psychiatric disorders in the SCI patient have had an unusually high occurrence rate. In a study that encompassed 16 years of data collection and followed over 100 spinal cord-injured persons, the diagnoses of depression, suicide, psychosis, and alcoholism were evaluated. Depression was reported in 10 to 30% of all spinal cord injury patients, but its diagnosis was thought to be hindered by the physiologic effects of the injury. Suicide was most likely to occur during the first 5 to 6 years after the injury and accounted for approximately 10% of all deaths among the SCI group. Passive suicide, however, was stressed not to be overlooked as a cause of death and included behavior of self-neglect that may have ultimately led to devastating complications of immobility. True psychosis was rare in a SCI patient, but alcoholism was common and frequently life threatening.[8]

Of increasing interest in the literature is the fertility and pregnancy outcome of the female spinal cord-injured patient who desires a family. The cardiovascular changes of pregnancy include an increase in plasma volume, increasing in red blood cell mass, increase in cardiac output, and an increase in clotting factors. These changes, in addition to the pulmonary and hormonal alterations, increase the risk of complications in the spinal cord injury patient. As plasma volume increases in pregnancy, the red blood cells are delayed in their rise and produce a physiologic anemia of pregnancy in the midtrimester. Anemia can be a devastating factor in skin and tissue breakdown of immobilized patients. As blood volume increases, maternal arterial pressure decreases to accommodate the increase. This drop in blood pressure and decreased venous return to the heart due to increased pressure on the large leg veins produces increased edema and circulatory compromise that may increase the incidence of decubitus ulcer formation in the spinal cord-injured patient. As progesterone increases and estrogen decreases in pregnancy, decreased bowel motility may result, and the immobilized patient may have additional problems with constipation.

In a study that evaluated the long-term prognosis of female spinal cord-injured patients, Pinkerton and others[9] assessed the rehabilitation outcomes in 24 females with spinal cord injuries.[9] The most common cause of injury in the females was a motor vehicle accident, with the woman more likely being the passenger in the automobile. Nine women were married at the time of injury, and three married after becoming disabled. Four of the 24 patients had pregnancies that reached a term gestation with good neonatal outcomes. Stress factors of these women included bladder and bowel management, occupational training, stress on families, and related activities of independence. Complications of the pregnancy period were reported as increased spasticity, increased edema, and increased schedule of bladder catheterization. Although the study reported an excellent outcome in the women who became pregnant, the general population was noted to have significant depression, and 3 of the 24 women committed suicide.

A sample of four pregnancies in three patients was reported in the literature by Young et al., who identified the major complications of the antepartum period, including anemia, pyelonephritis, decubiti, and premature labor.[10] Despite the maternal complications, this study showed that all neonates were healthy and showed no signs of depression, although some of the mothers took muscle relaxants and diazepam to control spasticity.

More recently, a larger study and the most comprehensive to date evaluated the pregnancy outcome of 50 pregnancies in a total of 33 spinal cord-injured patients.[11] Of the 33 women, 15 were injured in car accidents, and 4 women were pregnant at the time of paralysis development. These 4 women delivered 3 normal babies, with 1 intrauterine death at 20 weeks gestation. Reported problems related to the pregnancy were edema, increased seizures, difficulty in transfer, thrombophlebitis, premature labor, urinary tract infections, pyelonephritis, anemia, and decubitis ulcers. Delivery complications were reported to be minimal except for autonomic dysreflexia. One patient with autonomic dysreflexia sustained a cerebrovascular hemorrhage and coma. Dehisence of the episiotomy due to impaired perfusion to the area, thrombophlebitis, and pulmonary emboli were all postpartum complications. Neonatal outcomes included one anoxic infant, one Valium withdrawal, and one possible Valium withdrawal. At the conclusion of the study, the authors recommended that a multidisciplinary team approach and attention to the specific needs of the patient are imperative in the positive outcome of the pregnancies.

During the labor and delivery process, researchers have emphasized that the woman with a spinal cord lesion above T5 is at risk to develop autonomic dysreflexia. To prevent this dangerous reflex from occurring during the labor and delivery process, special attention must be paid to preventing bladder and rectal distension and limiting the number of vaginal exams. Researchers recommend the use of epidural anesthesia in these patients to prevent autonomic dysreflexia by blocking the impulses that may trigger the devastating complication.[12–14] McGregor and Meeuwsen also recommended the use of epidural anesthesia in the management of spinal cord-injured women in labor.[15]

Also reported in practice was the use of topical anesthetic agents when Foley catheterization, rectal manipulation, or vaginal examination was performed. They encouraged caution in the use of oxytocin for induction of such patients and recommended the use of internal fetal monitoring to decrease pressure on the maternal abdominal wall caused by confining fetal monitoring belts.

The nursing literature is unfortunately void of management and outcome principles for the care of the spinal cord injury patient who is pregnant. As more women enter the work force and participate in contact sports, the SCI rate will continue to increase in the childbearing population and the knowledge base of the profession will grow. It is evident, however, that a successful pregnancy outcome for these women is dependent upon a multidisciplinary team approach and intensive care and monitoring in all stages of the pregnancy.

*   *   *   *   *

CASE STUDY

M.L., a 25-year-old gravida I, para 0, was a quadriplegic from an automobile accident 5 years before. She presented 10 weeks pregnant. Because of the unique nature of pregnancy the gestation will present additional complications to her immobility and physiologic stability.

At M.L.'s first antepartum visit, a complete history and physical was performed to assess current physical status and medical history. Blood pressure was 104/68, heart rate was 76, and respirations were 18 and regular. Fundal height correlated with dates, and an ultrasound was done to confirm the fetal age. Antepartum laboratory analysis included all routine measurements of initial pregnancy, with additional tests of a urine screen for bacteria and an indepth neurologic examination. A specific patient history on the spinal cord injury was taken to ascertain the level and extent of the lesion, to identify current independence and level of function, and to establish a baseline of data on persistent or previous complications from the injury.

M.L. was injured in an automobile accident 5 years previously; she was a passenger in a head-on collision. The impact of injury was at the level of T4, with a complete lesion at this level. She had the use and control of her neck muscles, trapezius, and diaphragm, and biceps. M.L. had some control of her arms and hands but had no control of her legs or feet. She used a wheelchair for mobility and could transfer without assistance. Chronic self-care included intermittent self-catheterization of the bladder and a daily bowel training program with rectal stimulation. Initially, M.L. attended a physical therapy center three times a week to develop upper body strength but, at the time of pregnancy, she exercised at home with hand weights twice a week. Previous complications of the injury included urinary tract infections approximately two times a year, one episode of skin breakdown that did not require surgical intervention, frequent constipation, and one serious fall during a transfer attempt that resulted in a broken left wrist.

Before the injury she had completed one year of college and had been employed as a secretary and office assistant in her husband's insurance company. Two years ago, she returned to college as a part-time student and did secretarial work for her husband on a part-time basis in her home. Her parents were alive and lived in the same city and were reported to be an excellent source of support for both M.L. and her husband, Tom. The pregnancy was desired and no birth control had been used for 5 months. Both M.L. and her husband were evaluated as highly motivated about the pregnancy.

The plan of care in this antepartum period included frequent observation and evaluation of M.L. to recognize any early complications. She was scheduled for a return visit in 3 weeks and was to return to the office at intervals of 2 to 3 weeks.

Before 22 weeks gestation, M.L.'s antepartum course had been uneventful. Serial hematocrits and hemoglobin levels had been within normal limits, weight gain had been appropriate, fetal growth had been in the 50th percentile, and no complications appeared. At 22 weeks, M.L. presented with malaise, fever, and chills. Temperature was 102.8, blood pressure was 100/60, heart rate was 102, and respirations were 24/min. A sterile, catheterized urine sample was analyzed and showed large amounts of white blood cells (WBCs) and occasional red blood cells (RBCs). Culture showed *Escherichia coli*. M.L. was admitted to the hospital for observation and treatment of a urinary tract infection. Intravenous ampicillin and gentamycin produced an immediate improvement in her temperature and energy level within the first 24 hours. The intravenous antibiotics were administered for a total of 72 hours, at which time M.L. was discharged home on oral dosages. Discharge teaching included the importance of completing the antibiotic course, increasing fluids in her diet, and adding one additional self-intermittent catheterization to her daily schedule to reduce urine stasis in the bladder and reflux into the kidneys.

M.L. had no reoccurrence of the urinary tract infection and continued to gain weight appropriately. At 32 weeks gestation, her obstetrician began cervical examinations to monitor for any effacement and dilatation. At 36 weeks, M.L.'s cervix was found to be 2 cm dilated and 60% effaced, and she was scheduled to return to the office in 4 to 5 days for repeat exam. Teaching at this time included instructing M.L. to identify the signs and symptoms of labor to prevent an uncontrolled birth out of the hospital. Specific topics included self-palpation of uterine activity, signs indicating rupture of fetal membranes, periodic checking for vaginal bleeding and the sudden onset of profuse sweating, headache, or anxiety that may indicate autonomic dysreflexia in response to cervical change and uterine contractions. M.L. was encouraged to contact the primary care provider immediately if any of these symptoms occurred.

At 38 1/2 weeks M.L. discovered upon awakening that she was lying in a small pool of clear fluid. She suspected that her membranes had ruptured and presented to the labor and delivery unit. Upon admission, the nurse assessing M.L. performed a complete history and physical examination and obtained access to her antepartum records. On admission, blood pressure was 112/74, heart rate was 98, and respirations were 20/min. Fetal heart rate was 128 to 140 beats per minute. Vaginal examination revealed a 4-cm dilated cervix 100% effaced, and nitrazine paper test of the fluid was positive for rupture. M.L. was placed in a labor room with a birthing bed that avoided the need for patient transfer before delivery. An external electronic fetal monitor was applied and showed a fetal heart rate baseline of 126 to 144 beats per minute with multiple accelerations and no decelerations. Uterine contraction frequency was every 4 to 6 minutes, duration was 60 to 70 seconds, strength was moderate, and resting tone was soft to palpation.

An intravenous solution of 5% dextrose in lactated Ringer's solution (D5LR) was started with an 18 gauge catheter in her left forearm. No enema was administered because of the increased risk of autonomic dysreflexia. An "egg crate" mattress was applied to the bed because of the increased risk of poor circulation and decubitus formation. M.L.'s position was changed a minimum of every 2 hours and was documented in the nursing record. An indwelling Foley catheter was inserted to prevent distension of the bladder and to decrease the risk of autonomic dysreflexia. M.L.'s vital signs were assessed and recorded very 15 to 30 minutes. Tom remained at her bedside and offered emotional encouragement and support.

Four hours after admission, M.L.'s blood pressure increased abruptly to 178/126, heart rate was 120, and respirations were 26. She complained of a headache and was diaphoretic. Autonomic dysreflexia was diagnosed, and 10 mg hydralazine was administered intravenously to decrease the blood pressure. The fetal heart rate was 172 to 176 with no accelerations. Repeat blood pressure was 180/122. Twenty minutes after hydralazine administration, M.L.'s blood pressure began to respond and was recorded at 164/112. After 5 more minutes the blood pressure was 164/114. An additional 10-mg dose of hydralazine was administered and successfully lowered the blood pressure to 120/84 within 30 minutes. Once M.L.'s blood pressure and other vital signs returned to normal, the fetal baseline also decreased and demonstrated reassuring characteristics once again.

Six hours after admission, M.L. experienced one additional episode of acute-onset hypertension and was treated with hydralazine. In an attempt to prevent further occurrences of autonomic dysreflexia, an epidural catheter was inserted below the spinal lesion and dosed with marcaine. Labor continued without further complications.

A vaginal examination showed a completely dilated cervix and +1 station of the fetal head. M.L. was instructed to begin pushing using her upper abdominal and intercostal muscles. A noninvasive blood pressure monitor was applied to M.L.'s arm to assist the nurse in monitoring her blood pressure every 5 minutes during the second stage. After 40 minutes of pushing, the head began to crown at the perineum. The egg crate mattress was removed, and the birthing bed was positioned into a modified lithotomy position. Her legs were placed in stirrups and towels were used as padding to prevent pressure areas from developing. The nurse noted the time of stirrup placement and changed the position of M.L.'s legs every 30 minutes.

As the head started to crown, the Foley catheter was removed for delivery. Low-outlet forceps were applied and an episiotomy was performed to aid in delivery of the head. The baby was born approximately 7 hours after admission and had Apgar scores of 9 and 9 at 1 and 5 minutes, respectively. After delivery of the placenta and repair of the episiotomy, a Foley catheter was reinserted into the bladder to prevent distension during the time of postpartum physiologic diuresis. Vital signs were taken every 15 minutes, and postpartum recovery examinations began.

Two hours after delivery, M.L. was transferred to the postpartum floor. During the first 24 hours postpartum, vital signs were assessed every 2 to 4 hours. Postpartum assessments for bleeding, fundal tone, bladder distension, and episiotomy site were done every 2 to 4 hours. At 4 hours postpartum the intravenous catheter was removed. Every 2 hours, M.L.'s position was changed and documented. At 3 hours after delivery, the infant was brought to M.L. for rooming-in and breast-feeding.

The nurse reviewed breast-feeding techniques with M.L. and stayed in the room to support her during her first attempt. Because M.L. had good arm control and strength, she was able to position the infant and was pleased after the baby nursed for the first time.

The following afternoon, the indwelling catheter was removed and M.L. began her self-intermittent catheterization schedule. On the third postpartum day, the family was discharged home with instructions to return in 7 to 10 days for a checkup. Birth control pills were not prescribed because of the increased risk of thrombophlebitis in the spinal cord patient, and contraception control was foam and condoms. For follow-up care, M.L. was visited by a nurse at her home to continue postpartum and infant teaching and to assess the home environment for suggestions and improvements in caring for the newborn.

*   *   *   *   *

CASE ANALYSIS

Nurses responsible and involved in the perinatal care of the spinal cord injury client must base their practice on the identification and rapid treatment of known hazards of pregnancy in this population.

Antepartum Period

History and Baseline Examination. The nursing history of the patient should include not only the obvious area of injury and adaptation to the injury, but also the identification of support systems for the new family. Pregnancy may further limit independence of the patient, requiring the mother to become more dependent on significant others. Care of a neonate may also require additional support, and early problem solving for these couples is prudent. Physical examination is critical in the early trimesters of pregnancy to determine any current complications of immobility and to establish a definitive neurologic baseline.

Prevention of Anemia. The immobilized patient is at increased risk for poor tissue perfusion and cellular oxygenation. The physiologic changes of pregnancy may produce a physiologic anemia due to the increase in plasma volume before an increase in red blood cell mass. Anemia in the spinal cord-injured patient can predispose the patient to tissue hypoxia and breakdown and chronic decubitis ulcerations. To prevent this complication, patients are instructed to take vitamins and iron during the entire pregnancy. Evaluation of iron and hemoglobin levels needs to be performed each office visit.

Prevention of Constipation. The endocrine changes in pregnancy increase the possibility of constipation in the immobilized patient. Increased iron in the diet may also contribute to the problem. To prevent constipation, the nurse may instruct patients to add a mild laxative to bowel training procedures. This should be evaluated each visit for the outcome of this regimen.

Prevention of Urinary Tract Infection. Self-catheterization programs on an intermittent time schedule are usually satisfactory in preventing bladder distension and reflux. Before pregnancy, spinal cord injury patients frequently acquire urinary tract infections. Women should be instructed to continue the catheterization schedule and are taught the signs and symptoms of urinary tract infection to promote early reporting of the complication and early treatment.

Prevention of Decubitus Ulcers. Decubitus ulcers are the end product of decreased perfusion and oxygenation to tissue that is externally compromised by pressure or trauma. A constant concern of any spinal cord-injured individual, this complication may increase in pregnancy due to the increased venous stasis in the lower extremities and decreased blood pressure of the second trimester. To prevent the formation of an ulcer, individuals are counseled to increase position changes during the pregnancy, increase protein and carbohydrates in the diet (a registered dietitian consult), and evaluate themselves for signs of tissue breakdown along areas of bony prominence.

Intrapartum

Prevention and Early Detection of Autonomic Dysreflexia. Many of the routine nursing functions in the intrapartum may trigger autonomic dysreflexia resulting in hypertensive crisis, seizure activity, cerebral hemorrhage, and possibly death. The nurse responsible for the care of spinal cord injury patients in labor is encouraged to limit the amount of vaginal and rectal stimulation, prevent bladder and rectum distension, avoid abdominal pressure, and monitor the patient's response to contractions. Hydralazine should be readily available at the bedside to administer in the event of hypertensive crisis.

Regulation of Temperature. High cord injury patients have poor thermoregulatory control of basal temperature, relying on environmental temperature to maintain body heat. Patients should labor and deliver in rooms with independent temperature controls, and all attempts should be made to keep the room warm and dry.

Difficulty with Pulmonary Secretions. High cord injury patients may have difficulty clearing pulmonary secretions in stressful states such as labor and delivery. Equipment needed to establish, oxygenate, and suction an airway should be readily available. The use of central nervous system depressants that decrease respiratory effort should be substituted with other pain-controlling agents in the high lesion spinal cord injury patient.

Prevention of Fatigue. Because labor and delivery increase the workload on the cardiovascular, pulmonary, and musculoskeletal systems, fatigue of the patient may be a significant complication if the level of the spinal injury dictates the use of accessory and abdominal muscles to maintain ventilation. The nurse caring for the client must constantly assess breathing efforts and attempt to prevent exhaustion.

Prevention of Skin Breakdown. Maintaining the same position for more than 2 hours is enough to alter oxygenation to tissue and predispose to tissue breakdown in the immobilized patient. Developing a turning/repositioning schedule is imperative for the dependent patient and can easily be overlooked in the excitement of labor and delivery.

Postpartum Period

Prevention of Infection. The spinal cord-injured postpartum patient is at increased risk for episiotomy breakdown and infection due to decreased circulatory effort below the lesion. Nursing actions to prevent this complication include teaching perineal care, including frequent sitz baths and the prevention of fecal contamination of the area. A diet high in protein and carbohydrates is encouraged to promote healing at the site. Frequent position changes are scheduled to prevent dependent edema of the labia and perineum. Nursing assessments will include a physical description of the site and any signs of infection or breakdown.

Prevention of Postpartum Hemorrhage. Because the spinal cord-injured patient may not have sensations below the level of the lesion, it may be difficult for her to identify that she is having vaginal bleeding. Assessment of the patient frequently during the first 12 to 24 hours after delivery to prevent an unwitnessed hemorrhage is mandatory.

Prevention of Constipation. The NPO status of most labor patients may predispose the spinal cord injury patient to constipation. All efforts should be made to return the patient to the predelivery regimen of bowel training and function. Often the use of stool softeners is needed during the first 2 to 5 days postpartum. Evaluation of the patient's previous bowel techniques and schedule of elimination is performed to promote a smooth return to the schedule before discharge.

Prevention of Bladder Distension. The first 24 hours postdelivery are when the body begins its diuresis of intracellular volume. Many spinal cord-injured patients will have an indwelling catheter during this period to prevent distension of the bladder. After the first 24 hours, the catheter may be removed and the patient may return to the predelivery technique of bladder emptying. Attention should be given to the volume of urine emptied with each attempt; additional emptying schedules may be needed during the first postpartum days.

Promotion of Parent-Infant Bonding. The spinal cord-injured patient experiences all the needs and emotions of any new mother. Immediate parent-infant bonding should begin at delivery if the neonate's condition warrants. The mother is encouraged to look at the infant, touch, and hold the infant. If the patient has a high lesion, one should touch the baby to a place on the mother's skin where she can perceive touch sensations.

Promotion of a Return to Independence. The spinal cord-injured mother is encouraged to return to her level of predelivery independence before discharge from the hospital. New techniques to be addressed with the mother are infant care tasks, transferring during infant care, and emergencies that may arise in the home. It is imperative that the medical and nursing staffs encourage independence over dependence to promote increased confidence in mothering skills and self-esteem.

IMPLICATIONS FOR PRACTICE

M.L. was typical of the thousands of spinal cord-injured patients who are injured before starting or completing a family. Childbearing should not be proscribed in these women, but rather addressed in preconceptional counseling with the primary health care provider. Most spinal cord injuries do not alter fertility, and pregnancy may occur.

Of extreme help in the nursing care of M.L. was the use of unit-based education to prepare for her hospitalization and multidisciplinary team meetings to monitor her pregnancy progress and labor/delivery/postpartum plan of care. The pregnant spinal cord-injured patient is a challenge to all health care team members.

REFERENCES

1. US Department of Health and Human Services. *Spinal Cord Injury Hope through Research.* Washington, DC: US Government Printing Office; 1981:1–33.

2. Castillo RG, Bell J. Cervical spine injury: stabilization and management. *Postgrad Med.* May 15, 1988; 83(7):131–138.

3. Whiteneck GG, et al. Initial and long-term costs of spinal cord injury. *Paraplegia.* 1988;26:135.

4. Guha AB, Tator CH. Acute cardiovascular effects of experimental spinal cord injury. *Trauma.* 1988;28:481–490.

5. Dillingham TR. Prevention of complications during acute management of the spinal cord-injured patient: first step in the rehabilitation process. *Crit Care Nurs Q.* September 1988;11:71–77.

6. Nemeth L, Kiljanczyk HR. Intensive care of the spinal cord-injured patient: focus on early rehabilitation. *Crit Care Nurs Q.* September 1988;11(2):79–84.

7. Pierce DS, Nickel VH. *The Total Care of Spinal Cord Injuries.* Boston: Little, Brown & Co.; 1977:90–194.

8. Steward TD. Psychiatric diagnosis and treatment following spinal cord injury. *Psychosomatics.* Spring 1988;29(2):214–220.

9. Pinkerton AC, et al. Rehabilitation outcomes in females with spinal cord injury: a follow-up study. *Paraplegia.* 1983;21:166–175.

10. Young BK, et al. Pregnancy after spinal cord injury: altered maternal and fetal responses to labor. *Obstet Gynecol.* June 1983;62:59–63.

11. Verduyn WH. Spinal cord injured women, pregnancy, and delivery. *Paraplegia.* 1986;24:231–240.

12. McCunniff DE. Pregnancy after spinal cord injury. *Obstet Gynecol.* 1984;63:757–758.

13. Gimovsky ML. Management of autonomic hyperreflexia associated with a low thoracic spinal cord lesion. *Am J Obstet Gynecol.* 1985;153:223–224.

14. Spielman FJ. Parturient with spinal cord transection: complications of autonomic hyperreflexia. *Obstet Gynecol.* 1984;64:147–148.

15. McGregor JA, Meeuwsen J. Autonomic hyperreflexia: a mortal danger for spinal cord-damaged women in labor. *Am J Obstet Gynecol.* 1985;151:330–333.

Chapter 13

Cognitive Coping Strategies in Labor and Delivery

Christine Williams Burgess

Severe anxiety has been shown to be associated with prolonged labor and decreased fetal well-being.[1,2] Consequently, nursing experts have stressed the importance of psychosocial intervention in labor to minimize anxiety. Coping strategies in labor and delivery are a critical component of the mother's ability to defend against overwhelming anxiety. Strategies taught in childbirth education classes such as breathing techniques, progressive muscle relaxation, and comfort measures such as massage are helpful in preventing the escalation of anxiety. In addition, cognitive coping strategies lend themselves readily to the labor and delivery situation. These methods are useful in reducing the perception of threat in a variety of life situations. This case study demonstrates one woman's effective use of cognitive coping strategies to alter the meaning of the stressful situation and therefore reduce her perception of threat and the accompanying anxiety.

REVIEW OF THE LITERATURE

Coping methods can be defined as any behavior designed to reduce threat by avoidance or mastery.[3] Cognitive coping techniques are one approach to dealing with a threat by changing the way one thinks about the event to promote adaptation. Examples of such coping methods include the use of positive self-statements, cognitive distraction, negative thought-stopping, and imagery.[4]

Cognitive theory views the emotional response to a threatening situation as resulting from the perception of the threatening event. Lazarus stated that "cognitive processes determine the quality and intensity of an emotional reaction."[5(p21)]

Individuals respond to situations in a specific manner because of their ideas about the meaning of the situation for them. If their emotional response is detrimental to their well-being, as in severe anxiety, the cognitions about the event must be examined to intervene effectively. For example, the mother's emotional response to the labor situation will depend on not only the actual events of labor but also the interpretation of those events. Even in the case of a labor in which everything seems to go wrong, the degree of maternal emotional distress will vary based upon the mother's cognitions about those events.

Lazarus and Folkman referred to two types of appraisal of a threatening event, primary and secondary appraisal.[6] Primary appraisal occurs when the individual answers the question: "Am I okay or am I in trouble?" An event may be evaluated as irrelevant, benign-positive, or stressful. When the situation is judged irrelevant, the individual may ignore it. If it is judged benign-positive, it is seen as beneficial or desirable. When it is perceived as stressful, it is further judged as involving either harm-loss, threat, or challenge. Harm-loss involves damage already sustained such as "incapacitating injury or illness, recognition of some danger to self- or social esteem, or loss of a loved or valued person."[6(p32)] Threat refers to damage that has not yet occurred but that is anticipated. If a woman anticipates that either physical or psychologic harm awaits her in the process of labor and delivery, she will respond with anxiety. The value of threat to survival is that it allows the individual to plan for the future and to prepare for handling the anticipated event.

Challenge also involves anticipating and planning for difficult events. Challenge differs from threat, however, because the event is viewed as manageable and the possibility for positive outcomes is the focus of the individual's attention. Emotions that accompany a challenging situation include "eagerness, excitement, and exhilaration, whereas threat centers on potential harm and is characterized by negative emotions such as fear, anxiety, and anger."[6(p33)] Some situations, such as labor and delivery, may contain elements of both threat and challenge. It would be important to assist patients to view labor as more challenging than threatening because "challenged persons are more likely to have better morale . . . ," higher quality of functioning, and better somatic health.[6(p34)]

Secondary appraisal also occurs when the individual is facing a difficult situation. This part of the appraisal process involves answering the question: "What can I do about it?" This is accomplished by assessing not only what coping strategies are available but how likely they will be to bring about the desired outcome. The person must also answer the question: Will I be able to perform the necessary coping behavior? Although some situations allow less personal control than others, one can still be challenged "by the task of maintaining a positive outlook, or tolerating pain and distress without falling apart."[6(p36)]

The following statements were made by women who had recently delivered and demonstrate the effects of different appraisals of the labor experience.

Threat Appraisals.

- "I thought I was going to explode; I thought my body was going to blow up. When a contraction started, I started to cry."

- "I thought pushing was going to hurt the baby and it terrified me. I wanted a C-section so bad."

Challenge Appraisals.

- "I realized I wouldn't be given more than I could handle. I was able to relax and realize the contractions were for a reason. I tried not to fight them."
- "I felt whatever happens, I'm ready to have the baby come out. I thought about what I should do to keep myself relaxed and to get myself through it."

In the threat appraisals, the patients anticipated harm or damage either to themselves or to the baby. In both cases the patients did not see themselves as having coping options. The first woman seemed to feel helpless in the face of the threat and gave up. The second wished passively for someone to remove the threatening situation for her.

The patients who saw labor as a challenge were confident. They did not see themselves as overwhelmed by the situation. They saw that there were opportunities for coping and they felt able to perform those coping behaviors (Table 13-1).

Another prominent theorist who writes about modifying feelings by altering an individual's patterns of thinking about events is Albert Ellis.[7] He is noted for his ABC theory of irrational thinking. His theory states that there are three components that must be considered to understand how the individual reaches life goals. They are (A) the **a**ctivating events, (B) the **b**eliefs one has about these events, and (C) the **c**ognitive, emotional, and behavioral consequences of events.

The beliefs one has about important life events will influence the outcome of those events. Furthermore, rational beliefs will lead to self-helping behaviors and irrational beliefs will lead to self-defeating behaviors. In other words, what the patient believes about the events of labor will determine her willingness to help herself, and thus her beliefs influence the outcome of labor. The patient who sees herself as failing, for example, believes she can do nothing to help herself and will not try.

Rational thinking is characterized by objective observations, descriptions, and perceptions. For example, "The contractions were a little bit more intense than I

Table 13-1 Comparison of Behavioral Responses to Labor and Delivery

Patient feels challenged	*Patient feels threatened*
Active participation in labor and delivery	Withdrawal
Joy, excitement	Anger, tearfulness
Sense of control	Powerlessness
Competence	Helplessness

expected." Extremely negative evaluations are one form of irrational thinking. One patient's statements about her labor demonstrate this type of thinking: "At different points I'd think "Oh, I'm doing awful. I thought, I'm failing! It's going to be on the chart. It was like I was doing it totally wrong!" This example reflects self-criticism, overgeneralization, and all-or-nothing thinking. Even in the face of an unusual activating event, such as a difficult labor, irrational beliefs will increase feelings of anxiety and depression.[4]

Coping strategies that promote rational thinking can minimize negative emotions associated with a difficult task such as labor and delivery. Positive self-talk is one such coping strategy. Self-talk is the internal dialogue that is an integral part of our ongoing evaluations and interpretations of events. It includes "subjective value statements" that lead to self-enhancing or self-defeating behavior.[8(p13)] Positive self-talk is characterized by neutral or positive observations, descriptions, or perceptions. One example might be a laboring woman reminding herself that the increasing intensity of the contractions is bringing her closer to the desired event, delivery.

Visual imagery can also be used to transform a threatening experience such as labor contractions into a familiar experience that can be viewed as a challenge. One recently delivered woman described how she pictured herself in a situation where she was swimming to save a drowning child. This woman was an expert swimmer and felt confident about her ability to perform in that situation. She was able to transform the sensations associated with labor to sensations that held a different meaning for her. She imagined that her breathing techniques during contractions were actually the controlled breathing she would use if she were racing toward the child. She was also able to incorporate the physical discomfort of contractions in her imaging because this discomfort is not unlike the pain an athlete experiences in a race. In this way she was able to transcend the experience of labor as a threat to herself and improve her performance by placing herself in a more familiar, challenging situation.

Imagery can also be used to change the threat appraisal to one that is benign-positive. One patient described how the experience of an intense contraction was similar to being swept up by a wave. She did not associate feelings of threat with this experience; therefore, it was helpful for her to use imagery to picture herself going under the wave. She could then manage to "hold on" without anxiety until the contraction passed.

Another use of imagery is to attack the threatening situation directly by picturing oneself coping effectively in the specific situation. The woman who dreads delivery throughout labor may benefit by visualizing the delivery experience. She could be taught to image herself performing well and the delivery proceeding smoothly.

Negative thought-stopping involves catching oneself in the act of thinking irrational thoughts and refusing to allow oneself to continue. An example of this technique is seen in the following quote: "I wouldn't let myself anticipate the birth in terms of going over it and over it." Another patient described this technique in the following way: "I was worried about what I should feel. Then I'd say to myself: I'm the one having the baby. I'm not going to worry what I 'should' do!"

Cognitive distraction is a technique that can be used in labor to divert the patient's attention from anxiety-provoking thoughts. Breathing techniques and the use of a focal point can be said to be forms of distraction; however, there are many other opportunities for the use of this technique. One patient described her own creativity in using distraction as follows: "I'd look at holes in the ceiling. I'd look at the hole and think, how deep is it?" Having the opportunity to watch television or to look out a window to an interesting view also provides distraction during labor (Table 13-2).

*   *   *   *   *

CASE STUDY

The following case presentation will serve to illustrate one woman's effective use of cognitive coping strategies to promote adaptive behavior in labor. D.B. was a 26-year-old gravida I, para 0 occupational therapist. Her husband worked in sales and was studying to become a minister. She was 40 weeks gestation and 3 cm dilated on admission to the labor unit. She described herself as feeling "confident" and "at ease" at the time of the admission assessment. Her prenatal history was unremarkable. After an uncomplicated labor and delivery lasting approximately 7 hours, she delivered a normal infant.

D.B. attributed her positive experience in labor to her ability to engage in "heavy duty concentration." She stated: "Right from the start I knew I was going to have to use my mind to really help me through it." She elaborated on this with the following example: "There was one little thing in our book that said 'Go past the pain, go past the pain' and that's what really did it for me." The breathing techniques played an important role in this process: "The breathing helped me to realize I had to concentrate. The breathing was important because it gave you something to concentrate on. I only used the relaxation breathing and a few counter-blowing."

Table 13-2 Cognitive Coping Strategies

Coping Strategy	Example
Positive self-talk	"I just kept telling myself it won't be much longer."
Imagery	Picturing yourself delivering a healthy baby
Negative thought-stopping	"I wouldn't allow myself to dwell on what could go wrong."
Distraction	Looking out the window and concentrating on the view

"Logic is how I basically got through it. Saying 'Okay, we'll just get through this one.' Reason, logic, that's about what it amounted to. I didn't ask for medication; I thought we'll wing it. Let's just see how we can take it." Thinking "I'm going to get through this one, it hurts, but just go past it. Don't just sit there and say to yourself 'I can't believe this hurts.'"

D.B. described how she coped with anxiety-provoking stimuli in the following examples: "The fetal monitor made me nervous. I wish in a way that I couldn't see it because you could see the numbers rising and before I was even ready I knew one was coming. That's why I didn't look because I noticed that, when I did, I would tense up so much more." "When I saw the fetal heart rate going up and down, I just thought to myself 'I'm not going to ask . . . If something was wrong I'm sure they'd be running around doing something.' "

When D.B. experienced the urge to push before dilation was complete, she handled this by saying to herself: "You just want to get through this next contraction. You really don't want to push." Her own evaluation of this coping strategy was that it "really helped." Another helpful technique at this stage she described as follows: "It was just unbelievable concentration. There was a glove and it said 'size 7.' I can remember focusing on that for two urges that were really intense. It was like trying to stop something . . . trying to stop an urge."

*   *   *   *   *

CASE ANALYSIS

Lazarus' two part appraisal requires the individual to examine the significance of the event in reaching life goals as well as the coping resources available in that specific situation. In labor and delivery the stakes are high and the possibilities for harm are very real. D.B.'s description of herself in early labor as confident suggests that she saw the situation as one of challenge and that she felt prepared to handle it. She believed that she had coping strategies in her repertoire that would be effective and that she had the ability to perform them. This appraisal created very positive conditions under which to approach the labor experience.

Several cognitive strategies are possible to enhance self-helping behavior. Among them are positive self-talk, distraction, and negative thought-stopping. D.B. used positive self-talk throughout her labor. She compared her own thinking about contractions, "I'm going to get through this one . . . ," with the possibility of thinking, "I can't believe this hurts." She recognized that the latter would be self-defeating.

Distraction is also a technique D.B. relied on consistently during labor. She viewed the breathing techniques as a way to facilitate "concentration." She focused her attention away from more anxiety-provoking thoughts such as her overall progress in labor by concentrating instead on the rhythm of her breathing or on a size 7 glove that was a part of her immediate surroundings.

An effective technique for dealing with irrational thoughts when they do occur is negative thought-stopping. D.B. described her use of this technique when she began to worry about the meaning of the changes in fetal heart rate displayed on the monitor. She stated: "I just thought to myself, I'm not going to ask . . . . If something was wrong they'd be running around doing something." She did not allow herself to dwell on thinking of the worst possible meanings of this external event. She used logic to interrupt these self-defeating thoughts.

Ellis and Grieger wrote that it is normal and natural to respond to a difficult and painful life experience with feelings of frustration and displeasure.[4] Feelings such as severe anxiety, despair, inadequacy, and worthlessness however, tend to make a difficult situation worse. The approaches used to think about the event will interact with the event itself to create either adaptive or maladaptive emotional responses.

IMPLICATIONS FOR PRACTICE

Nurses can be of assistance in changing self-defeating cognitions at the time that they are happening. The first step is to encourage the patient in sharing ongoing interpretations of the events of labor and delivery. This provides the opportunity to detect irrational thoughts and to correct misconceptions. Nurses may accomplish this by questioning the patient about her understanding of what is happening in labor and challenging her inaccurate interpretations.

Patients can be encouraged to examine and to question their own irrational ideas. Under careful scrutiny such conclusions as "I'm a failure" can be exposed as illogical and self-defeating. The nurse can best respond to extreme, negative self-evaluations not by arguing with the patient's statements, which may encourage her to defend her position, but by gently casting doubt with a questioning response. Such responses as "Is that really possible?" allow the patient to examine the validity of her conclusions.

When the patient overgeneralizes, the nurse can respond by asking for specific examples. This forces the patient to supply concrete evidence in the form of specific instances to back up her statements. Often, the patient can produce only one or two examples. At this point the nurse can remind her of conflicting evidence, therefore effectively demonstrating the inaccuracy of the overgeneralization.

Finally, when the patient attributes blame for external events to herself, the nurse can respond to these statements by summarizing the key points and asking the patient to validate that this is in fact what she meant. This approach allows the patient to hear for herself the illogical approach she has taken to interpreting her experiences and thus to question it (Table 13-3).

Patients should not be encouraged to discuss their anxiety-producing cognitions at length because this can lead to the escalation of anxiety. The nurse needs to

Table 13-3 Nursing Responses to Patients' Self-Defeating Thoughts

Dysfunctional Thought Pattern	Example	Nursing Response
Overgeneralization	"I'm never going to have this baby"	"Is that really possible?"
Extreme self-criticism	"I'm doing this all wrong"	"What exactly are you doing wrong?"
Attributing blame to self	"What did I do to deserve this?"	"You seem very hard on yourself"

intervene to help the patient to substitute cognitive coping strategies such as distraction, negative thought-stopping, and imagery for dysfunctional thought patterns. Modeling logical, rational thinking in interpreting the events of labor and in approaching decisions throughout the experience can be helpful as well.

The conventional psychosocial approach looks at characteristics of the person that are difficult or impossible to alter during labor and delivery (e.g., history of psychiatric treatment, self-esteem, and level of functioning in life roles such as occupational roles). By challenging what the patient is telling herself about the events of labor as well as her own performance in labor, the nurse has the opportunity to promote health by preventing the escalation of anxiety.

REFERENCES

1. Lederman R, Lederman E, Work B, McCann D. The relationship of maternal anxiety, and plasma cortisol to progress in labor. *Am J Obstet Gynecol.* 1978;132:495–500.
2. Lederman R, Lederman E, Work B, McCann D. Anxiety and epinephrine in multiparous women in labor: relationship to duration of labor and fetal heart rate pattern. *Am J Obstet Gynecol.* 1985;153:870–876.
3. Lazarus R, Averill J, Opton E. The psychology of coping: issues in research and assessment. In: Coelho G, Hamburg D, Adams J, eds. *Coping and Adaptation.* New York, NY: Basic Books; 1974.
4. Ellis A, Grieger RM. *Handbook of Rational-Emotive Therapy.* New York, NY: Springer Publishing Co.; 1986:2.
5. Lazarus R. Cognitive coping processes in emotion. In: Weiner B, ed. *Cognitive Views of Human Motivation.* New York, NY: McGraw-Hill Book Co.; 1974.
6. Lazarus RS, Folkman S. *Stress, Appraisal, and Coping.* New York, NY: Springer Publishing Co.; 1984.
7. Ellis A. *Rational-Emotive Therapy and Cognitive-Behavior Therapy.* New York: Springer Publishing Co.; 1984.
8. Goodman DS, Maultsby MC. *Emotional Well-being through Rational Behavior Training.* Springfield, Ill: Charles C Thomas, Pub.; 1978.

ADDITIONAL BIBLIOGRAPHY

Billings A, Moos R. The role of coping responses and social resources in attenuating the stress of life events. *J Behav Med.* 1981;4:139–157.

Beck N, Siegel L. Preparation for childbirth and contemporary research on pain, anxiety, and stress reduction: a review and critique. *Psychosom Med.* 1972;42:429–447.

Brailey L. Mothers' coping strategies: a feasibility study. In: Kravitz M, Laurin J, eds. *Nursing Research: A Base for Practice. Proceedings of the Ninth National Research Conference, October 12–14, Montreal, Canada.* 1983;85–94.

Childress A, Burns D. The basics of cognitive therapy. *Psychosomatics.* 1981;22:1017–1027.

Coelho G, Hamburg D, Adams J, eds. *Coping and Adaptation.* New York, NY: Basic Books; 1974.

Cohen S. Cognitive processes as determinants of environmental stress. *Issues Mental Health Nurs.* 1985;7(1):65–71.

Coyne J, Lazarus R. Cognitive style, stress, perception, and coping. In: Kutash I, et al, eds. *Handbook on Stress and Coping.* San Francisco, Calif: Gossey Bass; 1980.

Folkman S. Personal control and stress and coping processes: a theoretical analysis. *J Pers Soc Psychol.* 1984;46:839–852.

Folkman S, Lazarus R. If it changes, it must be a process: a study of emotion and coping during three stages of a college examination. *J Pers Soc Psychol.* 1985;48:150–170.

Lazarus AA. *Behavior Therapy and Beyond.* New York, NY: McGraw-Hill Book Co.; 1971.

Lazarus R, Alfert E. Short-circuiting of threat by experimentally altering cognitive appraisal. *J Abnorm Soc Psychol.* 1964;69:195–205.

Mullen B, Suls J. The effectiveness of attention and rejection as coping styles: a meta analysis of temporal differences. *J Psychosom Res.* 1982;26(1):43–49.

Musil C, Abraham I. Coping, thinking and mental health nursing: cognitions and their application to psychosocial intervention. *Issues Mental Health Nurs.* 8:191–200.

Perlin L, Schooler C. The structure of coping. *J Health Soc Behav.* 1978;19:2–21.

Scott D, Oberst M. A stress-coping model. *Adv Nurs Sci.* 1980;3(1):9–23.

Chapter 14

Postpartum Depression

Jeanne Watson Driscoll

The birth of a baby is perceived to be an exciting and happy time in the life of a woman. Some women, however, experience a depressive reaction and wonder, "Why don't I feel happy? I love my baby but I am not sure who I am anymore." The following is the presentation of a case study of a woman experiencing postpartum depression.

REVIEW OF THE LITERATURE

Postpartum depression occurs in 10 to 20% of childbearing women.[1] Its symptoms can range from moderate to severe (Table 14-1), and it occurs at any time within the first year after the birth of a baby.

Hamilton proposed that five syndromes of psychiatric interest can be distinguished after childbearing.[2] These include maternity blues, postnatal depression, puerperal psychosis, major postpartum depression, and postpartum psychotic depression. He went on to state that "throughout all syndromes there is a pervasive tendency for change: changes in symptoms and the patterns of symptoms, changes in severity, and sometimes apparent total remission followed by rapid exacerbation. Finally, postpartum symptoms and syndromes seem to change in tandem with changes in genital physiology." Metz, Sichel, and Goff identified postpartum panic disorder as a separate syndrome that may also occur during the postpartum phase.[3]

Affonso and Domino reviewed the literature and summarized the theories currently related to the causes of postpartum depression.[4] These theories were psychoanalytic, personality-based, and biophysical. The theories do not lead to consensus or proof of one school of thought. The authors concluded that the causes of pre- and postpartum depression will be found when research discovers whether depression in these periods represents a continuum or separate entities.

Table 14-1 Probable Symptoms of Postpartum Depression

tearfulness/weepiness
dysphoria
despondency
feelings of inadequacy
inability to cope with the care of the baby
increasing guilt about the birth and performance as mothers
generalized fatigue and complaints of ill health
oversensitivity
anxiety
feeling hopeless/helpless
compulsive thoughts
excessive dependency
tunnel vision
feeling a "change" in self
lack of drive/energy
loss of interest in sex
feeling that "life will never be the same"
irrational fears about baby's safety
changes in appetite
sleep disturbances
confusion
suicidal ideation
changes in energy
physical signs and symptoms: excessive fatiguability, fluid retention, dry skin, cold
    extremities, excessive loss of hair, excessive weight gain or loss

Petrick described several factors that predispose women to postpartum depression.[5] These included personality traits (anxious and/or obsessional); genetic factors (known affective bipolar disorders); psychosocial stressors of pregnancy (changes in body image, activation of unconscious intrapsychic conflicts, and the emotional reorganization required to become a mother); and finally physiologic factors (hormonal changes—rapid decrease in progesterone between the first and second stages of labor, decreased estrogen, steroids).

Hamilton supported the position that the "psychiatric illness that follows childbearing is an entity, or group of entities, distinct from other varieties of psychiatric illness. It has roots in the childbearing event and in chemical and hormonal changes unique to the puerperium."[6] This is in opposition to the current thinking of other clinicians who feel that psychiatric illnesses that occur after childbearing are basically the same as psychiatric illnesses that occur without the event of the birth. Based on the current confusion regarding the diagnosis and etiology of postpartum psychiatric syndromes, many women find themselves in conflict with the medical/psychiatric communities when they are most vulnerable and in need of support and adequate treatment. Women often feel anger at the fact "that they (mental health professionals) wanted me to think that I was depressed because my father died seven years before the birth of my son. I had spent time working out my father's death; I knew that this had nothing to do with my current feelings." Rates of postpartum depression may be higher than documented secondary to fears of women being "labeled mentally ill" and being told that they "should be happy." The responsibility is now on women to try to cure themselves as a result of the confusion faced when admitting the need for help.

The treatment of postpartum depression varies depending on the symptoms presented. Usually the treatment includes supportive psychotherapy (group, individual, and/or couple), medications (antidepressants), and practical supports, such as home care, new mother support groups, and telephone support networks.

* * * * *

CASE STUDY

J.W. is a 35-year-old woman who presented to the author at 5 months postpartum. She was an attractive women who sat on the couch crying during most of the first meeting. She was concerned that she was "losing my mind." She went on to say: "No one believes this is postpartum depression . . . . I was feeling fine up until 6 weeks postpartum when I had my first panic attack."

When she experienced her first "panic attack," she called her obstetrician, who referred her to the local community mental health center. "At the center, I was evaluated and given a sedative. I was told that I was having an adjustment reaction and that, if I went back to work, I would probably feel better." She went to the clinic for prescription refills, "but I didn't feel I was getting any better. After 5 weeks, the panic attacks were still occurring and I was feeling more and more anxious." At this point, she called her internist. "He was great; he did some training in England and he believed that my symptoms were related to postpartum. He prescribed Deseryl [an antidepressant] and Ativan [antianxiety agent]." She began to take the medication but, again, did not feel she was getting better and felt she needed to talk to someone. "I told my internist I thought I needed to see someone to talk to and he told me he did not have faith in the psychiatric community regarding the management of postpartum depression. I pushed him and he referred me to a psychiatrist." She saw one psychiatrist, who wanted to switch her medications. "I was not comfortable with him and I did not like the side effects of those medications, so I made an appointment with a psychiatrist who was a woman. I liked her but I was still not feeling any better. She kept me on the Deseryl and requested that I have blood levels drawn. . . . . My levels were not in the therapeutic range and I was not feeling any better. In fact, I was worse; I was crying all the time and I was afraid."

She went on to discuss how she kept calling support groups in the community and looking "for people to believe me." At that time, she contacted the author and her collaborating psychiatrist. A medication consult was arranged, and it was recommended that J.W. be switched to Norpramin (antidepressant) and Klonopin (antianxiety agent).

This was a time of acute crisis for J.W. She called the author many times in panic, "I can't stop crying and I am so anxious; I just sit on the couch . . . I do feed the baby, but I don't like this feeling . . . what is happening to me?" She spoke about having trouble with sleep and having "bad dreams" when she was asleep. "I want to go to sleep and never wake up; that would be fine with me."

While the medication levels were being managed by the psychiatrist, J.W. decided to terminate with one psychiatrist and receive treatment from the author while having medications prescribed by the consulting psychiatrist who was the author's colleague. At this point, the original psychiatrist was contacted and the case was discussed. It was mutually agreed that J.W. would see the author in treatment (5 1/2 months postpartum). The treatment plan included individual psychotherapy, group therapy with her husband (the author and psychiatrist were coleaders of a group for couples who were experiencing postpartum depression), and medications. The medication regime included Norpramin, 100 mg at 6 P.M. and 125 mg h.s.; Klonopin, 0.5 mg t.i.d.; and Elavil, 25 mg h.s.

Utilizing the nursing process assessment format, the therapist collected the data pertaining to the holistic aspects of the client. She was currently having problems with sleep, although "the Elavil seems to be helping." Before the birth of the baby, she denied problems with sleep. "We go to bed at about 10:00 P.M. and I would wake at 6:00 A.M. feeling rested." Before the initiation of the Elavil, "I would go to sleep and wake at 3:00 A.M. and not be able to get back to sleep . . . . I would wake panicky and scared; I am having horrible dreams."

She had no problems with elimination. When questioned about nutrition, she said, "I have only lost 20 lb; I gained 30 with the pregnancy and I can't seem to lose this weight." She described eating three meals a day, paying attention to the four basic food groups. She does not drink caffeinated beverages.

J.W. described herself as "type A with compulsive tendencies." She felt that she was a good listener and a good friend, "although I don't feel like myself anymore." She stated that she "intellectualizes rather than talking about feelings." She coped by reading and talking about her problems. She felt that it was through reading and talking that she had found support. She stated that, before the postpartum depression, "I never cried; that sounds funny since I haven't stopped crying for the past few weeks. I need to be in control and this experience is frightening me, yet I feel that I am opening up more to Tim (her husband)." She took pride in her appearance. "I shower and do my hair and makeup every morning, even with this depression."[5]

J.W. had been married to Tim for the past 2 years. Prior to that, "we lived together for 5 years." She felt that he was a good friend and listener. "I am concerned for him with all this; he is so concerned." She described her inability to disclose to him "all the times that I am feeling really down; I don't want to ruin his day at work." She felt that her baby was "the joy of my life; he is such a good baby and so cute."

She had a successful breast-feeding relationship with her son that was terminated abruptly secondary to the necessity to take the medications. "I wanted to feel better and I did not want to put him at risk with the drugs."

J.W. is the youngest of four children (two sisters alive and well and one brother). Her mother is alive and "a bit angry since my father died." Her father died 2 days after he was diagnosed with pancreatitis and peritonitis on 27 December 1980.

When asked about her family's reaction to depression, J.W. said, "I think that they are all concerned for me . . . . I was the strong one up until this depression." J.W. had been employed by the same hospital for the past 10 years. "I was the charge nurse in the Coronary Care Unit prior to the baby. I was planning on going back to work part-time as soon as I was able after the baby; it may take a bit longer now. I enjoy work, although things have really changed; all my friends are working part time and the nursing shortage is beginning to affect where I work."

J.W. had no problems with menstruation and used a diaphragm, condoms, and foams for contraception. "I don't want to get pregnant. I am not sure we will have any more children after this experience." She resumed menses at 5 months postpartum and had noticed that, "when I got my period, the crying stopped; I wonder if I now have PMS (premenstrual syndrome). I was always regular, about 28 days; now it seems to be 38 to 40 days." She described increased intimacy with her husband currently but went on to say that she felt that sex had been more free and easy before their marriage. "It was as if I was afraid of being that close to someone. I felt very vulnerable." She is sexually active presently. She had no history of urinary tract or vaginal infections, routinely has a Pap smear, and performs self breast exams.

J.W. attended preparation for childbirth classes with husband. She had hoped for a vaginal birth but, "after 12 hours of labor with contractions every 3 minutes, they discovered that he was a frank breech position and did a cesarean. I knew something wasn't right, but I didn't want to make waves because I worked there and I was a nurse." She described the cesarean birth as being performed under spinal anesthesia with no complications. "I was up and walking that night."

J.W. denied any suicidal/homicidal ideation at this time. "I did think a few times that it would be nice to go to sleep and never wake up. I think that was because I was so tired." When asked about her past psychiatric history, she stated, "I did see someone for about 6 weeks after my father died. I was so angry at the care that he received and I thought that I should have been able to do more. After all, I am the nurse. That helped, as did talking with my friends. I don't think that this feeling has anything to do with my father's death, although one of the psychiatrists told me that it was all related . . . . I don't believe it. I worked that out and I was functioning well until I had my first panic attack." She did state that one of her sisters had panic attacks, "but she just gets the medication; she doesn't want to talk to anyone."

J.W. was an engaging woman who demonstrated insight and the ability to verbalize her concerns. Her ability to problem solve and seek solutions to her dilemma (specifically, treatment for her postpartum disorder) was impressive. She stated that she "wants this all to be over, so that I can get on with my life."

Based on the assessment, it was determined that the diagnosis was "atypical depression secondary to the birth of a baby." This diagnosis was determined by the psychiatrist for billing purposes. The nursing diagnoses included postpartum depression with panic attacks, sleep/rest disturbance, evolving maternal role development, and adaptive coping mechanisms.

The therapy was based on an eclectic model of interpersonal theories. The primary focus was the utilization of interpersonal therapy, journal keeping as well as behavioral approaches: walking 1 hour per day to increase exercise and the sense of well-being, jumping rope when feeling anxious as a behavioral method, and psychoeducation. Assertiveness techniques were learned and practiced. These were to help gain insight into her value as a person and, with that, the "right" to express her thoughts, concerns, and needs. She had, for "most of my life, taken care of other people." She was encouraged to read The New Mother Syndrome for validation and education regarding postpartum depression,[7] as well as Feeling Good by David Burns.[8] This book utilizes cognitive techniques regarding "cognitive dysfunctions" and learning how one's thoughts can affect one's emotions.

J.W. was able to integrate the therapy constructively. Meetings were held biweekly for 3 months and then monthly for 5 months. At 11 months postpartum, J.W. began to wean herself from the Konopin (with the supervision of the consulting psychiatrist). This was done over a 2-week period. She then began to wean from the Norpramin. "I decided that I was feeling better and I wanted to get off these medications."

At 9 months postpartum, J.W. returned to work, part-time. She negotiated an orientation program for her re-entry "because so many of the technologies have changed." She wanted to go "back to being a nurse. I like myself in that role and I know that I am good; besides, we could use the money." She spoke about how she was careful to whom she disclosed her postpartum depression because "so many people don't believe that it exists." At the same time, she became involved in a Mothers' Group, "Gymboree" (gym for kids), with her son and started a play group in the neighborhood. Also, she called the employee assistance program at her place of employment and told them that, if they heard of any other women who experienced postpartum depression, to have them call her. She feels that it is necessary and part of "getting better" that she "educate the health care providers. If I wasn't a nurse and didn't know how to play the health system, I don't know where I would be today."

At 1 year postpartum, J.W. is off all medications and feels "great." In looking back over the experience she feels "that the past year has been significant in that I have learned that it is all right to have needs and to get help. I am feeling like myself again." She terminated treatment after 8 months, when she was 13 months postpartum. She felt that she was doing well and would contact me in the future if there were other issues she needed to talk about. J.W. has concerns about having another child but feels that she will think about that in another year. "Right now, I just want to enjoy my son. It seems as though I missed the first few months of his life and now we are having a good time."

*   *   *   *   *

CASE ANALYSIS

Postpartum illness has two unique distinguishing features.[6] They are its acute onset and the fact that, from the patient's viewpoint, there is no apparent cause of the symptoms and the illness. This case adequately supports these features. J.W., before the birth of her baby, was a highly functioning woman, wife, friend, and nurse. She and her husband had anticipated the birth with excitement. However, she knew that she had postpartum depression and utilized her ego strengths to seek out and obtain appropriate treatment.

Medications were used to alleviate the symptoms of the depression and anxiety/panic and to promote sleep. Antidepressants can be safe medications. They have side effects but no life-threatening ones. They are not addictive. A person without biologic symptoms to the depression will tend not to respond to these medications, so there is little risk of abuse. Once the biologic event of the depression is over, people under treatment with medication will, on their own initiative, request that the medication be terminated.[9] This was demonstrated by J.W.

IMPLICATIONS FOR PRACTICE

Postpartum depression often goes undetected and untreated. Many women struggle with the feeling that something is wrong, only to be told by "helpful people" that, for example, "it will go away once your hormones balance; you'll be fine" or "pull yourself together, you have to take care of a baby." Feelings and concerns are negated and devalued. It is no wonder that women will not talk about how they feel. This case demonstrates the confusion in the health care system in response to this woman's cry for help. Fortunately, she had enough system savvy to fight her way through the maze of subjective opinions, but what about the other women who are suffering from this disorder?

It is necessary for health care providers, specifically nurses, to become informed about postpartum disorders. When they are informed, they can provide education regarding the existence of the postpartum syndromes and also perform case finding. J.W. felt very strongly, as did her husband, that it would have been comforting to have heard during prepared childbirth classes about what might happen.

Nurses concerned with the adaptation and adjustments of new parents can provide information and referral. It is professional responsibility to provide anticipatory guidance regarding the psychosocial issues inherent in becoming a mother. All too often, the focus of concern is on how to have the baby, and the tasks of learning to live with the baby are neglected.

The postpartum experience involves significant losses, specifically of dreams and expectations.[10] Nurses need to help women integrate birth experiences and to provide additional support to women on the journey to becoming mothers.

REFERENCES

1. O'Hara MW, Engeldinger J. Postpartum mood disorders: detection and prevention. *Female Patient.* 1989;14:19–27.

2. Hamilton JA. Postpartum psychiatric syndromes. *Psychiatr Clin North Am.* 1989;12:89–103.

3. Metz A, Sichel DA, Goff DC. Postpartum panic disorder. *J Clin Psychiatry.* 1988;49:278–279.

4. Affonso DD, Domino G. Postpartum depression: a review. *Birth.* 1984;11(4):231–235.

5. Petrick JM. Postpartum depression: identification of high-risk mothers. *J Obstet Gynecol Neonat Nurs.* Jan/Feb 1984;37–40.

6. Hamilton JA. Guidelines for therapeutic management of postpartum disorders. In: Inwood DG, ed. *Recent Advances in Postpartum Psychiatric Disorders.* Washington, DC: American Psychiatric Press, Inc; 1985: chap 5.

7. Dix C. *The New Mother Syndrome.* New York, NY: Pocket Books; 1985.

8. Burns D. *Feeling Good.* New York, NY: William Morrow; 1980.

9. Fernandez R. The role of medication in PPD & PPP. *Depression after Delivery Newsletter.* Winter 1988.

10. Driscoll JW. Maternal parenthood and the grief process. *J Perinat Neonat Nurs.* 1990;4:1–9.

ADDITIONAL BIBLIOGRAPHY

Affonso DD, Arizmendi TG. Disturbances in post-partum adaptation and depressive symptomatology. *J Psychosom Obstet Gynaecol.* 1986;5:15–32.

Arizmendi TG, Affonso D. Research on psychosocial factors and postpartum depression: a critique. *Birth.* 1984;11:237–240.

Braverman J, Roux J. Screening for the patient at risk for postpartum depression. *Obstet Gynecol.* 1978;52:731–736.

Chalmers BE, Chalmers BM. Post-partum depression: a revised perspective. *J Psychosom Obstet Gynaecol.* 1986;5:93–105.

Cox JL, Holden JM, Sagovsky R. Detection of postnatal depression. *Br J Psychiatry.* 1987;150:782–786.

Dalton K. *Depression after Childbirth.* New York, NY: Oxford University Press; 1980.

Formanek R, Gurian A, eds. *Women and Depression: A Lifespan Perspective.* New York, NY: Springer; 1987.

Handford P. Postpartum depression: what is it, what helps? *Can Nurse.* January 1985;30–33.

Hams A. Postpartum assessment: the psychological component. *J Obstet Gynecol Neonat Nurs.* 1986;15:49–51.

Harris B, Johns S, Fung H, et al. The hormonal environment of post-natal depression. *Br J Psychiatry.* 1989;154:660–667.

Inwood DG, ed. *Recent Advances in Postpartum Psychiatric Disorders.* Washington, DC: American Psychiatric Press, Inc.; 1985.

Martell LK. Postpartum depression as a family problem. *Am J Maternal Child Nurs.* 1990;15:90–93.

Pitt B. "Atypical depression" following childbirth. *Br J Psychiat.* 1968;114:1324–1335.

Saks BR, Frank JB, Lowe TL, et al. Depressed mood during pregnancy and the puerperium: clinical recognition and implications for clinical practice. *Am J Psychiatry*. 1985;142:728–731.

Werman DS. *The Practice of Supportive Psychotherapy*. New York, NY: Brunner/Mazel; 1984.

Chapter 15

Peripartum Cardiomyopathy

Tina Weitkamp

Cardiomyopathies are a group of myocardial diseases of unknown etiology which are classified according to the structural and functional changes that occur. There are three classifications of cardiomyopathies: dilated, hypertrophic, and restrictive. Dilated, the most common form, is characterized by cardiac enlargement, dilatation of the ventricles, and impaired systolic function. Dilated cardiomyopathies are frequently seen in people with chronic high alcohol intake, viral infections, pregnancy, or an autoimmune process. Hypertrophic cardiomyopathy seems to be genetically transmitted, resulting in marked hypertrophy of the cardiac muscle without dilatation of the heart chambers, resulting in a decreased diastolic function. The rarest form of cardiomyopathy is restrictive, which results in a decreased ability of the ventricle to expand, thus decreasing the filling of the ventricles.

During pregnancy, a dilated cardiomyopathy known as peripartum cardiomyopathy can develop. This rare form of a dilated cardiomyopathy develops during the last trimester of pregnancy or within the first 6 months postpartum. It is seen in 1/1300 to 1/4000 deliveries, with the majority of the cases occurring during the first 3 months postpartum.[1] The diagnosis of peripartum cardiomyopathy is based on the following criteria.

1. development of cardiac failure in the last trimester of pregnancy or within 6 months of delivery
2. absence of determinable etiology of cardiac failure
3. absence of demonstrable heart disease before last trimester of pregnancy.[2]
4. dilated, poorly contractile myocardium[3]

REVIEW OF THE LITERATURE

Those women at greatest risk for developing peripartum cardiomyopathy are black, living in a tropical or subtropical climate, over 30 years of age, with twin gestation and a history of hypertension.[2,4,5] The role of nutrition in the development of disease is unclear. The research of Hull and Hafkesbring speculated that the development of this disease is associated with malnutrition.[6] However, others have been unable to establish a role for nutrition in disease development.[2,5,7]

Although the cause of peripartum cardiomyopathy is unknown, there is a relationship between the development of the cardiomyopathy and the pregnancy. It is thought that peripartum cardiomyopathy is a multifocal disorder involving environmental, hemodynamic, metabolic, and hormonal changes of pregnancy.[7] Szekeley and Julian noted that pregnancy may predispose a woman to viral myocarditis and that this may be the cause of peripartum cardiomyopathy.[8] Although viral infections have yet to be proven, Melvin et al. felt that the diagnosis should be ruled out or proven with an endomyocardial biopsy and that treatment should be based on these findings.[9] Other speculated causes include fetal production of antimyocardial antibodies; sensitization of the mother by fetal tissue, which inhibits maternal response to foreign tissue; an interaction between nutritional factors and genetics; and drug intake.[7,10]

Predisposing factors that play a key role in the development of peripartum cardiomyopathy include hypertension, a family history of peripartum cardiomyopathy, geographical location, nutritional status, and anemia (both chronic, related to iron deficiency, and acute, such as hemorrhage at delivery). All of these factors affect the heart in various ways, resulting in a decrease in functional cardiac activity. These changes are to be found during pregnancy because of the normal cardiovascular adaptation that occurs (Table 15-1).

The patient diagnosed with peripartum cardiomyopathy often complains of chest pain, fatigue, increasing dyspnea on exertion, edema, hemoptysis, coughing, and tachycardia. A physical examination may reveal elevated blood pressure, elevated jugular venous pressure, pulmonary rales, cardiomegaly, S3 gallop, mitral regurgitation murmur, hepatic enlargement, and peripheral edema.

Table 15-1 Cardiovascular Changes of Pregnancy

Blood volume increase 40–50%
Blood pressure: slight drop in systolic and diastolic pressures, lowest at midpregnancy
Pulse rate increase 10–20%
Presence of a systolic murmur
Exaggerated splitting of S1
Increase in fibrinogen, fibrin, and clotting factors VIII, XI, and X

Diagnostic testing may reveal the following:

1. chest film displaying cardiomegaly, often with pulmonary venous congestion and occasionally with pleural effusion
2. electrocardiogram showing abnormalities including nonspecific ST and T wave changes or evidence of left ventricular hypertrophy
3. echocardiography showing evidence of left ventricular and left atrial dilatation with a decrease in left ventricular systolic function
4. hemodynamic investigation demonstrating elevated right-heart and left-heart filling pressures with decreased cardiac output and a low pulmonary arterial oxygen saturation
5. normal coronary arteriograms
6. endomyocardial biopsy specimens showing a loss of myofibrial fibers and an increase in collagenous fibers; electron microscopy may show fibrous structures in the sarcoplasm.

Most women who are diagnosed as having peripartum cardiomyopathy will exhibit clinical symptoms of progressive heart failure. In addition, 25 to 40% develop thromboembolic complications due to the hypercoagulable state of pregnancy.[7] As a result of the above immediate therapy to control heart failure, the prevention of thromboembolic complications is necessary. Immediate therapy may include the use of diuretics, digitalization, and anticoagulant therapy.

Burch et al. demonstrated that prolonged bed rest did alter the course of peripartum cardiomyopathy.[11] In addition to bed rest in the acute phase, they advocated bed rest for at least 3 months after the heart size returned to normal. In those diagnosed women whose heart size had not returned to normal after 6 to 12 months of bed rest, ambulation was gradually initiated. Burch et al. found that the heart size in 50% of the women returned to normal after prolonged bed rest if bed rest was initiated early in the disease process.[11] Demakis et al. showed that the heart size returned to normal within 1 year without the need for prolonged bed rest.[12]

The use of prolonged bed rest is unresolved in the literature, but the use of bed rest during the acute phase of the disease is commonly agreed by researchers.[2,7,8,11] If symptoms appear in the third trimester of pregnancy, a woman should be on bed rest to prevent overloading of cardiac status. During the third trimester, the basic circulatory needs of the woman and fetus must first be met. After meeting these basic needs, other activities that place additional demands on the heart may be undertaken.

Placement in the left lateral position allows an increase in blood return from the lower extremities and better uteroplacental circulation. Elevation of the head allows more complete expansion of the lungs by decreasing the uterine pressure on the diaphragm.[8,13]

Sodium dietary restrictions are not imposed unless severe heart failure is present. Elimination of high-salt foods and table salt decreases the sodium intake to approximately 2 to 3 g/day.[14] Excessive restriction of sodium may lead to an intravascular volume depletion.[13,14]

The caloric intake for pregnant women should be increased above the normal nonpregnant requirements by approximately 300 calories/day.[13] The avoidance of excessive caloric intake prevents an excessive weight gain, which can further compromise cardiac performance.[13–16]

Both dietary and medical supplementation of iron is advised in the pregnant women with a cardiac complication. During pregnancy, the body needs approximately 18 to 21 g of iron per day.[14] To meet this need a woman's caloric intake would most likely be greater than the allotted calories; therefore, iron supplementation is necessary. For maximal benefit from iron therapy, it should be administered with folic acid.[8]

When there is inadequate blood circulating to meet the metabolic needs of the woman and fetus, digitalization is begun slowly. Digitalis increases myocardial contraction, resulting in an increased effectiveness of each heartbeat. Because of the increased sensitivity to digitalis by a woman with peripartum cardiomyopathy, digitalis levels must be closely monitored.[11] Electrolyte status must also be evaluated, since hypokalemia and hypomagnesemia may induce digitalis toxicity.[7] Digitalis readily crosses the placenta and is safe for the fetus.[8] The major side effect that the pregnant woman may experience from digitalization is premature labor and a shortened labor.[17] This is thought to be due to the action of the digitalis on the uterine myometrium.[17]

The use of diuretics in the treatment of peripartum cardiomyopathy is limited. Diuretics are used for emergency treatment of heart failure, but long-term usage should be avoided. Long-term usage of diuretics could result in reduction of plasma volume, which may affect the uterine blood blow and placental perfusion.[7,8] A potassium-sparing diuretic should be utilized because hypokalemia induces digitalis toxicity. Potassium-sparing diuretics have not been proven safe for use in pregnancy, so the benefit of their usage must be closely monitored.

Vasodilating agents are used in the treatment of severe heart failure. They function by dilating the venous system and relaxing the arterioles, or both. The major side effects with the usage of these agents during the antepartal period are a possibly decreased uteroplacental perfusion and potentially toxic effects to the fetus.[7]

The use of steroids and immunosuppressive agents has been advocated based on the possible immunologic etiology of peripartum cardiomyopathy. Since an immunologic etiology is still speculative, the use of steroids or immunosuppressive agents without the histologic proof of myocardial inflammation is not recommended.[18]

With a diagnosis of peripartum cardiomyopathy, the risk for development of pulmonary and systemic emboli increases.[7] Leg exercises will increase the venous return from the lower legs and decrease the incidence of systemic and pulmonary emboli.[7,8] Another method of increasing venous return from the lower extremities is the utilization of elastic support stockings.[19]

Because of the high incidence of both pulmonary and systemic emboli, anticoagulants are used while cardiomegaly is present. Treatment involves the use of both oral and parenteral routes. Since oral anticoagulants cross the placenta, they may cause tissue damage and fetal hemorrhage. Fetal abnormalities associated with oral anticoagulants include hypoplasia of the nasal bones, chondrodysplasia punctata, and mental retardation.[7] The use of oral anticoagulants is not recommended during pregnancy, but they can be used during the puerperium for an indefinite length of time. Use of oral anticoagulants during lactation is controversial.[7,20]

Heparin is the anticoagulant of choice during pregnancy. Because of its higher molecular weight, it does not cross the placenta; hence, there are no fetal effects. However, the major problem of heparin therapy during pregnancy is the need for someone to administer the medication and, at the time of delivery, to have the antidote (protamine sulfate or fresh frozen plasma) readily available.[7,8,16] After delivery, these women need to be closely monitored for postpartum hemorrhage.

Until recently, most of the literature recommended the use of medications and bed rest for the treatment of peripartum cardiomyopathy.[2,7,21] Selected, more recent articles recommended consideration of a cardiac transplant as one method of treatment for the nonpregnant patient.[22–24] O'Connell et al. suggested that, if medical management is inadequate for the patient, an early cardiac transplant should be considered.[22] Research conducted by Aravot et al. showed that, of 468 transplants performed, 6 were performed on women with peripartum cardiomyopathy. Of these 6 women, 2 died: 1 from early rejection and another from septicemia. At the time of their article, 4 had been alive 4 months to 4 years post-transplant.[23] It now appears that a cardiac transplant is a feasible option for the postpartum women with peripartum cardiomyopathy, and it can be performed in a tertiary center with cardiac transplant capabilities.

Women with heart disease will often display signs of anxiety, depression, withdrawal, anger, or increased fear. These signs of stress are often manifestations of fear for themselves and their fetuses. Frequently, these women have been healthy until the development of peripartum cardiomyopathy, and they are suddenly faced with a serious illness that they may not fully understand. Because stress places an increased demand on the heart and may divert blood from the uterus, an important part of therapy is an attempt to minimize stress and to teach effective coping skills.[16] Frequent explanations of the treatment and disease process, as well as family support, are often needed.

Management of labor should include hemodynamic monitoring of the mother along with continuous fetal monitoring. Pain control can be through the use of relaxation techniques and psychoprophylactic methods of childbirth in addition to epidural anesthesia. Anesthesia without epinephrine is preferable.[1] The delivery should be in a left lateral position with possible shortening of the second stage of labor by the use of forceps. Cesarean sections should be performed only for obstetrical complications. After delivery, normal obstetrical monitoring and hemodynamic monitoring should continue until the maternal condition is stable.

* * * * *

CASE STUDY

A.T., a primigravida who lives in a rural area of a midwestern state, was referred to a perinatologist during the first trimester of pregnancy. Past medical history showed that in 1977 she had had an acute episode of rheumatic fever. At that time she had an elevated anti-streptolysin O level and also a streptozyme level indicating a recent group A ß-streptococci infection. She also had symptoms of Sydenham's chorea, a nervous disorder characterized by involuntary grimacing and jerky and purposeless movements. She did not show symptoms of carditis or arthritis. A.T. made a complete recovery from the acute episode. Her clinical findings were normal except for a nonspecific systolic ejection murmur.

During the next couple of years A.T. was lost to follow-up. She was not seen again until 1980, when she presented with a history of systemic hypertension. This was treated and, when seen next in 1982, she had a normal physical examination. In 1983, the first change in her electrocardiogram (EKG) was noted, a left bundle branch block. In 1984, she was found to have a prominent systolic ejection murmur, a developing left bundle branch block, and a widely split S2 that moved paradoxically. Her echocardiogram was negative for mitral stenosis with incomplete or annual calcification. At this time she was placed on Minipress (prazosin HCl), an ∂-adrenergic antihypertensive; Aldactone A (spironolactone), an aldosterone antagonist diuretic; and guanabenz monoacetate (Wytensin), an ∂-adrenergic agonist, sympathomimetic, and antihypertensive. There is no documented discussion relative to pregnancy planning or contraceptive counseling.

A.T. was next seen in March 1985, at 9 weeks gestation. At that time, her blood pressure was 130/75 and her cardiac assessment was unchanged. Current medications included captopril (Capoten), an antihypertensive, and Lopressor (metroprolol tartrate), a ß-adrenergic blocking agent and antihypertensive. Because of her history, she was referred to a perinatologist for continuing care during the pregnancy and also to her cardiologist.

When first seen and evaluated by the perinatologist, A.T. was found to have a blood pressure of 150/105 sitting and a pulse of 105. Cardiac assessment showed both S3 and S4 heart sounds, along with a long middiastolic rumble. An echocardiogram displayed a normal right atrium and ventricle; the triscupid valve and the left ventricle were also normal. The posterior leaflet of the mitral valve was less mobile than expected and could possibly have been thickened. The anterior leaflet of the mitral valve was normal, and mitral regurgitation was present. The aortic root and aortic valve were normal, but there was no aortic regurgitation. The ventricular septal motion was abnormal and showed a left bundle branch block. Because of the hypertension Apresoline (hydralazine HCl), a peripheral vasodilator and antihypertensive, was added to the list of medications. In addition, she was given prenatal vitamins and ferrous sulfate.

Pregnancy progressed normally for the next several months. In June she began a monthly dose of Bicillin (penicillin). At 31 weeks gestation, antepartum fetal heart rate testing was begun. A nonstress test (NST) was nonreactive. However, it was followed by a negative contraction test (CST). At this time, the fetus was diagnosed as having intrauterine growth retardation. During the next month the blood pressure gradually increased, and it was 180/120 when A.T. was admitted to the hospital at 35 weeks gestation. Three days later she was discharged home with blood pressure controlled at 140/100. Medications included Lopressor, Apresoline, prenatal vitamins, and ferrous sulfate.

At 39 weeks a lecithin/sphingomyelin (L/S) ratio was mature, and a decision was made to deliver because of the elevated blood pressure. A.T. underwent a cesarean section because of failure to progress when induced. She delivered an infant girl with Apgar scores of 8 and 9, respectively. At the time of discharge she was on captopril, an antihypertensive. At the postpartum check-up, she decided to use a barrier method of contraception.

A.T. then became pregnant with a second child 7 months later. This pregnancy was considerably more difficult. At approximately 10 weeks gestation, she was taken off captopril, an antihypertensive. At 14 weeks gestation, her blood pressure was 135/88 and her weight was 192 1/2 lb. As pregnancy progressed the blood pressure remained fairly stable. Early in the pregnancy she had a rapid weight gain but, as the pregnancy progressed, she lost weight. At term she had lost more than 29 lb.

It was during this pregnancy that the diagnosis of peripartum cardiomyopathy was made. It was felt that she had this disease even though she had a history of rheumatic fever. This diagnosis was made based on the fact that she had no major cardiac involvement from the rheumatic fever that could be responsible for the cardiac problems. In addition, progress during the first pregnancy was taken into consideration when the diagnosis of peripartum cardiomyopathy was made.

A.T. was admitted to the hospital at 32 weeks gestation for stabilization of her cardiac condition. Before delivery, she was discharged only once during hospitalization for 3 days at Christmas.

The echocardiogram done on admission showed severe left ventricular dilation with a left ventricular ejection fraction of 35 to 45%. Severe mitral regurgitation and mild aortic regurgitation were noted. Physical examination on admission showed rales over the lower half of the posterior lung fields, jugular venous distension of 8 to 10 cm, and an S3 gallop. She did not have any pitting edema. She was started on Lasix (furesemide), a diuretic, and digoxin, a cardiac glycoside, for control of the congestive heart failure. Upon readmission after Christmas, she was in pulmonary edema and had a urinary tract infection.

On 1 January, during a nonstress test, spontaneous uterine contractions were noted. After careful obstetrical and cardiac evaluation, it was decided to initiate oral ritodrine therapy. At this time basilar rales were present, and she was treated with Lasix and digoxin.

The following day the uterine contractions were still every 3 to 4 minutes, with a reactive fetal heart rate tracing. Basilar rales were present, and it was decided to initiate intravenous magnesium sulfate at 1 g/hr. She remained on the magnesium sulfate for 24 hours. During this time there was no change in her physical assessment or that of the fetus. Five days after the preterm labor began, an amniocentesis was performed and the L/S ratio was 1.2:1 and phosphatidylglycerol (PG) negative. A.T. was no longer having contractions, and she was transferred to the antepartum unit. Both maternal and fetal status remained fairly stable until day 9 of hospitalization.

At this time she was nauseated with vomiting, complaints of back pain, a temperature of 101°, and a pulse in the 120s. A diagnosis of a urinary tract infection was made. She was treated with intravenous ampicillin. She also experienced some pulmonary congestion, which was treated, and her condition stabilized.

During the next week the cardiac condition gradually deteriorated. Because of the deteriorating condition, it was decided to perform an amniocentesis. The L/S ratio was 1.6:1 and PG positive. Thus, it was decided to induce labor. However, before labor induction a Swan-Ganz catheter was inserted in the left subclavian vein to evaluate pulmonary and cardiac pressures during labor.

Throughout the antepartal period, A.T.'s nursing care was directed toward support of the medical therapy. She was allowed frequent rest periods during the day and also encouraged to lie in a left lateral position with head elevated to promote placental perfusion and complete lung expansion. During this period there was little structured support given toward the prevention of depression or working through the developmental tasks of pregnancy.

Labor management included the use of antibiotics, digoxin, Apresoline, and minimal fluids. During labor, approximately 3 hours after Pitocin was begun, an epidural was administered. Five hours after the Pitocin was begun, it was stopped because of questionable late decelerations on the fetal tracing. At this time the membranes were ruptured, clear fluid was present, and a fetal scalp electrode was applied. Eleven hours after the initiation of labor, A.T.'s cervix was completely dilated and a low forceps delivery was performed. The baby was normal, with mature lungs. Two hours after delivery A.T. was transferred to the coronary care unit. The next day she was transferred to the postpartum unit, and 3 days after delivery she was discharged home on digoxin and Apresoline.

One week after delivery she was seen for follow-up. Physical examination showed a blood pressure of 124/80 and a weight loss of 36 1/2 lb since the first prenatal visit. No rales were present, but mild edema was present in the lower extremities, and the jugular veins were less dilated. Auscultation of the heart revealed an audible S3 followed by a rumble until the beginning of systole.

Two weeks postdelivery A.T. was readmitted to the hospital for congestive heart failure, and the possibility of a heart transplant was discussed with A.T. and her husband. Approximately 6 weeks after delivery she had an orthotopic cardiac transplant. The procedure was uncomplicated except for the need for a pacemaker 12 days after the transplant. Four days later A.T. was discharged home. She was the earliest-discharged post–cardiac transplant patient from the institution.

One month after the transplant A.T. was readmitted to the hospital with rejection. The following day she experienced a cardiac arrest related to cardiogenic shock. Over the next week her condition gradually worsened. Her family decided not to have her connected to life support devices, and she died a week after the cardiac arrest.

*   *   *   *   *

CASE ANALYSIS

According to the criteria for the diagnosis of peripartum cardiomyopathy, A.T. did not have peripartum cardiomyopathy because of the history of rheumatic fever at age 14. However, she did have a dilated, poorly contractile myocardium during the second pregnancy, which Roth included as a diagnostic criterion for peripartum cardiomyopathy.[16]

A.T. developed congestive failure and did receive appropriate therapy for that based on treatment for peripartum cardiomyopathy. She was on medication to increase the contractility of the myocardium, antihypertensives, diuretics, and antibiotics. She was not placed on anticoagulant therapy, nor did she develop a thromboembolic complication. She maintained strict bed rest for the majority of the time she was in congestive failure. Furthermore, her diet was inadequate in caloric and nutritional intake (she lost 29 lb during the pregnancy). Throughout the last part of her pregnancy, she was unable to eat, insisting that eating required too much energy.

A.T. did not receive documented psychologic support during the last trimester of pregnancy, even though it was noted that she was depressed. However, she did have a special relationship with one of the clinic nurses, who visited her every day that she worked. A.T. would have benefited greatly from a more structured, day-to-day consultation with a clinical nurse specialist, therapist, or social worker with whom she could have discussed the pregnancy, her current disease state, the prolonged hospitalization, separation from her family, the coping skills needed, and the depression that developed. The only time a counseling session was scheduled for A.T. was after the discussion about a heart transplant. This was not done to work through her depression but as part of the protocol for a heart transplant.

A.T.'s main support person was her grandmother. Frequently during A.T.'s hospitalization, the grandmother was present, and it was noted that her presence was relaxing for A.T. During these visits A.T. talked to her grandmother but very little to her parents or husband. Her family might also have benefited from counseling, since there was little communication among family members.

At no time during the pregnancy was early termination discussed. When she entered the second pregnancy, it was thought that she would have an uneventful pregnancy because she had not developed any major complications with the first pregnancy. In addition, during the first and second trimesters she did not show signs of developing congestive heart failure. However, as the second pregnancy progressed and the cardiac condition deteriorated, termination of the pregnancy might have decreased the workload of the heart and thereby decreased the heart damage she experienced.

IMPLICATIONS FOR PRACTICE

Nursing must be supportive of the strict medical care that is necessary to minimize heart damage in a woman with peripartum cardiomyopathy. In addition, nursing provides a unique service to the patient and family. The nurse's role is not only that of caregiver and practitioner, but also that of patient advocate and educator. In fulfilling each of these roles the nurse develops a special relationship with the patient and her family.

Since a woman is frequently healthy until the diagnosis of peripartum cardiomyopathy, the nurse must work with the woman and family in grieving the loss of health and normal pregnancy status. After this, the woman must begin to progress through the developmental tasks of a high-risk pregnancy. Since the nurse is the most constant health professional in this woman's day-to-day life while hospitalized, the nurse has a responsibility to assist her in acceptance of the disease process and her health status. In addition, as a practitioner the nurse must be skilled in the areas of perinatal and cardiovascular assessment so that subtle changes might be detected early and immediately acted upon.

As an educator the nurse describes for the woman and family the disease process, medications, treatments, and their effects on the fetus. At the same time, she is responsible for educating the woman in the area of normal pregnancy and childbirth. Often childbirth classes will need to be conducted on a one-to-one basis by the nurse at the patient's bedside. After this education the nurse works with the woman relative to family planning within the confines of her medical condition.

In addition, the nurse is an advocate for the patient and her family. The nurse knows the unique needs of this family and works with them to meet these needs. She helps to identify many of the needs for the family so that unasked questions do not develop into unidentified problems.

REFERENCES

1. Homans D. Current concepts: peripartum cardiomyopathy. *N Engl J Med.* 1985;312:1432–1435.

2. Demakis J, Rahimtoola S. Peripartum cardiomyopathy. *Circulation.* 1971;44:964–968.

3. Roth R, Edwards W, Reeder G. Peripartum cardiomyopathy: diagnosis and management. *Minn Med.* 1987;79:517–520.

4. Veille J. Peripartum cardiomyopathies: a review. *Am J Obstet Gynecol.* 1984;148:805–818.

5. Cunningham F, Pritchard J, Hankin G, Anderson P, Lucas M, Armstrong K. Peripartum heart failure: idiopathic cardiomyopathy or compounding cardiovascular events? *Obstet Gynecol.* 1986;67:157–167.

6. Hull E, Hafkesbring E. "Toxic" postpartum heart disease. *N Orleans Med-Surg J.* 1987;89:550–557.

7. Julian D, Szekely P. Peripartum cardiomyopathy. *Prog Cardiovasc Dis.* 1985;27:223–239.

8. Szekely P, Julian D. Heart disease and pregnancy. *Curr Prob Cardiol.* 1979;4(6):3–74.

9. Melvin R, Richardson P, Olsen E, Kaly K, Jackson G. Peripartum cardiomyopathy due to myocarditis. *N Engl J Med.* 1982;307:732–734.

10. Adler A, Davis M. Peripartum cardiomyopathy: two case reports and a review. *Obstet Gynecol Surv.* 1986;41:675–681.

11. Burch G, McDonald C, Wash J. The effect of prolonged bed rest on postpartal cardiomyopathy. *Am Heart J.* 1971;81:186–201.

12. Demakis J, Rahimtoola S, Sutton G, et al. Natural course of peripartum cardiomyopathy. *Circulation.* 1971;44:1053–1061.

13. Gilbert E, Harmon J. *High-Risk Pregnancy and Delivery.* St. Louis, Mo: C.V. Mosby Co.; 1986.

14. Worthington-Roberts B, Vermeersch J, Williams S. *Nutrition in Pregnancy and Lactation.* St. Louis, Mo: C.V. Mosby Co.; 1985.

15. Ouimette J. *Perinatal Nursing Care of the High-Risk Mother and Infant.* Boston: Jones and Bartlett Publishers, Inc.; 1986.

16. McAnulty J, Metcalfe J, Ueland K. General guidelines in the management of cardiac disease. *Clin Obstet Gynecol.* 1981;24:773–786.

17. Perloff J. Pregnancy and cardiovascular disease. In: Braunwald E, ed. *Heart Disease: A Textbook of Cardiovascular Medicine.* 3rd ed. Philadelphia, Pa: W.B. Saunders Co.; 1988.

18. McAdams S, Maguire F. Unusual manifestations of peripartal cardiac disease. *Crit Care Med.* 1986;14:910–912.

19. Ueland K, McAnulty J, Ueland F, Metcalfe J. Special considerations in the use of cardiovascular drugs. *Clin Obstet Gynecol.* 1981;24:809–821.

20. Metcalfe J, McAnulty J, Ueland K. Cardiovascular physiology. *Clin Obstet Gynecol.* 1981;24:693–710.

21. Nesbitt R, Abdual-Karim R. Coincidental disorders complicating pregnancy. In: Danforth D, ed. *Obstet Gynecol.* 4th ed. New York, NY: Harper & Row; 1982.

22. O'Connell J, Costanzo-Nordin M, Subramanian R, et al. Peripartum cardiomyopathy: clinical, hemodynamic, histologic and prognostic characteristics. *J Am Coll Cardiol.* 1986;8:52–56.

23. Aravot D, Banner N, Dhalla N, et al. Heart transplantation for peripartum cardiomyopathy. *Lancet.* 1987;2:1025.

24. Joseph S. Peripartum cardiomyopathy—successful treatment with cardiac transplantation. *West J Med*. 1987;146:230–232.

ADDITIONAL BIBLIOGRAPHY

Fuentes F, Sybers H. Peripartum cardiomyopathy: the value of endomyocardial biopsy in diagnosis prognostication and therapy. *Tex Heart Inst J*. 1988;5(1):55–58.

Gianopoulos J. Cardiac disease in pregnancy. *Med Clin North Am*. 1989;73:639–651.

Goodwin J. Mechanisms in cardiomyopathy. *J Mol Cell Cardiol*. 1985;177(suppl 2):5–9.

Malinow A, Butterworth J, Johnson M, et al. Peripartum cardiomyopathy presenting at cesarean delivery. *Anesthesiology*. 1985;63:545–547.

Sirignano R. Peripartum cardiomyopathy: an application of the Roy adaptation model. *J Cardiovasc Nurs*. 1987;2(1):24–32.

Walsh S. Cardiovascular disease in pregnancy: a nursing approach. *J Cardiovasc Nurs*. 1988;2(4):53–64.

Chapter 16

The Support System of One Primipara following Preterm Birth

Diane J. Angelini

In this chapter, the support system of a primipara after the birth and eventual death of her premature infant are discussed. The purpose in examining this concept of "support system" is to understand the critical dynamics of what "support" means and to identify the support system network for this mother during a critical life event. In this discussion, social support systems and a systems theory framework are utilized, along with selected cybernetics concepts.

REVIEW OF THE LITERATURE

Support, social and otherwise, has long been a concept in clinical nursing practice. The need for social support and the actual support that is available have been shown to be jointly determined by properties of the person and properties of the situation.[1] The need for and availability of support are weighed to determine the level of support necessary to meet the particular need.[1]

Social support schemes can be viewed vis-a-vis the roles that key network members have in relation to a particular individual. A sociogram, for example, is one way to visualize who the social support members are and how their roles change over time. (Figure 16-1).[2]

Norbeck discussed a general guideline for support intervention, which is to produce minimal disruption or alteration in the natural support system, unless it is a pathologic system, while enhancing the capacity of that system to provide support.[1] She further maintained that an individual may need assistance to develop, maintain, or utilize that support network. A key member of the network may be the entry point for enhanced functioning of the support network.

Norbeck's model provides a framework for incorporating social support concepts into clinical nursing practice. She incorporated the nursing process into a social support model that identifies the need for social support, the actual social

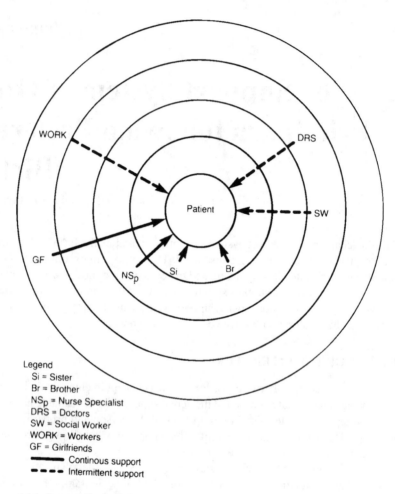

Legend
  Si = Sister
  Br = Brother
  NS$_p$ = Nurse Specialist
  DRS = Doctors
  SW = Social Worker
  WORK = Workers
  GF = Girlfriends
  ━━━ Continous support
  ▬ ▬ ▬ Intermittent support

Figure 16-1 Support Sociogram

support available, and the nursing process of planning, intervention, evaluation, and actual outcome.

Pregnancy, complicated by preterm labor and preterm birth, can be viewed as a situational crisis requiring additional social network supports to assist in amending or resolving the crisis. Pregnancy provides a vivid opportunity to study social support structure and social systems during a critical life event. Cronenwett looked at network structure, social support, and psychologic outcomes in pregnancy.[3] Fifty primigravid fathers and mothers were studied using a tool measuring social network characteristics and perceived social support during the third trimester of pregnancy. At 6 weeks postpartum, this same sample was administered the Postpartum Self-Evaluation Questionnaire (PSQ) developed by Lederman et al.[4]

Cronenwett defined the following types of support as utilized in her study.[3] Emotional support is defined as the person communicating love, caring, trust, or concern, and instrumental support is where the person directly assists through gifts of money, help with chores, help with work, etc. Informational support is when the person communicates things you need to know and helps to solve problems by sharing information or finding out things. Appraisal support is when the person assists in helping you learn about yourself just by being someone in the same situation.

The social network of both men and women was dominated by relatives in the Cronenwett study. Access to emotional and instrumental support was positively associated with 6-week postpartum outcomes; informational and appraisal support were not as significant at this time. However, access to information might be important but may have been sought from professionals and not relatives during this period.

Aaronson studied perceived and received support and their effect on health behavior during pregnancy.[5] Received support was found to be a facilitating factor for positive health behaviors.

Mercer and Ferketich looked at measurements of social support (i.e., perceived support, received support, and network size).[6] Perceived support was the more salient intervening factor in distress responses among the pregnant population studied. A significant positive correlation was noted between network size and perceived support, suggesting that larger networks contribute to the individual's perception of greater support availability.

Social support, however, has not yet been found to affect physical outcomes specifically. Studies are currently under way in preterm birth prevention programs to correlate the role of social support with that of physical outcomes such as preterm labor or preterm birth.[7] It is hypothesized that enhanced social support could reduce preterm birth. Clinical trials of prenatal intervention utilizing supplemental home visits and specific nursing care are currently under way.[7]

General System Theory and Cybernetics

General system theory is concerned with "wholeness" and is defined as a set of elements standing in inter-relations. Miller defined a system as a set of interacting units with inter-relationships among the units.[9] The structure of a system is the arrangement of its subsystems and components in three-dimensional space at a given moment of time. Process is seen as change over time of matter/energy or information.

Information, as defined by Wiener, is "the content of what is exchanged with the outer world as we adjust to it and make our adjustment felt upon it.[10] Utilizing and receiving information is a process of adjusting to the outer environment and interacting with the environment. To live effectively is to live with adequate information. Thus, communication and control of information are basic to one's inner life.

Singer utilized Wiener's informational concepts in defining an open system (i.e., the extent to which boundaries are permeable to information and energy from its environment or from other systems at the same level of analysis.[11] All living systems are considered to be open systems to some extent. In a closed system, there is no exchange of matter, energy, or information with the environment. In a closed system there exists a tendency for entropy or disorder to increase.

Within every system, it is possible to identify one unit or units that carry out a particular process. A subsystem, therefore, seems to be defined by the process it carries out. The structures or structural units carrying out processes are known as components.

The system for this primipara is considered to be an open, living system containing multiple subsystems who carry out critical support processes. The structural components who carry out these processes are composed of health care workers, members of her family of orientation, and personal friends. The goal of the system is to enhance the ability of this primipara to cope with the potential and eventual loss of her infant and to readapt to the environment.

The critical processes of the support subsystems or social networks were:

1. holding system components in appropriate positions and carrying out linkage processes among system members
2. transmitting information regarding the infant's condition
3. processing and decoding information relative to the importance of items
4. providing for affection and empathy
5. assisting in putting decisions into action, interacting with the environment on behalf of others, and increasing the interaction of this primipara with the external environment

* * * * *

CASE STUDY

One mother was in her mid-20s and single. Her infant, who weighed 2 lb 5 1/2 oz, died within 60 hours of preterm birth. The data comprise maternal perceptions of those individuals felt to be part of her support network during the time from birth until 6 weeks postpartum.

One necessary function is to hold the system components in appropriate positions and carry out linkage processes among system members. On the first postpartum day, the social worker helped to maintain system components in contact so they could easily interact. Miller calls this the supporter.[9] "[Social worker] came to see me today . . . . I told her about you [nurse], and she took your name. I guess she called you."

Being confined to a restricted space, this mother relied on others to carry out linkage processes for her. On the second postpartum day, the following inquiry was made, "Do you think the doctor might come today? . . . I just wanted to talk to him. . . . It would be good if you could get a hold of him. I want to know why this happened." In this instance, the nurse was used to acquire information regarding the causation or search for meaning as to why the birth had been premature.

On the third postpartum day, the nurse was further used as a link to other health care workers. "Will I get a copy of the birth certificate, do you know? How about the record of the baptism? Do they give you that? Could you check on it for me?"

One month postdelivery, the nurse was utilized again to acquire autopsy results. This mother acknowledged use of the nurse in linkage to significant others. "I wouldn't have been able to talk to the doctor [regarding autopsy results] if it wasn't for you [nurse]."

Another function is to transmit information regarding the infant's condition. On the first postpartum day, the mother noted, "I'm able to call the nursery whenever I want and go down there as long as someone goes with me. . . . I guess if there's any change [in the baby's condition] they'll call me. . . . I couldn't sleep last night. . . . I worried so I called [NICU] in the middle of the night." The NICU staff were accessible by phone providing information about the infant's condition. For the mother, the telephone was a vital channel in transmitting information.

One month postdelivery, the neonatologist called to provide information regarding autopsy results. "Dr. _____ called me. She didn't tell me much that I didn't already know. She said there was bleeding into the head. . . . She was very nice. She said if I have any other questions to just call her and she'd be happy to talk with me."

The nurse can process information and decode it relative to the importance of items. On the second postpartum day, the mother noted, "I can't understand everything she [neonatologist] says. I know she cares about the baby, but when she's talking, I'm trying to listen and look at the baby, and I can't understand her. I can't hear half of what she's saying." The nurse then decoded the information that had been transmitted so that it would have meaning. Miller defines the decoder as part of the information-processing subsystem.[9] "The decoder alters the code of information input to it through the input transducer into a 'private' code that can be used internally by the system."[9] The nurse thus became the decoder of medical information supplied by others.

On the third postpartum day, there was felt to be a distortion of information, based on memory of past events relative to the baptism record. "Look at the time. The baby wasn't baptized until 8:00 P.M. I think they [hospital] told me that the baby was baptized after the delivery [handing the baptism record to the nurse]." The patient, in this situation, is both the associator and memory as Miller defines them in system theory.[9] The associator functions by making enduring associations among items of information in the system; the memory stores various sorts of infor-

mation in the system. It was perceived that some distortion of information had occurred as it passed through different communication channels. The information
given in the baptism record didn't fit with memory, and some decoding was necessary by the nurse.

On another occasion, the mother commented about the physician. "I still don't
understand everything she [physician] says. It's so technical." The interpretation of
meaning strives for clarity and verifiable accuracy of both insight and comprehen-
sion.

The system also provides for affection and empathy. The system components
involved in carrying out this process comprised the family of orientation and close
personal friends. "One of my friends called to tell me that she is giving a Mass for
the baby. She heard about me and wanted to do something. She's going to give a
Mass for the baby. . . . She said she called the priest and told him about the baby
and how she wanted to pay for the Mass, and he said, 'Nothing doing. This one is
on me.' That was really nice of him."

The phone was a vehicle by which information was given out to others regarding
the condition of the baby and through which sympathy and understanding were
received.

"I called work yesterday. C. ____ answered. He was really surprised to hear from
me. . . . I told him that I was in the hospital and had the baby. He didn't know. He
was really surprised, and he felt really bad."

Within the first week postpartum, following the death of her infant, this mother
received empathetic input from people at work. Both inputs included gifts of money.
She noted: "A. ____ wrote me this nice letter. She said she knew how it was and
what an adjustment it was and everything. Well, she gave me money to buy a ticket
to a dance at work. It was really nice of her to do it."

Another friend at work also gave her a gift. "K. ____ came over last night. She's
one of the girls I work with. Well, she brought me an envelope with money in it from
the people at work. I was really surprised. . . . That was certainly nice of the people
at work."

The support system assists in putting decisions into action. It interacts with the
environment on behalf of others and increases interactions with the external environment. Major components here are family members and close personal friends.

On the third postpartum day, the day of the infant's death, the mother wanted a
Mass said for the infant. She utilized her sister to carry out the arrangements. The
mother made the decision to have the Mass on a day she could feel well enough to
attend. She noted, "Oh, I want to have a Mass for the baby. I don't know when to
have it. I want to feel good enough to go . . . but I want one and I want to be there."
The decision was the mother's, but she utilized the sister to put the decision into
action and interact with the environment in her behalf.

The brother was also utilized to pick up the baby later that day and bring it to the
funeral home. "My brother's going to take care of that for me." In commenting 1
month later, the mother noted: "I didn't know about it [the children's plot at the
cemetery], but my brother has a friend who's a mortician, and he knew about

it. . . . My brother took care of it for me." She later commented, "I went up to the cemetery the other day to plant some grass. I brought J. along with me."

In moving out into the external environment a couple of weeks after the preterm birth, she noted: "I have a girlfriend who lives in Toronto. She's invited me up for a few days. . . . It'll be nice to get away for a while."

Gradually, this mother utilized close personal friends more and began to increase her spatial dimensions within the environment.

*   *   *   *   *

CASE ANALYSIS

This particular woman seemed to be searching for information that would help in coping with her loss and that would assist her regarding events surrounding that loss. Support system components were utilized to serve as the linkage in passing on or acquiring information from each other or from and to the environment. Information may have been decoded by other network components as necessary.

System members were utilized for empathy and affection and to carry out decisions as they involved interaction with the external environment in behalf of this mother and infant. Such interaction consisted mainly of using support members to interact in her behalf.

The environment placed constraints on the system. A channel (e.g., the telephone) caused an overload of inputs at times, but it also provided a vital link in the information communication network.

On the third day of hospitalization, in which the infant died, the mother utilized certain system components (i.e., the nurse, the sister, and the brother) to carry out supportive measures in interaction with the external environment.

She relied heavily on the inner structure of her support system network. It was not an extensive network, but the components were consistent over time and were utilized to carry out critical supportive processes. She made most of her own decisions and, in that sense, monitored or steered the system herself. She relied on system members to supply information and to assist in carrying out decisions. The information channeled to her provided knowledge and control for decision making.

IMPLICATIONS FOR PRACTICE

The elaboration and specificity by which critical support processes were carried out by network components demonstrated just what types of support were needed or solicited and who provided that support for the mother of a preterm infant. Close interaction by family members can be evidenced.

The degree to which system members were significant changed at different times. Health care workers were utilized within the hospital setting; family members bridged the gaps among hospital, home, and immediate environments; and close, personal friends assisted in increasing her interaction with the external environment. The nurse was involved with much of the linkage of system components and information gathering and decoding early in the process, specifically within the hospital environment.

REFERENCES

1. Norbeck J. Social support: a model for clinical research and application. *Adv Nurs Sci.* July 1981;3:43–59.
2. Rich O. The sociogram: a tool for depicting support in pregnancy. *Matern Child Nurs J.* 1978;7:1–9.
3. Cronenwett L. Network structure, social support and psychological outcomes of pregnancy. *Nurs Res.* March–April 1985;34:93–99.
4. Lederman R, et al. Postpartum self-evaluation questionnaire: measures of maternal adaptation. In: Lederman R, et al., eds. *Perinatal Parental Behavior: Nursing Research and Implications for Newborn Health.* New York, NY: Alan R. Liss; 1981.
5. Aaronson L. Perceived and received support: effects on health behavior during pregnancy. *Nurs Res.* January–February 1989;38:4–9.
6. Mercer R, Ferketich S. Stress and social support as predictors of anxiety and depression during pregnancy. *Adv Nurs Sci.* January 1988;10:26–39.
7. Blyce R, et al. The role of social support in the prevention of preterm birth. *Birth.* March 1988;15:19–23.
8. Lumley J. Commentary: rethinking social support in preterm birth prevention. *Birth.* March 1988;15:23–24.
9. Miller J. Living systems: basic concepts. *Behav Sci.* July 1965;10:193–237.
10. Wiener N. *The Human Use of Human Beings.* New York, NY: Avon Books; 1954.
11. Singer JD. *A General Systems Taxonomy for Political Science.* New York, NY: General Learning Press; 1971.

ADDITIONAL BIBLIOGRAPHY

Brown M. Social support during pregnancy: a unidimensional or multidimensional construct? *Nurs Res.* January–February 1986;35:4–9.

Richardson P. Women's important relationships during pregnancy and the preterm labor event. *West J Nurs Res.* May 1987;9:203–217.

Symposium. Social support: critique, retrenchment and refinement. *West J Nurs Res.* February 1987;9:7–73.

Von Bertalanffy L. *General System Theory.* New York, NY: George Braziller, Inc.; 1968.

Chapter 17

Puerperal Mastitis and Breast Abscess

Gayle L. Riedmann

The recent resurgence in the popularity of breast-feeding has resulted in a re-examination of associated complications and recommended treatments. Infectious mastitis of the breast occurs in approximately 10% of women who elect to breast-feed and is almost exclusively a complication of the lactating woman. Breast abscess is a major complication evolving from puerperal mastitis and is usually associated with abrupt weaning during the illness or with a delay in the institution of antibiotic therapy.[1-4] The reported percentage of women developing abscess from mastitis ranges from 4.6%[2] to 11%.[5] Effective treatment usually requires hospitalization with incision and drainage as well as subsequent antibiotic therapy based on culture and sensitivity.[6] The incidence of breast abscess can be greatly reduced by early recognition and treatment of infectious mastitis. Recent changes in the diagnosis and treatment of infectious mastitis and current recommendations for management are discussed.

REVIEW OF THE LITERATURE

Mastitis is an inflammation of the breast. It is often referred to as *sporadic puerperal mastitis* when discussing breast infection in lactating mothers. It results from an invasion of the breast tissue by bacteria, usually *Staphylococcus aureus*.[2,7] The most common etiologic factors are milk stasis secondary to weaning or missed feeding and fissure of the involved breast.[2,3] Other contributing factors include improper positioning of the baby at the breast, prolonged periods between feedings, supplementary bottles or overuse of a pacifier, too-tight bras, anemia,

---

The case study described in this chapter is dedicated to the memory of Dr. Michael Newton, a pioneer in breast-feeding research who provided expert consultation in the management of the patient and assistance in the drafting of this case study.

stress, and fatigue.[8–10] Onset of symptoms is often abrupt. The affected breast becomes hot, flushed, and painful, with a localized hardness or lump. Fever, often exceeding 102°F, is accompanied by chills, malaise, and headache. The average onset is 2 to 3 weeks after delivery, peaking again at 6 weeks.[1,2,11]

Breast abscess results if the inflammatory reaction persists because of delayed or inappropriate treatment of mastitis. A large, hard mass in the affected breast which is painful, red, and warm to touch with edema of the overlying skin assists in the diagnosis. An area of fluctuation may be noted and, if far advanced, "pointing" may be seen. Needle aspiration may demonstrate the presence of pus. The most commonly cultured organism in breast abscess is *S. aureus*[3] although *Salmonella, Pseudomonas, Eschericha coli*, and *Proteus* may be found.[6] Treatment should be undertaken rapidly, as excessive destruction of breast tissue can occur by the time the abscess shows obvious fluctuation or skin involvement.

Prior to the development of antibiotics, the maternal morbidity associated with puerperal mastitis and subsequent breast abscess was considerably higher. Penicillin therapy had a significant influence in reducing the incidence of breast abscess. A classic 1950 study by Newton and Newton analyzing cases of breast abscess in lactating women occurring from 1940 to 1949 reported a decline from 0.82 per 100 deliveries before penicillin to 0.47 after the advent of penicillin.[3] This key study linked the development of breast abscess with lactation failure, specifically a failure in the let-down reflex due to pain, emotional upheaval, or fear. Inhibition of the let-down reflex and subsequent milk stasis combined with exposure to pathogenic bacteria predisposed to the development of mastitis and breast abscess. Trauma to the nipple was reported to occur in 23% of patients developing breast abscess, although this figure should probably be much higher as it is difficult to determine the presence of small fissures or cracks in the nipple. Forty-two percent of women reported some difficulty with their breasts during the first 2 weeks postpartum. In the 1940s, the time of this study, it was customary to discontinue lactation when infection occurred due to suspected danger of infecting the baby or delaying breast healing. Subsequent studies have refuted this belief.[1,2,5] However, this has remained controversial, as many present-day obstetricians and breast surgeons continue to advise women to stop nursing when mastitis or abscess are diagnosed.[12]

Only a few studies examining the appropriate management of mastitis have been done in recent years,[1,2,5] but they have had a major influence on current recommendations. Two aspects of ongoing debate have emerged: continued breastfeeding in the presence of mastitis and the value of leukocyte count and culture and sensitivity of breast milk to direct treatment.

Devereux studied 71 cases of mastitis in 53 patients from 1948 to 1968.[1] Management included ice packs, breast support without binding, analgesics, antibiotics, and continued nursing. Forty-seven patients were able to continue lactation during and following mastitis. Eight abscesses occurred, comprising 11.1% of the total of 71 cases of mastitis. Six of the 8 patients developing abscesses had delayed treatment longer than 24 hours. Based on these findings, the author recommended prompt, early treatment of mastitis with antibiotics and continued nursing to prevent abscess. Development of abscess was considered a strict contraindication to breast-feeding.

A prospective study done by Marshall, Hepper, and Zirbel in 1975 significantly affected the recommended treatment regime of infectious mastitis.[2] Sixty-five separate cases of acute puerperal mastitis occurring in 2534 women who elected breast-feeding were evaluated to define the incidence, bacteriology, clinical features, and response to treatment. Particular interest was directed to the effect of continued nursing on the course of the illness. Upon diagnosis, milk was obtained for culture and all patients were treated with antibiotic therapy. The reported incidence of mastitis was 2.5%, with 41 women continuing to lactate for an average of 13 weeks. Fifteen women elected weaning at time of infection. Notably, 3 breast abscesses occurred in that group, for an incidence of 4.6%. Milk stasis secondary to weaning or missed feeding preceded 9 of 65 cases of mastitis; fissure of the involved breast was noted in 8 patients. S. *aureus* was cultured from 23 of 48 cultures obtained. No adverse effects of continued lactation were noted on the mother or infant. The authors concluded with their observation that "lactation can and perhaps should be continued during treatment, as it may speed recovery and will not adversely affect the infant."[2(p1379)]

In 1983 a prospective study by Thomsen, Hansen, and Moller examined the value of leukocyte counts and bacteriologic cultivations of milk samples in the diagnosis of puerperal mastitis in nursing women.[13] Because of the frequency with which inflammatory symptoms of the breast occur in nursing women, diagnosis and management was directed by the presence of leukocytosis and bacteria in the breast milk rather than by symptoms alone. In this study, inflammatory signs of the breasts (swelling, tenderness, redness, heat, disturbed lactation, and fever) were recorded for 3 weeks postpartum. Milk samples were collected weekly from all patients. A total of 491 milk samples were examined. In women with inflammatory symptoms, three separate groups were identified based on leukocyte counts and culture results: (1) milk stasis: leukocyte counts of less than 10^6/ml of milk; (2) noninfectious inflammation of the breast: leukocyte counts greater than 10^6/ml and sterile or skin contaminated culture of less than 10^3/ml; (3) infectious mastitis: leukocyte counts greater than 10^6/ml and bacterial count greater than 10^3/ml.

Significant variation in the duration of symptoms was noted. In women with milk stasis, the symptoms lasted an average of 2.1 days and were self-limiting. The average duration of symptoms in the noninfectious inflammation group was 5.3 days; in the infectious mastitis group, however, the average was 5.9 days. The primary purpose of this study was to form a basis for diagnosis and classification; therefore, appropriate treatment of these cases was left for future study.

Thompsen et al. in 1984 utilized the categories proposed in the previous study to estimate the duration and outcome of milk stasis, noninfectious inflammation, and infectious mastitis.[5] Treatments of breast emptying and antibiotics were based on leukocyte counts in the milk in addition to quantitative bacteriologic cultivation.

Milk stasis (leukocyte counts of $<10^6$/ml of milk) was of 2 days duration only, and the outcome was usually favorable regardless of treatment. Treatment of noninfectious inflammation of the breast ($>10^6$/ml leukocyte count with sterile or skin-contaminated culture) by emptying of the breast resulted in a significant decrease in the duration of symptoms (3.2 days) and a significantly improved outcome. Without treatment, the duration of symptoms was 7.9 days, with infectious mastitis (leukocyte counts $>10^6$/ml of milk and bacterial counts of $>10^3$/ml) treated with antibiotics and emptying of the breast resulted in normal lactation in 96% of the cases, with a mean duration of symptoms of 2.1 days. Antibiotic therapy initiated without sensitivity tests resulted in mastitis recurrence in 10%. Emptying of the breast without antibiotic therapy in cases of infectious mastitis reduced the rate of a good outcome to 50% and increased the duration of symptoms to 4.2 days. Without treatment, the outcome of infectious mastitis was poor, with only 15% of cases able to continue nursing and 11% developing breast abscess. This study's findings are consistent with those of Devereux regarding the incidence of breast abscess after mastitis.[1] Based on the results of their study, the authors recommend the following treatment regimen for inflammatory symptoms of the breast: (1) Leukocyte and bacterial counts of the milk and antibiotic susceptibility tests of isolated bacteria should be carried out. (2) Cases of milk stasis need no specific treatment. (3) Noninfectious inflammation of the breast should be treated with regular emptying of the breast and sensitivity-directed antibiotic therapy.

The issue of patient motivation to pursue emptying of the breast was not addressed in this study. In cases of noninfectious inflammation, the dramatic difference in the treatment group (continuation of normal lactation, 96%; duration of symptoms, 2.1 days) vs. the no-treatment group (normal lactation, 21%; duration of symptoms, 7.9 days) suggested the need for careful consideration of this issue. The nontreatment group also experienced a subsequent infectious mastitis rate of almost 50%. Therefore, early initiation of antibiotic therapy in patients who are identified as being poorly motivated may be wise.

The value of obtaining a culture of expressed milk has remained controversial. The result of the culture may be unreliable because the infection involves the periglandular structures and not the ducts. In addition, culture of all cases of mastitis may prove impractical because the infection is usually under control by the time the sensitivity studies are available. A recent study by Matheson et al. investigating clinical symptoms, bacterial content in breast milk, and treatment in 43 women with puerperal mastitis found no difference concerning the coagulase-negative staphylocci and overall bacterial counts, either between milk from affected and nonaffected breasts or between milk from nonaffected breasts and milk from healthy donors.[4] The authors concluded that bacterial examination of breast milk is of limited value in deciding who needs antibiotic treatment as it has no discriminating ability between patients with short-lived and protracted symptoms. However, in cases of severe, prolonged, or recurrent mastitis, culture may be useful to direct antibiotic therapy.

Antibiotic therapy is generally recommended for treatment of cases of mastitis, even though its necessity is uncertain. Matheson et al. reported that penicillin treatment is questionable in light of the fact that, in his study, untreated cases healed almost as quickly as treated ones and that 70% of the *S. aureus* strains proved resistant to penicillin anyway.[4] A survey of women attending breast-feeding conferences by Riordan and Nichols found that more than one-third of the respondents did not contact their physician when they developed mastitis and nearly half never used antibiotics for the infection.[10] This suggests that host defense mechanisms are effective in controlling the infection and that nonprescriptive remedies such as massage, heat, and continued breast-feeding should not be underestimated.

When puerperal breast abscess is diagnosed, the literature universally agrees that incision and drainage is necessary, with or without antibiotic therapy.[3,12,14–17] The issue of continued lactation in the presence of breast abscess remains controversial, generally due to unsubstantiated fears of infecting the newborn. Most recent recommendations encourage women to continue breast-feeding, as lactation inhibition may hinder the rapid resolution of the abscess by increasing secretions that tend to promote rather than decrease breast engorgement.[17] Lactation can be supported through the use of a breast pump, manual expression, or infant sucking.

*   *   *   *   *

CASE STUDY

M.S. is a 23-year-old gravida I, para I who had a normal spontaneous vaginal delivery of a 6-lb 10-oz infant girl over an intact perineum. The first day postpartum was uneventful except for some difficulty nursing the infant. The infant was described as a "reluctant nurser" with poor latch-on and suck reflex, frequently falling asleep at the breast. The uncertainty and lack of confidence of M.S. in her ability to nurse the infant exacerbated the problem, even though a sleepy infant is considered normal during the first 24 hours of life. The lactation consultant was requested to visit the patient to assist in appropriate positioning and feeding. Little improvement was noted the second day postpartum, as the patient continued to have difficulty despite frequent encouragement from the nursing staff and the lactation consultant. M.S. was well motivated, however, and continued to work with the infant until a successful breast-feeding relationship was established.

M.S. was discharged on postpartum day 3 with emphasis on instructions to notify the nurse-midwife if symptoms of mastitis occurred, along with the usual postpartum instructions. She complained of slight nipple soreness and a small suck blister on the left breast. Follow-up by the lactation consultant on day 5 and day 10 postpartum revealed improvement in the infant's alertness and suck; however, the patient reported becoming frequently engorged. Frequent emptying of the breast was re-emphasized to prevent engorgement, as well as a review of the symptoms of mastitis. M.S. stated that the suck blister of the left breast had healed and denied any tenderness or inflammation of either breast.

Approximately 4 weeks postpartum M.S. complained of a tender, hardened area of the left breast above the nipple. She denied fever or flu-like symptoms. She was seen immediately by the lactation consultant, and a blocked duct was diagnosed. M.S. was advised to continue breast-feeding with therapeutic heat, massage, and nursing on the affected side. No improvement was noted 4 days later, and the involved breast had become reddened and more painful. She remained afebrile, however, and no fluctuation was noted upon physical examination. Physician consultation was obtained. An antibiotic regimen of dicloxicillin, 500 mg p.o. q.i.d. for 10 days, was initiated because of the persistence of the blocked duct, despite the absence of fever. M.S. admitted to having difficulty following the plan of heat, massage, and frequent nursing, as it had become too painful. She had resorted to hand pumping the affected side but was unable to express any milk. A different model of hand pump was ordered, as well as an electric pump for greater ease and more effective suction. The patient was observed while she massaged and pumped the affected breast to assure complete emptying.

M.S. was re-examined in the office 3 days later, and a slight improvement was noted, with a decrease in size and tenderness of the induration. This, however, was followed by a worsening of symptoms a few days later, including fever and chills. Physical examination revealed a well-delineated breast mass with a 1-cm area of fluctuance. Needle aspiration of the involved duct was attempted, yielding approximately 10 ml of pus, which was sent for culture and sensitivity. Antibiotic therapy was changed to erythromycin, 500 mg p.o. q.i.d., while awaiting sensitivity studies. Due to successful needle aspiration, a delay of surgical incision and drainage was elected.

Three days later, the patient developed fever above 102°F. She was immediately referred to a breast surgeon, whereupon incision and drainage was performed. A circumareolar incision was made, yielding approximately 100 ml of pus from the left breast. Culture and sensitivity revealed penicillin-resistant *S. aureus*. The patient's fever resolved postoperatively, and her subsequent course was uneventful.

Although the surgeons were reluctant, M.S. was offered the opportunity to continue breast-feeding from the unaffected breast. Arrangements for bringing the baby to the hospital for feedings during the day were planned by her husband and mother. Despite this support, however, M.S. elected to discontinue breast-feeding at the time of surgery.

* * * * *

CASE ANALYSIS

Prevention of infection is the most important concept in the treatment of mastitis. Breast-feeding instruction should begin antepartum with careful examination of the breasts for flat or inverted nipples. Appropriate use of breast shields as necessary in such patients should be started prenatally to prevent trauma once nursing is initiated. A thorough discussion of attitudes and desire to breast-feed should be explored, as women who express dislike of or indifference to breast-feeding may be more prone to infection due to inhibition of the let-down reflex.[3] All pregnant women should be provided with adequate resources to support breast-feeding, including written materials, classes, and informative groups such as La Leche League. A hospital-based lactation consultant can be a helpful adjunct to a successful breast-feeding program.

Continued efforts at preventing mastitis during the immediate postpartum period are illustrated in the case of M.S. Early identification of her difficulty nursing the infant prompted referral to the lactation consultant and notification of the nursing staff. Appropriate instruction and assistance was provided in positioning for correct latch-on and awakening the infant for feeding to prevent engorgement. Careful examination of the breast was conducted to look for suck blisters, lesions, cracks, or scabs on the nipples, which provide portal of entry for bacteria. Such support and teaching assisted the patient in continuing her efforts to breast-feed and encouraged her to work with the infant. Prior to discharge, verbal and written instructions of the signs and symptoms of mastitis are of vital importance, as early diagnosis and treatment are necessary to prevent the development of breast abscess. Follow-up phone calls were also made to check on progress and reinforce teaching.

Despite efforts to prevent mastitis, some patients will develop the early signs, as in the case of M.S. The purpose of treatment of mastitis should be to prevent the serious complication of breast abscess and allow lactation to continue: Diagnosis of milk stasis or a blocked duct usually requires only the following therapy:

1. moist heat to the affected breast for 15 minutes prior to nursing
2. gentle massage of the involved duct while nursing
3. frequent nursing (at least every 2 to 3 hours) beginning on the affected side (engorgement to be strictly avoided)
4. bed rest
5. increased fluids

6. removal of constrictive bra if any question of it being too tight

M.S. was seen frequently in an attempt to forestall the development of infectious mastitis. She was observed using the breast pump to assure adequate emptying of the breast. However, if symptoms persist, as they did with M.S., the following actions should be added:

7. culture and sensitivity of milk sample from the affected breast
8. institution of antibiotic therapy as indicated by sensitivity study

Unfortunately, culture was not obtained on M.S. during initial therapy. Most cases of infectious mastitis will respond to dicloxicillin, but her infection proved resistant. Despite efforts to remedy the developing abscess with a change in antibiotics and needle aspiration, she ultimately required surgical intervention. M.S. was remarkable in her motivation to continue nursing despite a prolonged period of breast involvement. Her motivation ceased, however, with the decision to operate. The circumareolar incision prohibited breast-feeding from the involved breast. Although M.S. was provided the option to continue nursing on the unaffected breast, she declined.

IMPLICATIONS FOR PRACTICE

The proportion of women choosing to breast-feed is increasing. While the benefits derived from breast-feeding for the mother and infant are numerous, the risk of complications remains a disadvantage. Mastitis occurs in up to 10% of lactating women, primarily due to milk stasis secondary to weaning or engorgement and/or trauma to the nipple. Many cases of mastitis and subsequent breast abscess can be prevented by conscientious patient teaching beginning in the immediate postpartum period. Health care providers should be knowledgeable of measures to prevent the development of mastitis, as listed in Table 17-1.

Puerperal mastitis can be successfully resolved without interruption of breast-feeding by prompt recognition and appropriate treatment. The frequent withdrawal of milk with infant suckling may reduce the risk of breast abscess by removing invading organisms before they have the chance to multiply.[16] While the vast majority of current textbooks of general obstetrics and gynecology recommend the continuation of breast-feeding,[14-16] one of the most widely read texts still maintains the opposite view.[12]

When caring for the postpartum lactating woman, the old adage, "flu in the breast-feeding mother is mastitis until proven otherwise," provides the best advice to health providers. The serious sequelae of a breast abscess can be avoided by conscientious instruction of patients to recognize early signs of mastitis and by the institution of early therapeutic management.

Table 17-1 The Practitioner's Role in the Prevention of Mastitis/Breast Abscess

Action	Rationale
1. Promote early breast-feeding after delivery without restriction on time	Encourages early flow of milk and prevents engorgement
2. Instruct and observe patient in correct positioning of the infant while nursing	Avoids trauma to nipple
3. Review warning signs of mastitis prior to discharge and at postpartum visits	Allows prompt recognition and early treatment
4. Provide information for suggested reading, pamphlets, lactation consultant hotline, support groups	Provides support and additional resources to reinforce teaching
5. In cases of mastitis: emphasize importance of therapeutic measures: frequent nursing, heat, massage, rest, fluids	Promotes resolution without antibiotic therapy (if afebrile and <24 hr)
6. Careful patient follow-up and initiation of antibiotics if symptoms not resolved within 24 hr or fever develops	Risk of abscess is greater in cases of febrile mastitis not treated within 24 hr

REFERENCES

1. Devereux WP. Acute puerperal mastitis: evaluation of its management. *Am J Obstet Gynecol.* 1970;108:78–81.

2. Marshall BR, Hepper JK, Zirbel CC. Sporadic puerperal mastitis. *JAMA.* 1975;233:1377–1379.

3. Newton M, Newton N. Breast abscess: a result of lactation failure. *Surg Gynecol Obstet.* 1950;91:651–655.

4. Matheson I, Aursnes I, Horgan M, Aabo O, Melby K. Bacteriological findings and clinical symptoms in relation to clinical outcome in puerperal mastitis. *Acta Obstet Gynecol Scand.* 1988;67:723–726.

5. Thompsen AC, Espersen T, Maigaard S. Course and treatment of milk stasis, noninfectious inflammation of the breast, and infectious mastitis in nursing women. *Am J Obstet Gynecol.* 1984;149:492–495.

6. Johnsen C. Inflammatory lesions of the breast. In: Strombeck JO, Rosato FE, eds. *Surgery of the Breast: Diagnosis and Treatment of Breast Diseases.* New York, NY: Thieme, Inc.; 1986.

7. Sarkar DS, Agarwal DS, Mukherjee P. Bacteriological study of breast abscess with special reference to *Staph. aureus. Indian J Med Res.* 1979;70:384–390.

8. La Leche League International. *The Womanly Art of Breastfeeding.* 4th ed. La Leche League International Press; 1987.

9. Huggins K. *The Nursing Mother's Companion.* Boston, Mass: Harvard Common Press; 1986.

10. Riordan JM, Nichols FH. A descriptive study of lactation mastitis in long-term breastfeeding women. *J Hum Lactation.* 1990;6:53–58.

11. Niebyl JR, Spence MR, Parmley TH. Sporadic (non-epidemic) puerperal mastitis. *J Reprod Med.* 1978;20:97–100.

12. Cunningham FG, MacDonald PC, Gant NF. *Williams Obstetrics.* 18th ed. E. Norwalk, Conn.: Appleton & Lange; 1989.

13. Thomsen AC, Hansen K, Moller BR. Leukocyte counts and microbiologic cultivation in the diagnosis of puerperal mastitis. *Am J Obstet Gynecol.* 1983;146:938–941.

14. Danforth DN, Scott JR. *Obstetrics and Gynecology.* 5th ed. Philadelphia, Pa: JB Lippincott Co.; 1986.

15. Mishell DR, Brenner PF. *Management of Common Problems in Obstetrics and Gynecology.* Oradell, NJ: Medical Economics Books; 1988.

16. Phillipp E, Barnes J, Newton M. *Scientific Foundations of Obstetrics and Gynecology.* London, England: William Heinemann Medical Books; 1986.

17. Benson EA. Management of breast abscess. *World J. Surg.* 1989;13:753–756.

ADDITIONAL BIBLIOGRAPHY

Dilts CL. Nursing management of mastitis due to breastfeeding. *J Obstet, Gynecol Neonat Nurs.* 1985;14:286–288.

Dudley H, Carter D, Russell RC. *Atlas of General Surgery.* Boston, Mass: Butterworths; 1986.

Ezrati JB. Puerperal mastitis: causes, prevention, and management. *J Nurse-Midwifery.* 1979;24(6):3–8.

Keen G. *Operative Surgery and Management.* 2nd ed. New York, NY: Macmillan Publishing Co., Inc.; 1987.

Lawrence RA. *Breastfeeding: A Guide for the Medical Profession.* St. Louis, Mo: C.V. Mosby Co.; 1985.

Neville MC, Neifert MR. *Lactation: Physiology, Nutrition, and Breastfeeding.* New York, NY Plenum Press; 1983.

Rhode MA. Postpartum management. In: Barger MK, Lops VR, Fullerton JT, Rhode MA, eds. *Protocols for Gynecologic and Obstetric Health Care.* Orlando, Fla: Grune & Stratton; 1988:188–190.

Varney H. *Nurse-Midwifery.* Boston, Mass: Blackwell Scientific Publications; 1987.

Chapter 18

Postpartum Vulvar Edema Syndrome

Christine M. Whelan Knapp

The United States maternal mortality rate has decreased dramatically in the past 50 years. In 1985, the rate for all races was 7.8/100,000 live births.[1] All professionals dealing with pregnancy need to be vigilant in decreasing this statistic further. When a syndrome is identified that has an extremely high mortality rate, it should be examined closely. Postpartum vulvar edema syndrome is extremely rare but, in the five cases reported, it has been shown to have an 80% mortality rate.[2,3]

REVIEW OF THE LITERATURE

When postpartum vulvar edema was first identified, speculation existed that it could be necrotizing fasciitis.[2] Necrotizing fasciitis was first reported in the literature in 1871.[4] It is extremely rare, it has a high mortality rate, and the causative agents are many, including both aerobic and anaerobic bacteria. The outstanding feature is fulminating fascial necrosis. The treatment is surgical debridement of necrotic areas and antibiotic therapy.

Rea and Wyrick in 1970 reported 44 cases of necrotizing fasciitis in 15 years of a busy surgical practice.[5] They had a 30% mortality rate. All but one patient was older than 50 years and had either diabetes mellitus or severe arteriosclerosis.

The first report of necrotizing fasciitis in the gynecologic literature was by Roberts and Hester in 1972.[6] They reported six cases in diabetic women with Bartholin's abscesses and had a 50% mortality rate. In the obstetric literature to date, there has been only one report involving four cases of necrotizing fasciitis.[4] The report presents four cases in nine years at Los Angeles County/University of Southern California Women's Hospital, which has an extremely large obstetric population. The four patients, one of whom had a cesarean section, presented with fever and inflammation. They all had positive cultures and necrotic fascia. The mortality rate was 50%.

In 1979, Ewing, Smale, and Elliott reported four women who presented with a syndrome of unilateral postpartum vulvar edema.[2] Although their clinical courses were similar to that of bacterial gangrene, there were no positive blood or tissue cultures in three of the four women and, in the remaining case, the bacteria identified was not thought to be the cause of the patient's condition.[2] This syndrome is characterized by late-developing massive unilateral vulvar edema and compromised blood supply, as demonstrated by minimal bleeding encountered when intervention was attempted.

All cases will be reviewed here, as there are so few in the literature (Table 18-1). All of the women were healthy, pregnant patients without any complicating disease. Symptoms began on the second postpartum day or later.

Case 1 was a 19-year-old para I who had a normal antenatal and intrapartum course. Her term infant was delivered by low forceps with the use of caudal and saddle block anesthesia. She did sustain a fourth degree laceration of the perineum. On the second postpartum day, she had a sudden onset of unilateral vulvar edema. Her white blood count at this time was 33,000/cu mm with a left shift. The term *left shift* is derived from the practice of differential cell counting and indicates an increase in the proportion of cells with only one or few lobes; these younger forms suggest an increased release of young neutrophils from the bone marrow and are seen in association with acute infection and inflammation.[7,8] Her temperature was 39.4° Centigrade. She underwent incision and drainage of her ischiorectal fossa, but no abscess was found and bleeding was minimal. Treatment by antibiotics and steroids was started. On the fourth postpartum day, the patient had a cardiovascular collapse. Despite emergency treatment, the patient died. An autopsy was denied. All cultures were negative.

The second case was a 16-year-old para I with a normal antenatal and intrapartum course. She delivered at term with low forceps. Epidural anesthesia was administered. She had a median episiotomy with a third degree extension. Again, the sudden onset of unilateral vulvar edema began on the second postpartum day. Her white blood count was 32,500/cu mm with a left shift, and her temperature was 38.5°Centigrade. Urine and blood cultures were negative. Her lochia cultures revealed *Klebsiella*, *Aerobacter*, and *Bacteroides*. They were not deemed to have any significance as similar organisms can be cultured from asymptomatic postpartum patients.[2] Treatment consisted of local heat, antibiotics, and steroids. However, on postpartum day 4, she had an onset of vascular collapse and, despite emergency measures including pressor and volume therapy, she died. Autopsy results demonstrated marked hemorrhage, inflammation, and edema of perineal and vaginal tissues.

Case 3 involved a 24-year-old para II who spontaneously delivered a term infant. Pudendal anesthesia was administered, and a median episiotomy was performed. On the third postpartum day, she developed unilateral vulvar edema. Her

Table 18-1 Published Patient Data of Postpartum Vulvar Edema Syndrome

Case	Year	Age	Parity	Duration of Preg.	Mode of Delivery	Anesthesia	Type of Episiotomy	Admitting WBC* (no./cu mm)	Temp.* (°C)	Day of Vascular Collapse	Outcome	Autopsy Results
1	1969	19	1	Term	Forceps	Caudal/Saddle	4th degree	33,000	39.4	4	Died	Autopsy denied
2	1971	16	1	Term	Forceps	Epidural	3rd degree	32,500	38.5	4	Died	Inflammation, edema of perineum
3	1976	24	2	Term	Spontaneous	Pudendal	Median	30,200	38.2	4	Died	Inflammation, necrosis of perineum
4	1976	15	1	Term	Forceps	Saddle	4th degree	22,300	37.2	—	Alive	Discharged on 23rd postpartum day
5	1985	26	5	Term	Forceps	Epidural	Median	28,000	37.1	4	Died	Inflammation, necrosis of perineum

*At time of vulvar edema

Source: adapted by author from Ewing TL[2] and Finkler NJ.[3]

episiotomy was opened and drained. She also underwent an incision and drainage of her vaginal and gluteal areas. No bleeding was encountered. Antibiotics and steroids were administered. Her white blood count was 30,200/cu mm with a left shift and her temperature was 38.2° Centigrade. Despite treatment, she sustained a cardiovascular collapse and died on day 4. Her perineal and vaginal cultures revealed *Clostridium sordelii* and coagulase-negative *Staphylococcus*. However, they were not felt to be the cause of the patient's condition.[2]

The last case in this report involved a 15-year-old para I who delivered her infant at term with low forceps and saddle block anesthesia. She had a median episiotomy and a fourth degree laceration. On the third postpartum day, she developed unilateral vulvar edema. Her white blood count was 22,300/cu mm with a left shift and her temperature was 37.2° Centigrade. Her episiotomy was opened. Again, there was no bleeding from this procedure. All of her cultures were negative. She was treated with antibiotics, steroids, and pressor therapy. She was discharged on the 23rd postpartum day.

Finkler et al., in 1987, reported a case of bilateral postpartum vulvar edema associated with maternal death.[3] This case is presented here since the author had partially cared for the patient antepartally.

*   *   *   *   *

CASE STUDY

L.Q., a 26-year-old gravida VII, para IV, abortus II, had an essentially normal antenatal course. She had no significant previous medical, surgical, or obstetrical history. She denied any allergies. On physical examination, she was noted to have varicosities in her lower extremities. Her laboratory data revealed a hematocrit of 31%. L.Q.'s obstetrical history was as follows:

Year	Weeks Gestation	Weight	Mode	Anesthesia
1975	Term	8⁴	Forceps	Spinal
1977	Term	9⁵	Spontaneous	Epidural
1978	Term	7⁸	Spontaneous	Epidural
1980	Term (Twins)	7⁶, 5⁵	Spontaneous	Epidural
1981	Induced abortion, 13 weeks			
1983	Induced abortion, 13 weeks			

Her present pregnancy was at 42 weeks gestation with a reactive, reassuring nonstress test, when she was admitted in active labor. Her labor progressed rapidly.

9 A.M.	3/75%/−1	Vertex occiput posterior
		Spontaneous rupture of membranes
		Epidural requested and initiated
12 Noon	7/100%/+1	Occiput posterior
12:30 P.M.		Midforceps rotation with median episiotomy
		Delivery of female infant, 8 lb, Apgar 8/9

There was a reactive, reassuring fetal heart rate tracing throughout labor.

L.Q. had a normal postpartum course. She did complain of some discomfort from the episiotomy site. Progress notes record the area as slightly swollen but within normal limits. L.Q. was discharged home on her third postpartum day. She returned the next day complaining of severe perineal pain. Dramatic bilateral vulvar edema was seen with minimal erythema. The patient's vital signs were normal and her temperature was 37.1° Centigrade. The vulva was transilluminated and aspirated. This revealed minimal clear fluid which was gram-stained negative. The patient's white blood count was 28,000/cu mm with a left shift. Blood cultures were obtained and, at this time, a preliminary diagnosis of vulvar cellulitis was made. Triple antibiotics of ampicillin, gentamicin, and clindamycin were started. Demerol and Vistaril were ordered for pain.

Approximately 6 hours later, L.Q. had a cardiorespiratory arrest with electromechanical disassociation. Resuscitation efforts were without success.

The autopsy revealed marked vulvar edema with inflammation. All cultures taken pre- and postdeath were negative.

$$* \quad * \quad * \quad * \quad *$$

CASE ANALYSIS

This is the only case of a woman with bilateral postpartum edema associated with maternal death. This essentially healthy patient had a normal antepartal and intrapartum course. The massive vulvar edema was late in onset. She did have leukocytosis, but all cultures were negative. The cause of this disease process is unclear.

Unilateral vulvar edema differs from necrotizing fasciitis in that no causative agent has been determined. Necrotizing fasciitis is usually identified by skin necrosis and abscess formation; unilateral and bilateral postpartum vulvar edema syndromes, however, are characterized by edema that is *dramatic* and *massive* and by a compromised blood supply. As Ewing et al. stated, "The common histologic change found in all biopsy and autopsy sections is one of subcutaneous and soft tissue edema and inflammation beginning unilaterally in the area of the episiotomies. Edema was present not only in the vulvar tissues but also at autopsy to the retroperitoneal tissues and the mesentery."[2(p174–175)]

The four cases of unilateral vulvar edema demonstrate late onset and leukocytosis, and all but one had vascular collapse. Although temperature elevations were present in all case reports, three of the five women were ≤38.2° Centigrade.

Speculation has ensued over the presence of an endotoxin.[3] At present, none has been identified. It has been postulated that the source of the endotoxin could be the bowel, as all women were delivered vaginally with episiotomies.[2,3] Fever tolerance can also be a symptom of endotoxin sepsis.[9]

There has been considerable thought given to the hypothesis that postpartum vulvar edema syndrome could have an immunologic cause, although none has been identified to date.[2,3]

IMPLICATIONS FOR PRACTICE

Postpartum vulvar edema syndrome, with only five cases reported in the literature, is poorly understood and highly lethal. Review of the literature does, however, yield implications for practice.[2,3]

It is imperative to inspect all postpartum edema, particularly that which occurs on the second postpartum day or later. When this occurs, there should be frequent and aggressive monitoring of the patient's condition when unusual vulvar edema causes suspicion of this syndrome. A complete blood count and cultures, including blood and gram stain, should be obtained. Broad-spectrum antibiotics should be started. There is controversy over the usage of steroids in this syndrome. Ewing et al. began steroids after their patients began to lose intravascular volume, which was early in the disease process, and advocated their usage.[2] Others feel that steroids could interfere with the leukocytic response to the infection and do not recommend them.[2]

If an episiotomy is present, it should be opened to ensure that necrotizing fasciitis is not present. If it is present, the patient should be taken to the operating room for surgical debridement. Since the usual progression of postpartum vulvar edema syndrome is to cardiovascular collapse, aggressive hemodynamic monitoring may be needed. This will include both peripheral blood pressures and left heart filling pressures as measured by arterial line and Swan-Ganz catheter, respectively. The left heart filling pressures will indicate whether vasopressor, cardiac stimulant, or volume replacement therapy, or some combination of the three, is most appropriate. The peripheral blood pressures will help determine the response to therapy.

REFERENCES

1. Ellerbrock TV, Atrash HK, Hogue CJP, Smith JC. Pregnancy mortality surveillance: a new initiative. *Contemp OB/GYN.* 1988;31:23–24.
2. Ewing TL, Smale LE, Elliott FA. Maternal deaths associated with postpartum vulvar edema. *Am J Obstet Gynecol.* 1979;121:173–197.
3. Finkler NJ, Safon LE, Ryan KJ. Bilateral postpartum vulvar edema associated with maternal death. *Am J Obstet Gynecol.* 1987;156:1188–1189.
4. Golde S, Ledger WJ. Necrotizing fasciitis in postpartum patients. *Obstet Gynecol.* 1977;50:670–673.
5. Rea WJ, Wyrick WJ. Necrotizing fasciitis. *Ann Surg.* 1970;172:957–964.

6. Roberts DB, Hester LL. Progressive synergistic bacterial gangrene arising from abscesses of the vulva and Bartholin's gland duct. *Am J Obstet Gynecol.* 1972;114:285–291.

7. Marsh JC, et al. Neutrophil kinetics in acute infections. *J Clin Invest.* 1967;46:1946.

8. Wintrobe MM, et al. *Clinical Hematology.* Philadelphia, Pa: Lea and Febiger; 1981.

9. Milner KC. Patterns of tolerance to endotoxin. *J Infect Dis.* 1973;128:S237–S245.

Chapter 19

Rape Trauma Syndrome in the Pregnant Adolescent

Jane McManus Kenslea

REVIEW OF THE LITERATURE

Rape occurs more frequently than any other violent crime in the United States. Approximately one rape occurs every 6 minutes, thus making it the fastest growing violent crime in this country.[1] It is estimated that one in six women will be raped in her lifetime.[2] Studies in Washington, D.C., Dade County, Florida, and Ventura County, California, confirm national and regional surveys revealing that 47 to 58% of all rapes occur in victims less than 19 years of age, with a peak age range between 14 and 17 years.[3] Thirteen to 18% of all rapes nationally involve girls less than 10 years of age.[3]

Rape is defined as the "carnal knowledge," to a lesser or greater degree, of a female, without her consent and by compulsion through fear, force, or fraud, singly or in combination.[3] The following specific qualifications further define the rape laws: (1) the victim resists, but the resistance is overcome by "force or violence"; (2) the victim is prevented from resisting by threats of great and immediate bodily harm accompanied by apparent power of execution or by an intoxicating substance administered by or with the privy of the accused; (3) the victim is unconscious of the act, and this fact is known to the assailant; and (4) the victim is incapable through lunacy or mental instability of giving legal consent.[3]

Despite recent attempts at societal sensitization to this potentially devastating crime, more than half of all rapes continue to go unreported. Historically, society perpetuated the mythology that the rape victim invited the act of violence and human degradation against herself. She was viewed as a partner to the crime, responsible for her actions and the implications of those actions.

Medical and criminal justice systems would often negate the ideology respecting the victim's innocence. Societal beliefs regarding the violent crime of rape are reflective of the following mythology: prior sexual experience on the part of the unmarried victim was reasonable evidence of provocation; women asked for rape by seductive behavior and dress; nice girls don't get raped and bad girls shouldn't complain; and women can't be raped unless they want to be.[4]

Victims, aware of the prevailing societal attitudes toward rape, would often choose to suffer the consequences silently, refusing to report the occurrence to the law, the medical system, family members, friends, or lovers. Those victims who reported the crime often fell subject to further assault imposed by the medical, legal, social, and media systems.

Prior to the past decade, research and literary documentation focused on the psychodynamics of the rapist and medicolegal instruction inclusive of protection of the examining physician.[3] However, there existed a paucity of information about the psychodynamic considerations/implications of the rape victim. For many years, the somatic, psychologic, and emotional sequelae commonly experienced by the rape victim in the aftermath of the assault remained unknown. Today, there are several literary resources (Mezey GC, *Victimological and Psychiatric Aspects of Rape*; Wyer RS Jr, et al., *Cognitive Mediators of Reactions to Rape*; Devasto P, *Measuring the Aftermath of Rape*) reflective of in-depth investigation of the psychoemotional effect of rape on the victim.

Burgess and Holmstrom were the first to cite the existence of a rape trauma syndrome in female victims of forcible rape.[5] Their initial study, completed in 1973, included 92 adult women victims between the ages of 17 to 73 years. They described the syndrome as having two phases: (1) the acute phase of disorganization and (2) the long-term phase of reorganization. Both phases are dynamic and varied with respect to the rape circumstance, individual integration, and sequence. The acute phase lasts approximately 2 to 3 weeks after the attack. The first hours include the reaction of shock and disbelief. Styles of emotion displayed by the victims varied. The expressed style demonstrated fear, heightened anxiety, anger, and shock through sobbing, crying, smiling, restlessness, and tenseness. The second, more controlled style projected a composed or subdued reaction, thus masking feelings.[5]

Somatic reactions during the acute phase included physical ailments, musculoskeletal tension, gastrointestinal irritability, and genitourinary disturbance. Dysmenorrhea, vaginitis, diarrhea, headaches, general malaise, and anorexia were not uncommon manifestations of the acute trauma. Emotional reactions ranged from fear, embarrassment, humiliation, guilt, anxiety, and self-blame to indirect anger. The fear, anxiety, guilt, and shame appear to be a well-documented universal phenomenon despite the varying circumstances of rape. Initially, there seems to be little anger displayed by the victims.[6] However, this anger may later manifest itself in nightmares, explosive outbursts, depression, and sexual aggression as the victim attempts to master her response to the assault. During the period after the acute phase, the victim will make various attempts to reorganize her life. Mobility efforts include change of residence, telephone number, or immediate travel for change of environment.

The Compounded vs. Silent Reaction

Two common reactions of the victims studied have been identified as the compounded reaction and the silent reaction.[5] Those victims at risk for the compounded reaction often have a past or current mental health condition or physical or social limitation(s). The life-threatening attack may have exacerbated the pre-existing conditions, resulting in a compounded rape trauma syndrome. Symptoms for this group include more severe depression, psychotic behavior, conversion hysteria, psychosomatic disorders, and suicidal attempts and ideation. Acting out behavior include drug abuse, alcoholism, and sexual promiscuity.[5]

The victim reacting silently to the rape will not report assault. Many months and years will pass with the victim carrying a tremendous psychologically damaging burden. This victim is at risk for experiencing a significant loss of self-esteem, social isolation, separation, anxiety, sexual problems, and expression of aggressive or hostile behavior toward men.

Post-traumatic Stress Disorder

Many victims of rape have also been found to suffer from a post-traumatic stress disorder. The disorder is defined as:

> The development of characteristic symptoms after the experience of a psychologically traumatic event or events outside the range of human experience considered to be normal. The characteristic symptoms involve re-experiencing the traumatic events, numbing of responsiveness to, or involvement with the external world, and a variety of other autonomic dysphonic, or cognitive symptoms.[7]

Sleep disturbance, heightened anxiety, hyperalertness, memory impairment, difficulty concentrating, and detachment and estrangement from others are commonly found symptoms in victims during the post-trauma period.

The aforementioned symptoms reflect maladaptive responses developed by the victim to protect herself against further exposure to trauma. These responses are immediately effective defense mechanisms that later may prove psychologically costly, resulting in damage to the victim's pride and self-esteem.[6] It has been suggested that the degree to which the post-traumatic stress disorder manifests itself depends on immediate treatment and counsel of the victim at the time of the rape.[8]

Factors Influencing Recovery

Burgess and Holmstrom suggested that treatment received during the immediate post-trauma period can influence the recovery process.[9] They evaluated cognitive, verbal, physiologic, and psychologic strategies for coping with the rape during and immediately after the assault. Analysis of these strategies revealed their significance to both the rape victim and the counselor. Understanding the individual coping behaviors became imperative for successful crisis intervention and counseling. For the victim, a clear understanding of her own coping behavior facilitated complete recovery from the assault.

In a follow-up study of 81 rape victims over a 4- to 6-year period, coping strategies and responses were analyzed to determine which strategies resulted in less psychologic trauma.[10] Positive self-esteem and utilization of defense mechanisms—explanation (providing a reason for rape), minimization (reducing anxiety to a manageable content), suppression (gaining cognitive control over thoughts about rape), dramatization (repeatedly overexpressing anxiety in an attempt to dissipate it), and mobilization (changing residence or traveling)—were all cited as adaptive strategies for coping for rape.[10] Victims who employed or exhibited such responses were found to recover sooner than those victims displaying maladaptive responses. Maladaptive responses were often built on a person's framework of poor self-esteem. The victim had not developed or utilized the aforementioned defense mechanisms in the aftermath of this traumatic crisis. Drugs, alcohol abuse, suicidal attempts, and various self-destructive behaviors were recognized as maladaptive and meant a longer, more complex recovery for the rape victim.[10] Family support and the stability of one's partner also influenced the length of recovery. Those victims receiving support and continued stability from their partner relationship recovered more quickly.[10]

Long-Term Psychologic Effects

There have been few conclusive studies regarding the long-term psychologic effects on the victim of rape. One of the most thorough research projects on the long-term effects of rape covered a 24-month period immediately after the assault.[10] Statistical measures of anxiety, fear, and depression immediately after the assault were elevated to levels suggestive of marked clinical distress. Subsequent postrape assessments at 3- and 6-month intervals revealed that the initial distress had diminished.

Santiago et al. studied the long-term effects of sexual assault in 35 rape victims 2 to 46 years after the assault.[11] Anxiety, depression, and fear inventories were used to assess the victims' psychoemotional status. Scores were compared to those of 110 nonabused matched control subjects. The rape victims had significantly higher levels of anxiety, depression, and fear.[11] Notman and Nadelson confirmed these findings in their study of 41 women victims of rape.[6] The study was done at 1 and 2.5 years postassault. Fear, depression, suspicion of others, emotional disturbance, and sexual problems were self-reported by one-half to three-quarters of the women studied.[6]

Treatment

The majority of those victims of rape who seek psychologic help at the time of the assault receive short-term crisis intervention counseling. The therapy is issue oriented and supportive in nature. Mental health professionals have long supported the theory that a brief course of supportive counseling is the appropriate intervention for all victims of rape. Counseling includes reassurance, support of adaptive behavior, ventilation, and anticipatory guidance for the victim. Psychotherapy was advised only for those victims believed to have an underlying psychopathology. Recently, however, mental health professionals are experiencing an evolution of attitude and a clearer understanding of the devastating trauma of rape for the victim, her family, and spouse or sexual partners. Hours of clinical treatment and research have illuminated the extensive psychologic and emotional damage to these relationships that results in the disruption of several vital resources for the victim.[13]

Identification of psychosexual conflicts and of the psychodynamics of the sexual assault has resulted in a new appreciation of the value of psychotherapy for the rape victim.[13] For the majority of victims who are amenable to this mode of professional intervention, the recovery process may be abbreviated and may be more successful. A suggested treatment plan is shown in Figure 19-1.

* * * * *

CASE STUDY

The following case study reviews the clinical recognition, diagnosis, and management plan of a 19-year-old pregnant adolescent suffering from rape trauma syndrome. Behavioral symptoms and the young woman's factual history about a violent rape 2 years previous to the pregnancy confirmed the existence of crises in this young woman's life. Her labile emotional status suggested the existence of previous trauma. Of significance is the selectively limited factual information offered by the patient regarding her life crises. Her primary diagnosis and management plan were predicated upon this information. A later, more definitive diagnosis was based on more extensive information.

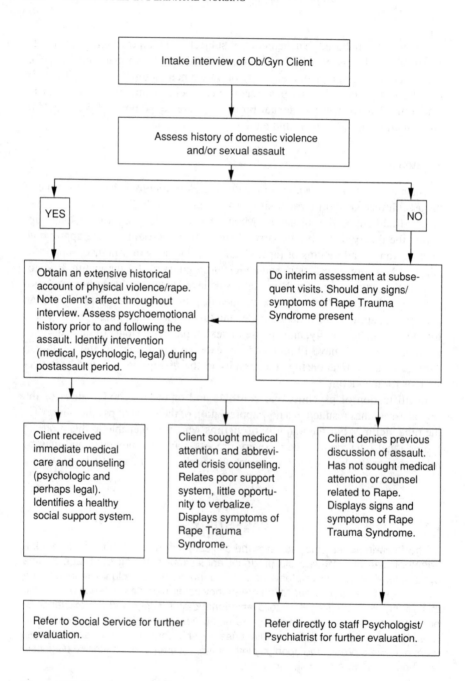

Figure 19-1 Suggested Treatment Plan

K.L., a 19-year-old black woman (gravida II, para I), presented for prenatal care at an adolescent midwifery service at 10 weeks gestation. The following information was obtained at the initial visit.

Her mother had died of ovarian cancer at age 29 in 1979. Her father had died at age 38 with acquired immunodeficiency syndrome (AIDS). Three siblings (one brother, age 20, and two sisters, ages 15 and 16) were all alive and well.

The patient denied allergies, smoking, alcohol, and/or drug abuse. She had had the measles, mumps, and chicken pox as a child with no known sequelae. Surgeries included removal of tonsils and adenoids at age 5. In 1985, the patient underwent an extensive surgical repair of throat and neck lacerations incurred in a stabbing. The postoperative course was uncomplicated. The patient denied any history of blood transfusions. Menarche occurred at age 12, and menstruation was regular at every 28 days for 5 days. She experienced dysmenorrhea for 2 years from 1984 to 1986. Her last menstrual period was 20 March 1987, with an expected date of confinement of 25 December, 1987.

The patient denied a history of sexually transmitted diseases. In 1982, she had a therapeutic abortion at 8 weeks gestation, without complication. Counseling prior to the procedure was confirmed.

In 1985, the patient was raped with forced vaginal and rectal penetration. A penicillin injection was administered for sexually transmitted disease prophylaxis after the rape incident.

The patient denied previous use of contraception. However, she did receive diethylstilbestrol (DES) per protocol after the 1985 rape.

The patient's blood type was O positive. Antibody screen was negative. A complete blood count was unremarkable with a nonreactive serology. Rubella status was immune. Hepatitis B and a tine test were both negative. Sickle cell screen was also negative. Urine, gonorrhea, and chlamydial cultures were all negative. The patient was offered but refused HIV III screening.

The patient lives with her boyfriend (father of baby), a 24-year-old full-time employee of the City Police Department. They share a small two-room apartment on the second floor of a well-maintained apartment building located within walking distance of the hospital. The boyfriend was described by the patient as helpful and supportive and was identified as her primary support person. The patient denied domestic violence/abuse. Educational goals included obtaining a high school diploma. The last year of school completed was the 10th grade. Financial status was limited to the boyfriend's income. The patient was waiting confirmation of Medicaid eligibility.

The patient's physical examination revealed poor dentition, with caried posterior molars, abundant plaque deposit, and discoloration. Her neck had an L-shaped scar extending to the upper chest (6 cm x 3 cm, well-healed). The lungs, heart, breasts, and abdomen were all within normal limits. The pelvic examination showed an anteverted, soft, nontender uterus at 10 week size. On the right was a 3-cm nontender corpus luteal cyst.

Throughout the initial interview and physical, the patient appeared depressed. Her affect was dull and withdrawn. Eye contact was infrequent. The following narrative is the patient's account of the violent rape, which was related during the physical examination when the nurse-midwife questioned the etiology of the extensive neck/chest scar.

The patient lived with her biologic parents and three siblings until the spring of 1979, when her mother died of ovarian cancer. Six months after the mother's death, all four children went to live with the maternal grandmother. The father lost a custody battle due to his long-standing substance abuse problems. The patient lived with her grandmother for a brief 2-month period and then set out on her own because of personality problems between herself and the grandmother.

The next few years were spent living with different relatives. In 1982 at the age of 14 she became pregnant and elected to terminate at 8 weeks gestation. Her boyfriend at the time did not know of the pregnancy. In 1984, she moved to her cousin's home. She lived with this cousin, his wife, and their three young children. In December 1985, the cousin, intoxicated, raped the patient vaginally and rectally at knifepoint and then proceeded to stab her several times after the rape. The patient was taken via ambulance to the nearest medical center for emergency surgery. Immediately after the surgery, the patient, unable to speak because of extensive edema and neck trauma, wrote of the rape in detail and submitted it to medical personnel and police.

The patient received prophylaxis for sexually transmitted diseases and pregnancy. The rape protocol was implemented and a social work referral was completed. The cousin was found guilty of the rape and stabbing and was incarcerated shortly thereafter.

After her recovery, the patient lived with a second, female relative. In 1987 she met her present boyfriend (the father of the baby), with whom she lived at the time of the interview. The patient stated that she continued to have nightmares and fearful days since her life-threatening assault. She did remember receiving counseling with a social worker daily for 3 weeks during her inpatient stay in 1985. However, she did not remember what she talked about. Both the patient and her boyfriend were happy about this pregnancy. If she were to have a girl, they had planned to name the child after the patient's deceased mother.

The initial psychosocial assessment was that of an adolescent primigravida who appeared depressed with a recent history of severe physical/sexual assault. An immediate referral was made to the Social Service Department.

A female social worker was assigned to work with the patient throughout the pregnancy. They met frequently for one-half hour sessions either before or after each prenatal visit. In the later months of pregnancy, the patient appeared more spontaneous and less depressed. She was interested and responsive to educational efforts regarding childbirth preparation. The pregnancy progressed and was uncomplicated. On 12 December 1987, the patient delivered a male infant (Apgar 8/9) after a 4-hour, uncomplicated labor. Both mother and infant were discharged on the third postpartum day. A social worker's note of the second postpartum day stated that the patient appeared slightly depressed. The plan to meet again with the patient at the 6-week visit was confirmed with the patient by the social worker. The patient did not return for her 6-week postpartum examination. To date, several outreach efforts to contact the patient have proved futile. Neither she nor her new-born have returned for health care. A close family contact confirmed that the patient relocated with her infant son and boyfriend 1 month following delivery.

* * * * *

CASE ANALYSIS

Several weeks following this patient's discharge with her infant, an extensive medical record review, inclusive of a previously misplaced inpatient record, revealed a documented assessment of this patient by a staff psychologist in December 1985. The patient had met with the psychologist during her inpatient hospital stay at that time.

The patient explained the rape incident in detail and hesitantly confirmed that she had also been raped at age 15 by an unknown assailant. This rape was never reported to legal authorities or family members. The patient's mother, whom the patient previously related had died of ovarian cancer, had been murdered in 1979. The patient, a young girl of 11 at the time, was a witness to the mother's murder. She was hospitalized for intensive psychiatric treatment for 1 week after the mother's death. The patient related suicidal ideation and one failed attempt in 1984. Frequent nightmares, crying spells, and angry outbursts were a common occurrence after the mother's death and increased after the first rape.

This young woman, at age 19, was pregnant and suffering a compounded rape trauma syndrome. Had there been better communication among the multi-disciplinary health care team members regarding the patient's complicated psychiatric history, referrals and treatments would have been different. The patient seems to have suffered a post-traumatic stress disorder after her mother's murder. Her subsequent pathologic silent response to the first rape reflected a compounded rape trauma reaction. The second, more violent, life-threatening rape further complicated an already pre-existing psychiatric condition.

An extensive psychiatric evaluation and perhaps protracted psychotherapy would be the preferred treatment of choice for this young woman given her past and current history of psychiatric/physical assault. Both she and her infant are at risk for continued psychiatric conflict as victims sharing the sequelae of her severe rape trauma syndrome.

IMPLICATIONS FOR PRACTICE

Appropriate diagnosis and treatment of the physical and psychologic injuries of the sexual assault victim are of paramount importance. It is not uncommon for the pregnant adolescent to share a previous or more immediate sexual assault incident during a prenatal visit. The questions of any prior history of domestic violence or sexual assault should be included in the initial prenatal interview. The patient may elect to share her answers later in the pregnancy once a relationship of trust is established with the practitioner.

The confirmation of a previous assault necessitates that a thorough history of the episode inclusive of the patient's emotional/physical response be obtained and carefully documented. Clinical management should be predicated upon the young woman's previous intervention during the postassault period.

If the victim was emotionally healthy before the assault and received crisis counseling that was issue-oriented and supportive, then perhaps a referral to social service is appropriate. However, psychotherapy continues to be viewed as the treatment of choice for the victim with a past or current history of psychiatric or physical difficulties. This mode of treatment would be available to all victims of sexual assault, should they request it.

In conclusion, any pregnant woman with a history of sexual assault is at risk for antepartum and/or postpartum depression. Thus, continuous psychoemotional assessment throughout pregnancy is the responsibility of the primary practitioner. A diagnosis or suspected exacerbation of the rape trauma syndrome should be considered when the practitioner observes any of the following symptoms:

1. signs of anxiety as the interview progresses, such as long periods of silence, blocking of associations, minor stuttering, and physical distress
2. reports of sudden marked irritability, avoidance of relationships with men, or marked change in sexual behavior
3. history of sudden onset of phobic reactions, fear of being alone, fear of open spaces, going outside, or being inside alone
4. persistent loss of self-confidence and self-esteem, an attitude of self-blame, paranoid feelings, or dreams of violence or nightmares[3]

Physicians, nurse-midwives, and nurses are often the first health care providers to be held in confidence of a young woman's sexual assault. Successful recovery from the life-threatening crime is a direct reflection of the appropriate assessment and management of the rape trauma syndrome in women of all ages.

REFERENCES

1. Hicks DJ. Rape sexual assault. *Obstet Gynecol Annu.* 1978;7:447–465.
2. Nelson C. Victims of rape: who are they? In: Warner CG (ed.). *Rape and Sexual Assault Management and Intervention.* Rockville, Md: Aspen Publishers, Inc.; 1980.
3. Woodling BA, Kossoris PI. Sexual misuse, rape molestation and incest. *Pediatr Clin North Am.* 1981;28:481–499.

4. Hilberman EMD. Rape: the ultimate violation of the self. *Am J Psychiatry*. 1986;133 (special issue).

5. Burgess AW, Holmstrom LL. Rape trauma syndrome. *Am J Psychiatry*. 1974;131:981–985.

6. Notman MT, Nadelson CC. The rape victim: psychodynamic considerations. *Am J Psychiatry*. 1976;133:408–412.

7. American Psychiatric Association Committee on Nomenclature and Statistics. *Diagnostic and Statistical Manual of Mental Disorders III*. American Psychiatric Association; 1980.

8. Martin CA, Warfield MC, Braen R. *Physicians Management of the Psychological Aspects of Rape*.

9. Burgess AW, Holmstrom LL. Adaptive strategies and recovery from rape. *Am J Psychiatry*. October 1979;136 (special issue).

10. Burgess AW, Holmstrom LL. Coping behaviors of the rape victim. *Am J Psychiatry*. April 1979;133 (special issue).

11. Santiago JM, McCall-Perez F, et al. Long term psychological effects of rape in 35 rape victims. *Am J Psychiatry*. November 1985;142 (special issue).

12. Sutherland S, Sherl DS. Patterns of response among victims of rape. *Am J Orthopsychiatry*. 1970;40:503–511.

13. Rose D. Worse than death: psychodynamics of rape victims and the need for psychotherapy. *Am J Psychiatry*. July 1986;143 (special issue).

ADDITIONAL BIBLIOGRAPHY

American Academy of Pediatrics Committee on Adolescence. Rape and the adolescent. April 1988; 81595–597.

Burt MR, Katz BL. Coping strategies and recovery from rape. *Ann NY Acad Sci*. 1988;528:345–358.

Dennis LI. Adolescent rape: the role of nursing. *Issues Compr Pediatr Nurs*. 1988;11(1):59–70.

Glaser JB, Hammerschlag MR, McCormack WM. Sexually transmitted disease in victims of sexual assault. *N Engl J Med*. September 1986;315:625–627.

Hall ER. Adolescents' perceptions of sexual assault. *J Sex Educ Ther*. Spring–Summer 1987;13:37–42.

Meyer CB, Taylor SE. Adjustment to rape. *J Pers Soc Psychol*. 1986;50:1226–1234.

Mezey GE, Taylor PJ. Psychological reactions of women who have been raped: a descriptive and comparative study. *Br J Psychiatry*. March 1988; 152:330–339.

Mims FH, Chang AS. Unwanted sexual experiences of young women. *J Psychosoc Nurs Ment Health Serv*. June 1984;22:7–14.

Shearer SL, Herbert CA. Long-term effects of unresolved sexual trauma. *Am Fam Physician*. January 1988;37:44.

Underwood MM, Fiedler N. The crisis of rape: a community response. *Community Ment Health J*. Fall 1983;19:227–230.

Vinogradov S, Dishotosky NI, Doty AL, Tinklenberg JR. Patterns of behavior in adolescent rape. *Am J Orthopsychiatry*. April 1988;58(2):179–187.

Chapter 20

Access to Perinatal Care: An Ethical Dilemma

Vanda R. Lops

The expansion of nursing practice has given rise to numerous conflicts and dilemmas for the practitioner. One area in which difficult decisions arise is that of ethics and clinical practice.

In this chapter, we present a case study that dramatically demonstrates lack of access to perinatal care. Nursing implications are discussed, and the use of an ethical decision model is demonstrated.

The ethical decision-making model consists of ten steps (Table 20-1).[1] Steps 7 to 10 in the model (i.e., determining who should make the decision, assessing the range of outcomes, implementing the decision, and finally evaluating the action) will be utilized in this case study.

Table 20-1 A Bioethical Decision Model

Step 1   Review of the situation to determine health problems, decision needed, ethical components, and key individuals.

Step 2   Gather additional information to clarify situation.

Step 3   Identify the ethical issues in the situation.

Step 4   Define personal and professional moral positions.

Step 5   Identify moral positions of key individuals involved.

Step 6   Identify value conflicts, if any.

Step 7   Determine who should make the decision.

Step 8   Identify range of actions with anticipated outcomes.

Step 9   Decide on a course of action and carry it out.

Step 10 Evaluate/review results of decision/action.

Source: Reprinted from *Bioethical Decision Making for Nurses* (p99) by JE Thompson and HO Thompson with permission of Appleton and Lange, © 1985.

REVIEW OF THE LITERATURE

Since 1966, according to the U.S. National Center for Health Statistics,[2] maternal mortality has declined 72% and infant mortality has declined 58%. During the 1980s, however, these rates of decline seemed to slow and, in 1985, maternal mortality among black and all nonwhite women rose, with black mortality four times as high as that of white mothers.[3]

Between 1984 and 1985, neonatal mortality increased nationwide by 3% among black infants and 1% among all nonwhite infants for the first time since the early 1960s, before the advent of Medicaid.[3] In 1985, the percentage of low-birth-weight (LBW) babies also increased and appeared to parallel the increase in the percentage of babies born to mothers who received late or no prenatal care.

These national trends are even more dramatic when viewed on the statewide level. White infant mortality rates increased in 19 states. The lowest increase was noted in Washington state (10%) and the highest increase was in Delaware (38%). Black infant mortality increased in 12 states. The lowest rise was seen in Kentucky (11%), and the highest increase (46%) was in Massachusetts.[3] In California, infant mortality is increasing, and each year nearly 40,000 babies begin their lives with significant health risks or die in infancy.

According to the Children's Defense Fund,[3] the percentage of low-birth-weight (5 lb 8 oz or under) babies increased in 1985 for the first time in 20 years. Simultaneously, the prematurity rate also increased. While the percentage of babies born at low birth weight was virtually unchanged from 1980 to 1984, it had declined by 13% from 1970 to 1979. Now this modest process is being reversed.

Access to and availability of prenatal care have also diminished. Most medical experts regard early prenatal care as critical to a good pregnancy outcome, with the gold standard of the future being preconceptual counseling. However, between 1984 and 1985, the percentage of babies born to mothers receiving no prenatal care increased. In 1985, three in every ten women of all races and one in every two black women did not receive adequate prenatal care. For example, in 1985 in New York City, more than 60% of nonwhite infants were born of mothers receiving inadequate prenatal care.[4] According to UNICEF, since 1985 the United States ranks 19th in overall infant mortality.[5]

These findings demonstrate an inherent deficiency in the American health care system's ability to provide perinatal care to all citizens. Historically, the concept of equality relative to access in health care has grown over the decades, nourished by the development of employment-related health insurance and the introduction of federal programs for the elderly and poor. However, current changes in health economics pressure health providers to cut back on obstetrical care. The American College of Obstetricians and Gynecologists estimates that 17.6% of obstetricians were decreasing the numbers of high-risk patients they managed and 9% were no longer taking any obstetrical patients.

Additionally, the widespread loss of private and group insurance created a health care structure that, although accounting for over 11% of the total government expenditures, provided health care for only 88% of the population. A 1983 study on access to health care done at the University of Chicago and funded by the Robert Wood Johnson Foundation reported that 12% of 20 million people in the United States do not have a source of health care.[3] The reason most often cited for this was lack of health insurance due to unemployment and lack of finances.

* * * * *

CASE STUDY

A visibly pregnant young women presented at the Obstetric Clinic on a busy afternoon requesting to see a physician. Several hours earlier, she had entered the main emergency room and was sent directly to the labor and delivery unit. Since no labor or labor-related problem was noted, she was referred to the clinic, which was now in session.

Initial nurse-patient communication revealed that, because of finances, the patient had not received medical care during the pregnancy. Further questioning revealed that the patient was an epileptic and was followed sporadically by a community physician. She was currently taking the medication he had prescribed and had not experienced seizures for the past 9 to 10 months. The patient complained of right-sided pain, which had been present for the past 4 to 5 days.

The patient's temperature was 102°, and a pulse of 104 was documented. From the last menstrual period, a gestational age of 31 weeks was calculated. The patient appeared pale and lethargic. Costovertebral angle (CVA) tenderness was elicited. A urine specimen was positive for 3+ protein. At this point in the assessment, the registration clerk entered the clinic and advised the nurse that, since the patient had no medical coverage and no finances, she could not be seen and no diagnostic or treatment procedures could be initiated.

* * * * *

CASE ANALYSIS

Although this case study is hypothetical, for many women seeking care it is a stark reality. Furthermore, these circumstances confront all the members of the obstetric team with an ethical dilemma. Within the framework of the ethical decision-making model proposed by Thompson and Thompson,[1] an attempt will be made to clarify and find a solution to this dilemma.

The first two steps of this model are concerned with reviewing the situation and gathering any additional information that may influence the decision. Some of the questions to consider include defining the health problems that are part of this dilemma and considering the decisions that need to be made. Part of this process includes identifying the ethical and scientific components of the decision and the individuals who will be affected by it. In this dilemma a number of people are involved, all of whom view the problem differently: the patient, the nurse, and the registration clerk. To the patient, the immediate problem is that she is experiencing pain and needs treatment. The nurse sees a number of problems: lack of prenatal care, a patient with signs and symptoms of pyleonephritis and anemia, and the use of potentially teratogenic agents during pregnancy. The registration clerk does not see the problem as a health care one but as lack of financial capability on the part of the patient.

Once the problems have been defined, the next step is to enumerate the decisions to be made. The primary decision is: Should the patient be seen? An extension of this decision must include provision for ongoing care.

Most decisions in health have both scientific and ethical components. Studies have demonstrated that early and consistent prenatal care yields improved fetal outcomes.[6] Data have demonstrated that untreated urinary tract infections in pregnancy are associated with preterm labor[7] and that certain anemias in pregnancy may be associated with increased maternal and fetal morbidity.[8]

The ethical components are defined by asking what should be done in this situation and what rights the involved individuals have. Even the medical novice would agree that an individual who needs care should be able to receive it. This raises a most basic issue: the right to health care. The ANA Code of Ethics (1981) states that the nurse provides services with respect for human dignity and the uniqueness of the client, unrestricted by the considerations of social or economic status. In this situation, the nurse has recognized abnormal findings, but can she demand treatment for the patient? As the health care facility employee, does she not have the obligation of loyalty to the employer by adhering to the decision to refuse care because of financial reasons?

Another person to consider in this situation is the fetus. Whether the fetus has the right to a safe pregnancy and a full-term birth is a hotly contested point. All of the individuals in this situation will be affected by the decisions made: the registration clerk representing the facility, the patient, and the nurse who must assess her responsibilities and duties and, based on these, make a decision as to what can be done.

To make the most efficacious, just, and acceptable decision, one must have further information. Demographic data as to place of birth, age, and marital status should be obtained. The presence of a significant other or family willing to assume financial responsibility will affect the decision process. Educational level will assist in determining the patient's ability to understand what is happening and the need for follow-up.

Legally, can it be established that the patient has a right to be seen and that, once care is initiated by a provider, that provider has the responsibility to continue with the care? Does an unborn child have legal rights, and, if so, who will act as the fetus' advocate? Last, are there other options for this patient, such as referral to other medical or financial sources?

The next several steps in the model involve the identification of the ethical issues involved, the historical basis of the question, the philosophical perspective, and the personal and professional values of the individuals. The ethical issues include autonomy, beneficence vs. malfeasance, allocation of resources, and the sanctity of life. All of these appear to lead us to the central question of the right to health care.

According to Sade,[9] autonomy, which is the right to choose for whom one cares, is an inalienable right of the health care provider. Humans are living, thinking creatures with the right to select values by which to live their lives. The right of a patient to demand care from a provider, therefore, is immoral because it denies the most fundamental of rights, that to one's own life and the means to support it. If each person has the right to be autonomous, can that right be extrapolated to the professional health care provider? If so, in this case, the health care facility appears to have the right to choose for whom it will provide care.

This leads to the issue of beneficence vs. malfeasance, that is, doing good and not doing harm. Might one ask, should not beneficence be a value by which humans would want to live their lives? In this situation, would not the care provider do good by providing care and harm by not doing so, and indeed is not the main purpose of the health care provider to provide care when needed?

If care is to be provided on the basis of need, should it be provided regardless of economic consideration? This raises the further ethical issue of justice and allocation of resources. It seems just that everyone be treated equally. If health resources are limited, then their allocation needs to be systematized. Should a system of fee for service in which the patient receives only what is paid for be instituted, or should there be a minimal level of health care for everyone, thus providing the greatest good for the greatest number? Within the issue of justice and allocation of resources, if it is just that everyone be treated equally, then health resources must be allocated accordingly.

The sanctity of life is nowhere more pertinent than in the pregnant patient who represents not only two lives, but also the potential of the generation to come. It is better to provide care with an eventual healthy outcome (vs. a negative outcome) which would affect not only the family unit, but society as well.

The issue of the right to health care is hotly debated and certainly cannot be definitively decided in this chapter. According to Fried,[10] a right invokes entitlements: those things that one must have and, if one does not, one may demand.

Rights are associated with equality, and in fact equality may be a right. If equality is a right, granting that right should not depend on whether it is at the time feasible or comfortable to do so. It can then be said that an individual may not be entitled to a particular item but is entitled to equality in respect or access to that item.

On the other hand, Sparer stated that the right to medical care exists only if there is a definable duty, such as a contract, on the part of the health care provider to give this care.[11] Then, and only then, does a person have a legal remedy that can be used to enforce the performance of care. There is no legal right to health care without these conditions. Lappe added a further dimension to this issue when he considered disease causation as a factor in this debate.[12] If the individual is responsible for his own well-being, then government's only role is to encourage good health habits. If, however, disease is predetermined by the interaction of social, environmental, and genetic factors that fall largely beyond the individual's control, then government has a high degree of responsibility in assisting people to cope with disease. In this instance, it can be said that the responsibility for getting pregnant lies with the patient. However, it must be ascertained if birth control was used, if the patient was indeed cognizant of any family planning methods, or if this could have been a birth control failure.

Even more basic is the right to live vs. the right to die. Does the unborn child have this right? At 31 weeks gestation, termination is not an option. If the patient does have pyleonephritis, is not treated, and subsequently delivers a premature infant, the infant may die or require prolonged, specialized care. Additionally, the untreated maternal infection may lead to increased maternal morbidity and even death. These facts appear to support the rendering of care.

As part of the in-depth investigation of the ethical issues, the historical as well as the philosophical perspectives need to be considered. Prior to this current period of dramatic technology, where real differences in restoring health and promoting life can be seen, medical care was rarely a cure. In fact, more was accomplished by public health measures such as improved sanitation, working conditions, and diet than by the medical ministrations of the time.[13] The ancient Greeks felt that humans were primarily responsible for their own health and that health was attained and maintained by proper diet and exercise. These ideas were adopted and continued by the Romans. Renaissance man thought of health in terms of body "humors," and illness was a disorder of these caused by intemperance.

In the United States, the 18th and 19th centuries witnessed the advent of paternalistic health regimens. The government enacted such legislation as the Indian Health Service Act of 1789 and the Quarantine Laws of 1878 and in 1898 established the Public Health Service. The 20th century saw the start of mass health screening programs sparked by the fact that, of the 3.7 million men screened for military service at the beginning of World War I, 500,000 were rejected, all for preventable conditions. During the early 1900s attempts were made to introduce a system of National Health Insurance. An example of such an effort was the Sheppard-Towner Act, which provided for maternal and child health funding. All efforts, due to physician opposition, were solidly defeated. In 1910, prompted by the widespread abuses of child labor, Workmen's Compensation was enacted. In 1935, the Social Security Act, health insurance amendment omitted, became a reality.

To assure provision of long-term and rehabilitative care for the returning World War II serviceman, the Hill-Burton Act was passed. This was the first in a series of acts, all part of a public policy aimed at assuring medical care for everyone regardless of finances. This act required that a reasonable volume of the services of a facility built with Hill-Burton funds be available to the indigent. This law was largely unenforced by federal or state agencies until 1974, when a law allowing litigation for failure to provide such care by Hill-Burton grantee facilities was enacted. In 1960, the Kerr-Mills Act, the forerunner of Medicaid, created new vendor payments to the medically needy, aged, blind, and disabled who were not on welfare. Additionally, hospitals providing free and below-cost service to indigents could, up to 1969, when this free service requirement was dropped, claim charitable organization status with the Internal Revenue Service.

Under the Johnson administration, the war on poverty became the rallying cry of government. The year 1965 saw the passage of Medicaid (MCA), which was available in all states and provided medical care for the poor and elderly with preset state eligibility requirements. Since its enactment, however, expenditures have escalated and, in an attempt to curtail costs, eligibility requirements have become increasingly stringent, benefit packages have decreased, and co-insurance and increased deductibles have been added.

Within the concepts of the new federalism of the 1980s, there was a reapportionment of MCA funds distribution, with a greater financial burden placed on the states, which, in turn, increased recipient requirements. At present, in many instances, this funding provides for little more than emergency medical care for much of the population. Additionally, although the number of children in families with no medical insurance had risen by 30%, federal funding to key sources of maternal care had dropped by one third.[14]

One of the philosophical systems to consider is utilitarianism postulated by John Stuart Mill and Jeremy Bentham in the late 18th and 19th centuries. The fundamental principle of this system is utility, which states that an action is right if it tends to promote the good, not just of the individual performing the action, but of everyone affected by it; the act is wrong if it produces the reverse. It is in opposition to egoism in that it espouses the greatest good for the greatest number. In these terms the uniqueness of the pregnant patient who presents not as one patient but as two supports a decision in favor of the provision of care. One can further state that such provision of care has perhaps the most far reaching of effects through the present generation as well as the generation represented by the unborn.

Within this philosophical stance, the end, getting the patient treated with an eventual safe pregnancy outcome, does justify the means. Additionally, health care providers cognizant of the risks involved, in terms not just of human wastage but of possible increased financial loss to society, must accept this as justification of any means necessary for the prevention of a negative outcome.

A component of utilitarianism is situation ethics, in which the situation determines whether the act is good. In this situation, a fellow human presents in need of care. Is not the most loving thing to do to provide that care? The consequences, if care is not provided, are immeasurable in terms of human potential never fulfilled. This appears further to justify the giving of care.

Theologically, the basic concepts of many of the world's great religions are the traditions of love for thy neighbor, the sanctity of life, and the golden rule, all espousing respect and love for others. To provide care out of love and respect for both of the lives involved regardless of the financial consideration appears to be an action congruent with these precepts.

In identifying the values of the key individuals, the assumption can be made that the patient, in seeking care, places a value on her life and may be demonstrating a concern for the life of her unborn child. The nurse, by virtue of her chosen profession, also values life and the benefits of health care. She concludes that medical care is needed. This decision vs. her sense of loyalty to the employer truly places her in a conflict situation. What value is placed on life by the health care facility? Is a greater value placed on financial solvency than on life? On one hand, the nurse, as representative of the facility, is saying that the patient needs to be seen. Concurrently, the other representative, the clerk, is saying that care must be financially compensated if the facility is to continue to function.

The next step in our model requires definition of problem ownership. Primary ownership belongs to the patient, but, in part, it can also be attributed to the care facility, the health care system, and society. Assuredly, individuals should be responsible for their own health status. Health behaviors, however, are multifaceted and not always self-volitional in character and, thus, are vulnerable to any number of external influences. Once the patient has entered the system and there has been "hands-on" care, is that facility legally liable if the patient is not treated and goes on to a negative outcome? Society, in part, owns this problem because it has failed to ensure access to care and because it very well may have to assume ultimate financial responsibility for any ongoing care.

The last two steps of the decision-making model involve assessing the range of actions and outcomes possible and reaching a decision. The actions include the rendering of care and the possibility of a good outcome or not rendering care with almost certainly a negative outcome. A third action may be to refer the patient to another care source, which would solve the dilemma for those involved. Be aware, however, that this new provider may also become mired in the same conflict situation. In the interim, the patient will still not have received the treatment needed.

The decision here, based on the use of this model and its ethical, philosophical, theological, and medical components, appears clear-cut. The only decision possible is to render the patient the necessary care.

IMPLICATIONS FOR PRACTICE

The implications for the nursing profession are numerous, and their effect can be felt in the political, economic, and ethical arenas. Nurses need to see themselves as members of a voting bloc, capable of bringing about change in the current political system. They must make their opinions heard on a variety of programs and issues on the federal, state, and local levels. Implicit in this is the mandate to become knowledgeable about the political model and how it functions. Affecting increased perinatal services within this model is a difficult task because short-term and rapid results are the desired ends rather than long-term considerations. It is easier, therefore, to lobby for a new Newborn Special Care Unit, which can be materially experienced by constituents, rather than for prenatal care, which extends over 9 months and, if successful, yields no dramatic results except a normal newborn.

Awareness of legislators and their positions on health care issues is essential, as is exercise of the voting privilege accordingly. Policy-makers recognize the importance of the opinions of their constituents; communications that express a stand on an issue are given serious consideration.

Participation in organizations having a reputation for affecting policy changes, as well as being an active member of one's professional organizations, is essential. These organizations keep members apprised of health care legislative issues and have the lobbying potential to effect change.

Economically, lack of access to or availability of perinatal care affects all health care providers not only as practitioners but in other societal roles as well. An article on premature and low-birth-weight infants in the 16 May 1989 issue of *Newsweek* reported that, according to the Office of Technology Assessment (OTA), 75,000 to 100,000 newborns enter intensive care units each year, primarily for prematurity and/or low birth weight.[14] It further stated that prenatal care more than pays for itself in that it cuts down on high technology rescues of preterm babies and on the expense of treating the approximately one in six newborns who leave the Newborn Special Care Units with a mental or physical disability. In Virginia alone, researchers estimated that, if prenatal care were universally available, that state would spend almost 50 million dollars less per year in treating mental retardation linked to low birth weight.[4] The OTA concluded that, for every low-birth-weight infant averted by early and adequate prenatal care, the United States health care system would save between $14,000 and $30,000. These savings could be used to finance actual prenatal care programs, with a considerable amount left over.

At the core of nursing practice are the elements of concern and caring for the patient and belief in the promotion and maintenance of health. Nurses are part of a profession that demands the highest standards of knowledge, discipline, and skills in clinical practice.

In the case study presented, it is easy to be outraged by the inadequacies of the present health care system. Because of the underlying principles upon which nursing is predicated, it is easy to find nurses faced with the ethical dilemmas inherent in such situations. Often, any attempt to analyze and rationally solve an ethical dilemma merely increases the ramifications of that dilemma to the consternation of those attempting a solution.

In conclusion, it can be said that the truest test of a society's status and progress is the manner in which it views its disadvantaged. Nurses can, and must, play an active role in ensuring this progress now and in the future.

REFERENCES

1. Thompson JE, Thompson HO. *Bioethical Decision Making for Nurses.* E. Norwalk, Conn: Appleton & Lange; 1985.

2. U.S. National Center for Health Statistics. 1984.

3. Hughes D, Johnson K, Rosenbaum S, Butler E, Simons J. *The Health of America's Children: Maternal and Child Health Data Book.* Children's Defense Fund; 1988.

4. Chiles L. *Death before Life: The Tragedy of Infant Mortality.* The Report of the National Commission to Prevent Infant Mortality. 1988.

5. National Commission To Prevent Infant Mortality. 1988.

6. Moore TR, Origel W, Key TC, Resnik R. The perinatal and economic impact of prenatal care in a low socio-economic population. *Am J Obstet Gynecol.* 1986;54:29–32.

7. Kass EH. Pregnancy, pyelonephritis and prematurity. *Clin Obstet Gynecol.* 1973;13:239.

8. Garn SM, Redella SA, Petzold AS, Falkner F. Maternal hematologic levels and pregnancy outcomes. *Semin Perinatol.* 1981;5:155.

9. Sade RM. Medical care as a right: a refutation. *N Engl J Med.* 1971;285:1288–1292.

10. Fried C. Rights and health care—beyond equity and efficiency. *N Engl J Med.* 1975;293:241–245.

11. Sparer EV. The legal right to health care: public policy and equal access. *Hastings Center Rep.* October 1976;39–47.

12. Lappe M. The predictive power of the new genetics. *Hastings Center Rep.* October 1984;18–21.

13. Reiser SJ. Responsibility for personal health: a historical perspective. *J Med Philos.* 1985;10:7–17.

14. *Newsweek.* 1989;May 16.

ADDITIONAL BIBLIOGRAPHY

American Association of Colleges of Nursing (AACN). *AACN Position Statement; Nursing Research.* Washington, DC: AACN; 1981.

Aroskar MA. Anatomy of an ethical dilemma: the theory. *Am J Nurs.* April 1980; 658–663.

Blattner P, Dar H, Nitowsky HM. Pregnancy outcome in women with sickle cell trait. *JAMA.* 1977;238–1392.

Bryant JH. Principles of justice as a basis for conceptualizing a health care system. *Int J Health Serv.* 1977;7:707–719.

Creasy RK. Preterm labor and delivery. In: Creasy RK, Resnick R, eds. *Maternal-Fetal Medicine.* Philadelphia, Pa: W.B. Saunders Co.; 1984.

Curtin L. The nurse as advocate: a philosophical foundation for nursing. *ANS/Ethics Values.* 1979;1–9.

Fried C. Equality and rights in medical care. Hastings Center Rep. 1976;6:29–34.

Guttmacher S. Immigrant workers: health, law, and public policy. *J Health Polit Policy Law.* 1984;7:503–514.

Kennedy EM. Surgery to save a wounded system. *Consumers Digest.* November 1985;13–120.

Rosenblatt RE. Rationing "normal" health care: the hidden legal issues. *Tex Law Rev.* 1981;59:1401–1420.

Rosenthal G, Fox DM. A right to what? Toward adequate minimum standards for personal health services. *Milbank Memorial Fund Q.* 1978;56(1):1–6.

Sher G. Health care and the "deserving poor." *Hastings Center Rep.* February 1982;9–12.

Smith SJ, Davis AJ. Ethical dilemmas: conflicts among rights, duties, and obligations. *Am J Nursing.* August 1980;1463–1466.

Toulmin S. The tyranny of principles. *Hastings Center Rep.* December 1981;31–39.

Weber LJ. Ethics commission access report urges adequate care for all. *Hosp Prog.* July–August 1984;62–65.

World Health Organization. *The Prevention of Perinatal Morbidity and Mortality.* Technical Report Series No. 457. Geneva, Switzerbland: WHO; 1970.

Index